KILLING
FAIRFAX

KILLING FAIRFAX

PACKER, MURDOCH
& THE ULTIMATE REVENGE

Pamela Williams

HarperCollins*Publishers*

HarperCollins*Publishers*

First published in Australia in 2013
by HarperCollins*Publishers* Australia Pty Limited
ABN 36 009 913 517
harpercollins.com.au

HarperCollins*Publishers*
Level 13, 201 Elizabeth Street, Sydney NSW 2000
31 View Road, Glenfield, Auckland 0627, New Zealand
A 53, Sector 57, Noida, UP, India
77–85 Fulham Palace Road, London W6 8JB, United Kingdom
2 Bloor Street East, 20th floor, Toronto, Ontario M4W 1A8, Canada
10 East 53rd Street, New York NY 10022, USA

ISBN 978 0 7322 9766 4
ISBN 978 1 4607 0017 4 (e-book)

Cover design by Matt Stanton, HarperCollins Design Studio
Cover photography by Steve Baccon @ Reload Agency
Front cover photograph of James Packer and Lachlan Murdoch, 2013
Photograph of Pam Williams by Steve Baccon @ Reload Agency
Typeset in Baskerville MT by Kirby Jones
Printed and bound in Australia by Griffin Press
The papers used by HarperCollins in the manufacture of this book are
a natural, recyclable product made from wood grown in sustainable
plantation forests. The fibre source and manufacturing processes meet
recognised international environmental standards, and carry certification.

6 5 4 3 2   13 14 15 16

To Jenni Hewett
and Warren Scott

CONTENTS

PROLOGUE

Blue skies threw an early spring day across Sydney as an extremely tall, instantly recognisable man with a buzz cut bounded up the steps to Rockpool, the fashionable lunch place for the business set on Hunter Street in the centre of the city. He was met at the front desk by the restaurant's maître d' and swiftly ushered past the noisy main room and up a set of back stairs that led to a small private dining room on the first floor. The table was laid and a waiter hovered. Another guest arrived soon after, and the need for a private setting was clear. The sons of two of Australia's great media dynasties, James Packer and Lachlan Murdoch, welcomed each other with the backslapping pleasure of old friends. Packer ordered a vodka and after a fleeting hesitation, Murdoch did the same.

It was 1 p.m., 16 August 2012. Packer, newly slim and fit, was in ebullient form. 'I walked to work this morning,' he told Murdoch. 'I went to the gym as well and I'm feeling good.'

Murdoch, nursing an injured ankle after a trampoline accident, wanted details and they chatted easily as they ordered white wine and small serves of calamari and ocean trout.

Then they turned the conversation — as they had so many times before — to Fairfax, the hallowed newspaper company and third force on Australia's media scene. Fairfax was in free fall. Media companies across the globe were in trouble, caught in the teeth of a new-media juggernaut that had brought once proud companies to their knees. It was an industrial revolution. The old guard was sagging under the double bind of high costs and the remorseless onslaught of social media, while the internet was cutting a sharp path through the classified advertising that had once been the monopoly of newspaper firms. Fairfax had fallen fast and far.

'They lost the classifieds to the internet,' said Packer scornfully. 'They just didn't see it and didn't understand it, and now they're finished.'

The previous day, Wednesday 15 August, the Fairfax-owned *The Australian Financial Review* had published a story headlined 'New media stocks put on weight'. It had not escaped Packer's eye. The report was illustrated with a graphic table showing media companies listed by their worth on the stock market. At the top was SEEK, the $2.2 billion online jobs site in which Packer had invested 10 years before. SEEK had decimated Fairfax's newspaper job ads. Next was pay TV company Consolidated Media Holdings, valued at almost $2 billion, and controlled by Packer with 50.1 per cent of the shares. ConsMedia, as it was known, held 25 per cent of Foxtel and 50 per cent of Fox Sports. Then at $1.77 billion came the publicly listed REA Group, operator of the realestate.com.au website and 61 per cent owned by the Murdoch family's News

Corporation after a small initial investment made a decade earlier by Lachlan Murdoch. It now dominated real estate advertising, smashing Fairfax's hold on that market. In fourth place, at $1.6 billion, was Carsales.com, an internet company in which Fairfax had once held a small cornerstone stake before selling out to James Packer. Carsales had destroyed Fairfax's monopoly on the car market. Together, these top four companies were worth almost $8 billion. They had a stranglehold on the growth sectors of the media — online advertising for cars, jobs and property, and subscription TV. In fifth place was Kerry Stokes Seven West Media at almost $1.5 billion. Fairfax itself was in sixth place on the list, valued at $1.3 billion, a number that would sink within days to less than a billion dollars. The table told the whole story of what had happened to Fairfax's classified print advertising; it was a shocking indictment of the company's inability to ride the internet wave.

'Lachlan, how much did realestate.com cost you?' Packer demanded, leaning forward and slapping the table.

Murdoch put down his fork. 'Well, I think it was $10 million. But don't forget, $7 million was in comp. And it's worth nearly $2 billion now.'

'Fairfax just didn't see any of this coming. They thought it was all beneath them. They thought we were idiots. You know, I think we killed Fairfax,' James Packer said.

The two men looked at each other for a moment.

'I think so,' said Lachlan Murdoch.

One lifted his glass in a toast. And then the other.

CHAPTER ONE

SEEK AND YE SHALL FIND

In March 2003, the phone rang in the Melbourne offices of the online recruitment company SEEK. It was an odd call. The woman on the phone said her name was Jacquie Murray and that she worked for James Packer. James, she said, would be in Melbourne in a couple of days and would very much like to meet the founders of SEEK. The call was met with hilarity. This was akin to a whale phoning a tadpole. At SEEK, they decided it must be a prank.

The Bassat brothers, Paul and Andrew, and their friend Matthew Rockman had built SEEK from a daydream. By 2003, five years after its launch, it was a serious company, worth $100 million, driven by the boom in online advertising. They were proud of what they had done, and they planned, if they could, to one day overwhelm the classified jobs advertising in Australian newspapers — and at one company in particular, the mighty Fairfax, which owned the greatest streams of classified advertising in the country. It might have seemed a fantasy, but they were focussed and confident, and they thought Fairfax was complacent about the structural challenges posed by the internet. They, on the other hand, were young and they got it.

After five years of starting up and surviving the dotcom crash of 2000 and 2001, when internet companies everywhere flamed out, the SEEK founders had hit their stride. They were used to the peripatetic interest of the big boys in the major media companies. Many had courted them off and on, kicking the tyres or threatening — though not in so many words — to rub them out further down the track. But the interest always seemed to peter out. Now James Packer had called. Or so someone said. They thought it could hardly be Packer: scion of the legendary media dynasty whose family owned the Nine television network, rafts of magazines, Melbourne's Crown Casino, and half shares in an online joint venture, ninemsn, with the global powerhouse Microsoft. The Packers also had a joint venture in Monster, a competitor to SEEK. The Packers were all billionaires. Why would a Packer be personally calling SEEK, except, perhaps, to push them around?

They were sure the phone message was a hoax, probably from their own side. Everyone at SEEK loved a killer practical joke. They had once sent a staff member on an hour-long drive to Frankston for a meeting. When he got there, there was no-one to meet. Everyone roared laughing. Someone was always doing something like throwing a rubber ball at someone else, hitting a coffee cup, spilling it over a hard drive. Andrew Bassat was the prime joker; his brother Paul was deemed the adult supervision. How embarrassing if they turned up at Packer's office and it was a

SEEK practical joke. Finally they rang back to check, to find that James Packer did in fact want to meet them.

A few days later, the two Bassats and Matt Rockman trotted down to the Crown offices for the appointment, not sure what lay ahead. The Packers' company, Publishing and Broadcasting Ltd, was one of the most powerful in the media world and the Packers themselves had a fearsome reputation. Kerry Packer, the patriarch, was the third generation in a line of uncompromising larger-than-life figures, prone to strike terror into those around him. He was known for shoving around governments and prime ministers, and for living his life as he saw fit. His son James was rumoured to be just as bad. The Packer mystique alone was enough to make the three men edgy.

If they expected to enter a lair fit for a king, they were surprised. They were ushered into a pared-back Melbourne office with biscuit-coloured carpet, blonde timber, half-full bookcases and grey velour sofas. The walls were hung with a series of photographs in ubiquitous gold frames — photos of Crown casino under construction. There was not much on the desk. It all looked like business.

James Packer was there, in jeans and a polo shirt, wearing a broad smile. Almost the first thing he said was, 'I really wanted to meet you guys. With ninemsn, we've got this investment in monster.com and it's fucking hopeless. I think you guys have won. Game over. And I'd like to invest in your business.'

Over the years, one or other of the Bassats had held talks on half a dozen occasions with Fairfax; they had talked with the PBL internet subsidiary, ecorp, with Telstra, with Village Ten Online, with Yahoo, and with the Murdoch family's News Limited. But no-one had ever before conceded that SEEK was the leader in online jobs advertising. Paul Bassat was amazed.

> The first thing James Packer says to us is that we've won, rather than, 'We're going to buy you or squash you.' It was totally disarming. In conversations with Fairfax and others it was always, 'Maybe if you like us we can go out on a date.' James was saying, 'Let's just get our gear off and have sex.' He said, 'I think you guys are building a business and I want to be in it. And you are winning.' He had identified the trend; it was 2003 and he clearly understood there was going to be a winner.

Packer told them about his father. Kerry had always wanted to buy Fairfax, he said. It was a company the family hated: its pioneering investigative journalism had targeted Kerry Packer over many years, with exposés of his business dealings and the private world of the very rich. James Packer himself had a visceral loathing of Fairfax for more than a few reasons, but a Fairfax takeover was not on his mind. He planned to take a different form of revenge. 'I think there's a better way: by being involved with the players who are going to take their business off them,' he told his three astonished listeners. Packer was convinced the Fairfax classified print advertising business was going over a cliff. And that was something he wanted to be part of.

James Packer had been avidly chasing internet deals since 1997, after meeting Steve Ballmer, Microsoft's then executive vice president of sales — and later CEO — at a technology conference in the US. James was a man of a different stripe to his father. He had a playboy instinct and a young man's zeal, but he was interested too in businesses outside the tight world of media that his father dominated. He was riveted by the potential of the World Wide Web and Ballmer told him that if he wanted to know more, there was a guy he should meet in Australia: Daniel Petre, who had worked for Microsoft for nine years. Returning to Sydney after meeting Ballmer, James Packer immediately sought out Petre and invited him to lunch, together with Jodee Rich, who was at that time still the most important influence on the young Packer's growing interest in technology.

After that first lunch, James soon invited Petre to another far more important summit: a meeting in a small private room at establishment restaurant Beppi's with James and his father, Kerry. 'Come and talk to me and my dad,' Packer had entreated. Petre was more than willing. A private audience with Kerry Packer to discuss the future as Petre envisaged it was not to be missed.

Petre told the father and son that the internet would take over everything and he explained his views on how quickly the web would transform advertising as well as news. Delighted to find a guru who could help work over his father's obsession with the old world, James Packer invited Petre to join their business and establish an online division. He was determined to push his father towards the internet.

In 1997, the Packer business founded a new company, known firstly as PBL Online and later ecorp, to carry them into the new world with Petre at its helm. One of its first initiatives was ninemsn, a joint venture between Microsoft and PBL that took content from Packer magazines and television and put it online.

With ninemsn, PBL was partnering one of the biggest companies in the world. In another joint venture, the company brought the international online auction site eBay to Australia in 1999 for an initial investment of $3 million. In that same year, ecorp brought Ticketek on board to generate much-needed revenue.

Not all of the companies and joint ventures inside ecorp would do well; some, like the online brokerage business Charles Schwab in which ecorp held a 50 per cent stake, were outright failures. Eventually, 20 per cent of ecorp would be floated in 1999 at $1.20 per share. It soared to a market capitalisation of more than $5 billion before the dotcom crash, and was finally privatised back into PBL at 55 cents a share.

Petre became a central figure in PBL's business and joined the PBL board in 1998. It was his mantra that the traditional media classified advertising model would be gone in two years, and that advertising would migrate to the web. He found that trying to persuade Kerry Packer to trust the web businesses was a lost cause, but James was different.

'Kerry Packer didn't get it,' Petre recalled.

> He thought eBay Australia was rubbish because he thought people wouldn't be honest with each other. And he just didn't get the internet. He was just supporting James. James Packer got it though, and he gave us air cover. The internet was a gold rush back then. Claims were being staked and if you didn't get a claim you were dead. And if you didn't get to be number 1 you were dead. Number 1 gets the very high margin, number 2 gets to do okay and number 3 is basically dead. By the end of the lunch at Beppi's in 1997 — well, you

can get starstruck a bit. And they asked me to join them.

The Packers were prepared to bet on this. James' great skill was that he knew something was happening, way back then.

The general public understood little of the online business developing behind the scenes at PBL. Profiles of ecorp chairman Petre and his deputy chairman Jeremy Philips — tagged 'the two wunderkinds' — stayed in the business pages. True to form, the Packers themselves remained in the background, giving out as little information as possible.

What the public did know all about was One.Tel, the mobile phone and internet company started by Packer's school friend Jodee Rich and Rich's friend Brad Keeling. Packer had invested 5 per cent of the initial seed capital of $5 million in 1995. The company floated in 1997; by February 1999, at James Packer's instigation, PBL and News Corp had invested close to $900 million for roughly 40 per cent of the company. A year later international giant Lucent Technologies announced plans to build a European network for One.Tel, and One.Tel joined the ranks of Australia's Top 50 companies. But the company regularly needed more funding. By early 2000, the dotcom crash was under way and One. Tel's costs (including huge salaries and bonuses for executives) and investments on mobile spectrum licences were out of control. As One.Tel struggled with debt, the share price crashed below $1. Still, in late 2000, James Packer gave Rich and Keeling his full-throated support. He would be publicly labelled a fool for it not long after, not least by his own father.

In May 2001, One.Tel blew up after the directors, including James Packer and Lachlan Murdoch, abandoned a $132 million capital-raising. Creditors were owed hundreds of millions of dollars, liquidators were brought in, and News Corp and PBL had lost their money. As directors, Lachlan Murdoch and James Packer declared they had been profoundly misled. It was the start of years of legal action, with damaging and embarrassing revelations gushing like water from a broken pipe. Loyalty and naivety, it seemed, had mixed with bad business practices, greed and ambition.

James would wear the stain of One.Tel for years to come, a hot red burn on his forehead. To the outside world, Kerry Packer seemed to take satisfaction from his son's failure. One.Tel consolidated a message the father had often conveyed: that his son did not know what he was doing. For all the court hearings that would follow, the real agony was the public castigation and the knowledge of the money lost. Other executives and directors across the telephony and internet spectrum of Australia and New Zealand might have overseen massive losses too, but what James Packer learned was that a media tycoon — with all the public exercise of power that entailed — was always under scrutiny, and more so when things went wrong. For James there was nowhere to hide. Lachlan Murdoch's father might have publicly put an arm around his own son to draw him back into the protective web of the family firm after One.Tel, but there was no such tenderness for James Packer. His father was in love with media and as far as Kerry was concerned, the Nine Network and the Australian Consolidated Press magazine empire were the biggest and best businesses in the world; the internet was a fool's game. A devastated James Packer, who had been chief executive of PBL from 1996 to 1998, and executive chairman since then, suffered a complete nervous breakdown. 'I told you you would fuck it up,' his father told him brutally.

Rupert Murdoch, however, spared a moment for Packer. Lachlan Murdoch and James Packer shared a birthday, 8 September. In 2001, four months after the One.Tel implosion, with people thrown out of work and the hounds baying, James was invited to Lachlan's 30th birthday party at a bar in New York. James Packer turned 34 that day. Amidst the speeches Lachlan wished his morose friend a happy birthday too.

At one point in the evening, Packer found himself alone in a corner, talking to Rupert Murdoch. 'I am so sorry,' he told the head of News Corp.

The elder Murdoch, a man from the sink or swim school, replied with more kindness than Packer felt he had a right to expect. 'It's okay, James,' Murdoch said. 'Just make sure you learn the lessons.'

After One.Tel, Packer fled to America to hide in Los Angeles, invited by a new friend, the actor Tom Cruise, who kept watch as he tried vainly to get back on his feet. Packer was at times suicidal. He had campaigned heavily to force his father into taking up a 25 per cent stake in the subscription television company Foxtel in 1998 and to buy Crown Casino in 1999, big investments which one day would define the future of the company. He had pushed hard, backing Petre in the internet ventures — ecorp, ninemsn, eBay and all the rest — through 1997, '98 and '99, and while ecorp might not have been profitable, these deals had firmly positioned PBL as a serious contender in the new web-based landscape. But James Packer would be remembered forever for One.Tel. The public shellacking, especially from the Fairfax newspapers, and the guilt of letting everyone down bit hard. He would never forget the toll it took, even ten years later. James knew the media coverage was partly because he was a Packer, but rather than take it on the chin, his desire for retribution against Fairfax grew, adding to the family lode with which he had been raised. Like his father, James Packer would never forget nor forgive Fairfax.

Packer had imagined that One.Tel could take on Telstra. Now all those dreams were burned. Packer's marriage to Jodhi Meares collapsed under the pressure in 2002, soon after the start of liquidator's hearings into One.Tel. It was a devastating blow.

Tom Cruise held him together on the worst and darkest days, and in Cruise's realm, he turned heavily to Scientology. Back in Australia, the Fairfax newspapers pounded him as every savage detail of the One.Tel debacle came out, amidst often-lurid speculation about Scientology and questions of whether James was suffering from depression. It would take Kerry Packer a year to understand that his son was in serious trouble.

James Packer was out of action for a total of 18 months, and in that interregnum Kerry Packer, who had eased back on the pedal, reasserted himself. In August 2002, eBay offered $120 million to buy out the 50 per cent of eBay Australia and New Zealand that was owned by ecorp. Daniel Petre had already resigned as chairman of ecorp and a director of PBL a year before, in October 2001. With James Packer hardly focussed, mostly in the US avoiding scrutiny and trying to recover from the One.Tel implosion, and Kerry gloating and pointing out the errors and the death of the web, Petre had had enough. But a year after his departure from ecorp, when he heard about the eBay offer, Petre still conveyed his opinion to Kerry Packer that it would be crazy to sell.

Kerry, though, was not interested in reasoned analysis. He had never formed any affection for the business and saw the chance to make a killing. He agreed to sell and did not bother to call his son. Instead, John Alexander, then CEO of PBL's two main media businesses, Nine and ACP, called James in Los Angeles. 'Your dad's sold eBay for over $100 million,' he said, trying to calm Packer by pointing out that after One.Tel, it looked good to make such a big profit with one of his internet plays. It had little impact. 'James' response was one of anger and he remained furious for years afterwards,' Alexander recalled.

Looking back later, James said he wondered at the time how his father would have reacted if his own father, Frank, had got rid of Kerry's cherished television licence two years after acquiring it. 'I thought, "Imagine if Sir Frank had sold out of Channel Nine in 1958",' he said.

James knew the eBay sale was not just about rationalising and striking a fat profit, but was knitted to Kerry's suspicion of a business model he could not understand. He was used to hearing his father shout: 'This is just bullshit.' James would patiently try to show him how to search the web, and then the PC would freeze and Kerry would erupt. When ecorp had been floated in June 1999 Kerry Packer had told John Alexander he didn't understand the business model but knew that PBL had to be in the space. After the dotcom crash, Packer was even more untrusting of these companies that seemed to flourish on nothing but thin air and imagination.

'To be fair to Dad, I'd always say these businesses are going to be huge,' Packer said later. 'But One.Tel had failed. My dad would always say, "You're living in the future, living in Dreamland".'

When James Packer finally returned to Sydney his mind was still on the web. SEEK was now making serious headway in classified jobs online and everyone was talking about it. It was making headlines.

> When I came back from the US, everyone was saying
> there's still this thing called SEEK. I kept hearing about it
> because we were in monster.com and we would do all these
> competitive analyses and SEEK was always better than us.
> Our people kept saying, 'We'll catch them, we'll catch them.'
> So I knew about SEEK. I said, 'Well, I want to meet the
> Bassats and Matt Rockman.' And they came in and we met
> at Crown. The meeting went well and they said they'd only
> consider doing 25 per cent, and they said they'd want a big
> price. And I basically just said yes. Everyone else wanted to
> buy into Fairfax, but I thought Fairfax was fucked. Daniel
> Petre had educated me.
>
> By 2000, I was thinking the internet is going to change
> the world. The classifieds are going online. It's Gordon
> Moore's [co-founder of the silicone chip company Intel]
> law that chip capacity doubles every two years. Rockefeller
> and Buffett talk about compound interest. Chip capacity
> is the same model, you double and double. Computers are
> 100 times more powerful every ten years. I was sitting there
> thinking about this in 2000 and looking at the invention of
> mobile phones, the internet and pay TV. The internet was
> nascent and everyone was saying this was just the beginning.
> And the people who influenced me at that time, like Daniel
> Petre and Jodee Rich, were saying, 'Your father is an old-
> fashioned monopolist.' Dad was still very worried about
> Fairfax. And I had Fairfax attacking me every day. John

Alexander and I did talk a lot in those days about how to screw Fairfax.

When they met in March 2003, Paul Bassat was struck by James Packer's personal antipathy towards Fairfax, without understanding what the battering and the guilt over One.Tel had done. Nor did he realise then that chasing SEEK was the first big deal Packer had pursued since returning from Los Angeles, or that Packer thought his reputation might never be retrieved. He was fascinated by Packer's determination to attack Fairfax from the outside.

> James had a fairly strong dislike of Fairfax. Basically from the very first meeting at Crown, James said his father always wanted Fairfax. But James thought there was no longer any reason to buy Fairfax. We said we were nervous that if we sold some of our business to him, he would then turn around and buy Fairfax. And he said, 'Why would we buy Fairfax when people like you guys are going to take their classifieds and take all their value?' I think he felt he could get the value without buying the Fairfax business.

Even so, Packer was hardly over the line in buying into SEEK. The SEEK founders demurred; Packer might be a big wheel, but this was their baby and they were on an upwards trajectory. For the first time in their brief history they did not need money, no matter who kicked their tyres. They had investors like the wealthy Besen and Lieberman families in Melbourne and a venture capital fund controlled by Bill Ferris, Joe Skrzynski and Su Ming Wong in

Sydney. A year earlier, they would have jumped at the opportunity; now, a link with the Packers would be a purely strategic play. Over the next week, the three founders talked over their options until finally they made a decision.

They decided they did not want James Packer investing in their business. They had felt bruised after negotiations with ecorp several years before. When the SEEK founders had retreated from a proposal to sell 25 per cent of their company to ecorp in 1999 — wanting to maintain their independence — SEEK was pushed off the ninemsn website. At the time, the two ecorp executives conducting the negotiations, Daniel Petre and Jeremy Philips, had glimpsed the impending threat to newspaper revenue that SEEK represented. They left a meeting with the Bassats fully expecting that one of the big companies would take care of SEEK in the end.

'We were in a cab going back to Tullamarine Airport,' Petre recalled, 'and we thought, these guys are so smart, so focussed. And we thought there was no way Fairfax and News were going to let these guys take out their classifieds. We thought they would squash SEEK. We thought it meant so much, even in 1999, that they would never let it survive.'

Back then, the Bassats had never met James Packer. Doing a deal directly with him now, in 2003, might get them back onto the ninemsn site, with its high traffic, but it mattered far more to stay in control of their own destiny. How to break this news, this rejection, to Packer — that was the challenge. Particularly as they liked him and could see he understood their business.

'James got our space almost better than us in terms of where it could go,' Andrew Bassat said later.

He could see the potential. He got that newspapers were under threat and the dollars were flowing online. He saw the future and the vision and the big themes. And he had nothing to protect. He did not have newspapers to protect. We got a really strong sense that he was a guy we could trust. But we wanted to keep our independence. He was very respectful and he said, 'You guys have built a great business and I'd like to be part of it and help you along the way.' He saw it could be a *really* great business in five years' time.

The three founders decided Paul Bassat, a lawyer with an effervescent personality who had first conceived the idea for SEEK, could have the job of breaking the bad news to Packer. Ten days after their first meeting at Crown, Bassat flew to Sydney to meet Packer at the Park Street headquarters of the family empire. Bassat had never been good at delivering bad news. He started cautiously.

'Well it was great to meet you, and if it was 12 months ago …'

Packer interrupted: 'I don't think the conversation's getting better from here,' he said.

'No,' said Bassat.

'Why?' Packer asked.

Bassat explained as best he could. They assumed the Packers would want control and they would lose the flexibility they enjoyed. Their views had been coloured by the original negotiations with ecorp, where tough contracts and legal constraints and controls were part of the picture.

'Okay,' said Packer. 'Have you got a couple of hours?'

Bassat did not have a couple of hours, but he agreed anyway. It was clear Packer was not taking no for an answer.

James Packer was positive and upbeat as he drove Bassat to the Nine Network at Willoughby, where he introduced him to one of his closest confidantes, John Alexander. A one-time top editor and publisher at Fairfax, Alexander had been kicked out of the company in 1998 amidst a power struggle. James Packer had phoned soon after to offer him a job and Alexander had risen rapidly at PBL, forming exceptionally close personal bonds with both Kerry and James Packer. Sitting in JA's office, as Alexander was universally known, they shot the breeze about the mutual benefits of a PBL–SEEK link-up, chatting about media and the online rush. Alexander, who had closely supported James in the two years after One.Tel, staying in touch daily, could have killed off any SEEK proposal in a flash with just a word to Kerry Packer. But he backed it from the outset.

It became ever clearer to the Bassats that Packer was not giving up. Over the next weeks the courtship intensified. 'You've said no because of these reasons,' Packer would say to them. 'So if we can address these issues, can we invest?'

'I said, oh well, maybe,' Paul Bassat recalled.

> We had numerous conversations about this: myself, my
> brother Andrew, Matt Rockman and the SEEK board.
> James finally convinced us. We found him motivated,
> passionate, very bullish about our business — possibly the
> only person as bullish about the business from the outside
> as us. When we indicated we'd be open to a conversation,
> James said, 'What do you think your business is worth?'
> We said about $100 million. We expected to make about
> $8 million that year and we thought 12 times earnings
> before interest and tax. We had talked about them buying

20 per cent of the company. It was going to be about $25 million. He accepted on the spot and we reached an in-principle agreement. But James had said all along, 'This is my father's company and this will require Kerry's approval. All investments need his approval.'

On Friday 2 May 2003, Paul Bassat and James Packer agreed on the terms by phone. The critical face-to-face meeting with Kerry Packer was set for the following Monday, 5 May. On the Sunday, Paul Bassat asked his brother Andrew what they should wear to meet the legend. Should they wear suits? Andrew Bassat said no, pointing out that every time they had met James Packer they wore casual pants and shirts. They flew to Sydney on the Monday, and sat waiting, somewhat nervously, outside Packer's office suite at his Park Street headquarters. Five minutes later the lift doors opened and Kerry Packer walked out, wearing a suit.

They were brought into Packer's office, with its orange carpet, green sofas, television screens and stuffed animals, the legacy of Packer's love of big game hunting. Pictures of lions and tigers lined the walls. The desk was at the end of the room, overlooking Sydney's Hyde Park. Before Kerry took over, this had been the office his father, Sir Frank Packer, had occupied.

But this was more than just meeting the Packers. Waiting in the room with Kerry and James were John Alexander, Peter Yates, then chief executive of PBL Ltd, and Ashok Jacob, joint CEO of the Packers' private company Consolidated Press Holdings.

The Bassats had expected to be in there for 20 minutes, but two hours later Kerry Packer was still asking questions. He was charming. Not once did he ask about SEEK's financial data.

Instead he wanted to know about and understand the business. He wanted to see how their website worked. Paul Bassat sat down and gave a demonstration on the big PC on Kerry's desk. When they explained the importance of market leadership in classified advertising, Packer cut them off. When he was a young man, he informed them, he had sold real estate advertising for his father against the competition from Fairfax. 'So you don't have to tell me the importance of being number one in classifieds.'

In a later meeting, Packer admonished the Bassats, warning they should be concerned about the power of Fairfax. 'You don't understand, you just don't understand,' he said. 'You're just kids. These organisations are much more powerful than you think.'

It was a theme he would come back to later, asking whether SEEK was worried about Telstra. Paul Bassat said no, earning a swift rebuke. 'Telstra is a very big organisation. I worry about Telstra,' Packer said coolly.

Bassat knew it was a putdown. 'So I said, "Well then, Kerry, *I* worry about Telstra." He was basically saying to me, "You young punks don't understand."'

At the end of that first two-hour meeting, Kerry Packer pushed hard about the size of the shareholding he wanted. The Bassats were interested in selling 20 per cent of SEEK; James Packer wanted 25 per cent. Kerry Packer wanted more, but certainly no less than 25 per cent. The Bassats pushed back cautiously, feeling more than a little outflanked by the feeling of contained power in the room. Suddenly Kerry looked at his watch and announced that he had to go. Could they come back in an hour? The hour gave them breathing space. They phoned Matt Rockman in Melbourne and regained their resolve.

When they returned there was no sign of Kerry Packer; it reduced the stress in the room. The Bassats announced they would go to 25 per cent but no higher. Someone said, 'Well, we'll sell that to Kerry.'

The following day, James Packer phoned again and the details were agreed. PBL would pay $33 million for a 25 per cent stake in SEEK and James Packer would join the board. But before the deal could be concluded, James would have to negotiate the conclusion of ecorp's joint venture with Monster.

It would be three months before the SEEK deal was signed and announced and it would be almost that long before Fairfax found out. During that time, James Packer never let go of the reins. He rang the Bassats almost every day, making sure everything was okay, checking that no-one was beating them up. He remembered the concerns they had conveyed about the 1999 talks with ecorp. They could see Packer was not going to let his fish slip away. Paul Bassat noted the attention to detail.

> I had said to Matt and Andrew, 'I bet we get the term
> sheet [from the PBL lawyers] and it'll have all sorts of
> employment things and warranties.' And it didn't. It was just
> half a page. It was the same story with the contract, it was
> just straightforward. The point is, James had made up his
> mind about the investment and he understood that it was
> our company and we didn't want to wake up and find we
> were working for someone else. For James, the big picture
> was getting the deal. The details were less important. He
> wanted the deal and he wanted to be sure nothing would
> get in the way. When he came onto the board he was always

pushing us to grow the business. He was very growth-oriented, very supportive.

For SEEK, in one respect nothing had changed. In other respects, everything had changed. They had the PBL aura now. They were a small dotcom in Melbourne but with the Packers involved.

The founders of SEEK had travelled a long way from the early days of the company, when they might be lucky to have a few hundred job ads on the site in a month, or would find themselves up late on a Friday night typing after an early corporate client faxed over a list of the ads they had placed in the next day's Fairfax metropolitan newspapers. SEEK had begun in the time-honoured way: not quite in a garage, but almost.

—————

It had been an early autumn day, six years before, in March 1997, when the brainwave for SEEK had first struck. Paul Bassat and his wife Sharon were waiting outside a house going to auction in Union Street, East Brighton, on the outskirts of Melbourne. Bassat suddenly realised how frustrated he was with the whole process of looking for houses in the classified pages of the newspaper, then driving around to see what the properties looked like.

Bassat, then 29, was a lawyer working in the commercial and corporate division at Arnold Bloch Liebler. His friend Evan Thornley had set up internet company LookSmart in late 1995 and had asked Bassat to act for him. Bassat knew nothing about the internet, but it encouraged him to find out. By the time he found himself house-hunting in Brighton in 1997, he was in the zone. Standing in the street he thought, 'Why don't we do real estate on the internet?' He headed to his parents' house to use their computer to check out housing on the web. To his astonishment, there were already lots of companies 'doing all this stuff'.

Bassat called his older brother to suggest they start putting together a business proposal. Andrew Bassat, 31, was a management consultant at Booz Allen. He was not an internet user but they were both excited to find advertising already online. They would spend nearly six months creating a plan. The brothers had three basic questions: firstly, was classified advertising a good business? With pens in hand they would comb through the huge Saturday edition of *The Age*, owned by Fairfax, counting the ads. They could see there was a dominant real estate agent in each geographic sector. It seemed to be a good business. Secondly, was classified advertising going to move from print to online? They believed they could see the start of a trend, mainly in the US. Thirdly, they asked themselves, 'Why us?'

Andrew Bassat played devil's advocate. Why would newspapers not be there? Why would newspapers not go online? Why, with their various monopolies carving up the country, wouldn't they just take it all online themselves? He kept thinking about the newspaper companies. They had all the jobs, all the money and all the newspaper brands. They had the revenue. The Bassats were absolutely clear in their minds that classifieds would move online. But they figured that for newspapers to make the same move, it would mean sacrificing revenue. It was expensive to put an advertisement in a newspaper, but it was cheap online. Would shareholders allow that for four or five years until the online model became established?

They convinced themselves there was no-one in a dominant position in the online market, and that the big newspaper companies would be concerned about travelling too far down that track and competing with their existing print revenues. They estimated there was $800 million per annum of revenue in employment classifieds in all papers across Australia; of this, they believed $300 million flowed to Fairfax. They guessed Fairfax's total revenue from real estate, jobs and car ads could be around $700 million. They could not be sure, but these were big numbers. If they could take just a small slice of that pie, it was worth it.

Then the Bassat brothers decided they preferred employment to real estate. It was a more fragmented market, with no huge players. And there were not just the big recruitment firms, but also hundreds of thousands of small and medium businesses that hired their staff directly. They decided in a landscape like that someone, hopefully themselves, could build a dominant player. They looked around at the competition. There were already around 100 players in employment: Fairfax, News Limited and the US company Monster, plus seven or eight other serious players and about 90 little ones.

Paul Bassat spoke to his boss, Mark Liebler, and asked for leave from work for a few months to pursue funding for the new venture. Liebler wanted to know what would happen if he got the funding. 'Well, I will go and run it,' Bassat replied cheekily. 'And if not, I want my job back.'

Liebler agreed. Paul's brother, Andrew, would keep his own job and work on the business plan at night.

In the end, the first and indeed the only people they approached were Matt Rockman, a friend the same age as Paul Bassat, and his father Irvin Rockman, a developer and hotelier known particularly for his Rockman's Regency Hotel in the heart of Melbourne.

The Rockmans invested $750,000 each. Matt Rockman, who had a background in property development and was sales director for Rockman's Regency, decided he too wanted to join the company, and with that they were off. They planned to launch their new website on 16 March 1998, a year after the idea was first conceived. They had no real understanding that they were on the cusp of a new era where the internet, technology, recruitment advertising and the media industry would all overlap. There were a lot of gaps in their plan: for starters, none of the three founders had any experience. Andrew Bassat had a modicum of IT knowledge but his brother Paul and Matt Rockman were fundamentally clueless as far as the technology was concerned. They outsourced the work of building the website to their detailed specifications. They examined sites around the world and agreed that they didn't want it to look like a newspaper. They wanted users to be able to search by type of job and location and to receive a daily email update; they wanted companies and recruitment firms to be able to come to the site and put up their own ads. As with so many start-ups, there were so many things that could go wrong. To anyone else it might have looked like madness, but they were young and they did not see the shades of grey. They had a young man's view of risk, they were hungry, and there was not a lot to lose.

For a month they worked from Irvin Rockman's office in South Yarra. He was supportive, but a little nervous. Over time he would grow to be passionate about the company and would remain chairman of SEEK for eight years. They took an office at St Kilda junction in a shabby building with nothing to recommend it, which they loved. Paul Bassat was nominally CEO, Andrew Bassat handled corporate and strategic development and Matt Rockman was in charge of sales. He would go out to visit recruitment firms and the first question they would always ask was, 'Who are you?' The second question was always, 'What's the internet?'

All three took credit for the SEEK name. Andrew Bassat had combed through thesauruses trying to find a word that worked and which still had a URL available. Given their original plan to cover jobs, real estate and cars, they needed something broad enough for all three. They reserved a few names: The Spot, Gusto and Fig Jam (inspired by the acronym 'fuck I'm good, just ask me'). Then they found SEEK.

When they were ready to launch the site they had a grand total of fewer than 400 ads, mostly from the recruitment firm Chandler & Macleod. They didn't charge much; the strategy was to cut deals wherever they could. 'You can have all the job ads you want for $500 a month,' they would offer. Chandler & Macleod would make photocopies of the ads they were running in Saturday newspapers and fax them over to SEEK on a Friday. The young founders would sit up typing like mad in their Wellington Street office. One of them could not spell very well and on the last night before the launch in March 1998, Andrew Bassat found he had to re-type 50 ads. By the time the site went live, they had already gone home, exhausted. Their first month's revenue was $6880. One year later it was $79,930. It would take four years — until 2002 — to make a profit.

Some days were crazy; someone would be looking for a job in Perth and SEEK would have only three jobs in Sydney. There were good days and bad days. In the first month there were 492 ads on the site and a total of 74 job applications for the month. Their very first job placement, though, happened quickly. They knew about it because they received an email from a young woman who wrote to tell them she had looked for a job as a personal assistant, found one on SEEK, applied successfully, and was now working in a fashion company. Two months later Paul Bassat visited the firm and after introducing himself, struck up a conversation with the woman. He told her she was the first person they knew of to land a job through SEEK. She was delighted. The managing director who had placed the ad, however, had a different view. 'This is fucking hopeless,' he told a protesting Bassat. He planned to stop advertising with them as no other ads had borne fruit. 'The rest isn't working,' he complained.

Every day they were bashed up. Sales staff left, clients left, it was an uphill struggle.

The initial funding provided by the Rockmans in 1997 before the launch was expected to last 12 months but they stretched it to 15 months. By late 1998 they were making $15,000 a month. They had estimated Fairfax had revenue of $250 million a year just from employment ads. SEEK had revenue of $180,000 a year.

Before the launch Andrew Bassat had approached both Evan Thornley at LookSmart and Steve Vamos, the chief executive of ninemsn, to get a presence on their sites. Ninemsn had the biggest online audience in the country, and any way they could reach that audience was worth the cost. Somehow, they had to attract eyeballs to SEEK. Within a month of the launch they had struck a partnership with ninemsn where they paid $7500 a month for a position on the site. A user clicking on 'jobs' would be directed to SEEK.

They finally gained a little momentum but they needed a capital injection, which they drew largely from private investors.

By early 1999 they had 20 people on staff. And then the buzz started and the big end of town came calling, in the person of the ecorp executives — landlords of the ninemsn site where SEEK was a tenant. Daniel Petre and Jeremy Philips were on the hunt for net deals and keen to buy 25 or 30 per cent of SEEK. But the Bassats and Rockman were not comfortable. They did not like the employment contracts they were given to look at, they wanted to stay in charge, and they felt the vibe was wrong. SEEK was valued at around $6 million and it was becoming a tidy little success story. Ecorp was interested in investing $2 million for 25 per cent.

'They were very open,' Paul Bassat recalled later.

> They said, 'We think employment is going to be one of
> the great categories online, and we want to be in it and
> a participant. And if you guys say no, we'll do a deal
> with someone else.' We knew we would lose the ninemsn
> distribution if we said no, but in the end we said no. We had
> a lot of conversations between the three of us — we were
> very informal — and there was Matt's father. We went back
> to the board and said, 'We don't really want to do this.'

PBL, the owner of ecorp, was an 800-pound gorilla. It had assets to leverage. It had none of the classified print muscle of Fairfax, but it had a great deal of heft given that a third of SEEK's traffic was coming through ninemsn. It was a big risk to reject the overtures, but it was just not a great fit. After to-ing and fro-ing for weeks, followed by a pause while ecorp worked on its own public offering, SEEK said no. Later, in March 2000, ecorp announced it was buying 50 per cent of the international job-site Monster in

Australia. Monster would never beat SEEK, but there was still a downside: SEEK was kicked off ninemsn and replaced by Monster.

SEEK's three big online competitors now were Fairfax's MyCareer site, News Limited's CareerOne, and Monster. None of the four was miles ahead of anyone else.

As SEEK became more visible, others came calling too. In 1999, Paul Bassat and Irvin Rockman had been invited to meet Fred Hilmer, the new chief executive of Fairfax at the Spencer Street offices of *The Age*. Hilmer had been appointed by Brian Powers, chairman of Fairfax since May 1998 and previously executive chairman of PBL and chief executive of the Packers' private company Consolidated Press Holdings. Powers' departure from the Packers to take up with their hated foe Fairfax was one of the more astonishing moves on the merry-go-round of Australian media, and it had provoked a regulatory inquiry into whether Powers was an associate of the Packers and whether he was in a position to control Fairfax — a breach of the laws which kept television and newspaper markets apart. In the end Powers was deemed not in control of Fairfax as he was only one on a board of ten.

Powers was a fast-talking American lawyer and investment banker from Hellman & Friedman in San Francisco with a big personality and ready wit. Hilmer was a former partner at the management consultants McKinsey & Company and Dean of the Australian Graduate School of Management. The choice of Hilmer, with his reserved personality and lack of media experience of any kind, was greeted with astonishment. Powers told one Fairfax editorial executive it was an experiment. Hilmer might have been a McKinsey-style analyst more than a businessman, but he was particularly close to one of the best-connected names on the Australian business scene, investment banker and Fairfax director David Gonski, and it immediately became company lore that Gonski had put Hilmer forward.

The SEEK founders decided meeting Hilmer would be interesting, but they were wary of disclosing too much detail to a company they thought was on the one hand a competitor, but which might also one day be a potential acquirer. Hilmer met them in the boardroom at Spencer Street, an old-style executive suite, wood-panelled and sombre. He told them that as a new media CEO, he had done the rounds of media proprietors to say hello. When he had met Rupert Murdoch, the News Corp boss had told him there were two things Hilmer needed to know about media. The first was that media grew faster than GDP, and the second was that media fragmented.

'I assumed that by quoting Murdoch's statement about the history of media, Hilmer was telling us that he thought there would be a fragmentation of media advertising in favour of the internet, but that it was not an existential threat for newspapers and they would continue to thrive. The meeting was very pleasant and it was the only time I met Fred,' Paul Bassat said later.

Hilmer was not in the business of personally chasing SEEK. Paul Bassat met him only the once; his brother Andrew not at all. In the ensuing years, the Bassats met both Nigel Dews, the intense young geek running Fairfax's digital business, f2 — who was so close to Hilmer that he was nicknamed 'Fred's love child'—and Alan Revell, a traditional newspaper editor who had crossed the boundaries by working as an editor and an executive at f2, and as publisher and editor-in-chief of *The Sydney Morning Herald*. In April 2003, Revell would be appointed commercial director of Fairfax.

'There were a couple of things that were most apparent about Fairfax,' Paul Bassat recalled.

They were never very aggressive about trying to drive an outcome in their conversations with us. We had a handful of friendly meetings with them with no real follow-up after each meeting. A period of six months or more sometimes passed between each of these meetings. That was a big contrast to our subsequent conversations with James Packer. In our first meeting at Crown, James explicitly said to Andrew, Matt and I that he wanted to invest in SEEK and help us build a bigger business. He then rang us almost daily over the subsequent few months to ensure that the negotiations were on track.

The second thing about our conversations with Fairfax is they never seriously tried to address the concerns that we had. Our goal was to build online at the expense of print and their goal was to defend their rivers of gold. Our interests weren't aligned. As a result, we weren't open to doing the sort of deal that they wanted to do with us: buying a strategic shareholding at a relatively low valuation with board representation and with veto rights.

I think in hindsight the only way Fairfax could have done a deal with us would have been to either buy the business outright at a price that reflected our growth potential, or by taking a passive minority stake that didn't carry with it veto rights or board representation. The combination of their sporadic dialogue with us and their unwillingness to put something on the table that satisfied our

requirements, meant there was no real possibility of a deal
with Fairfax being done.

SEEK however, was methodical in pursuing Fairfax's business.
After three years, they understood that job seekers would always
go to where they could do best, whether it was print or online.
They knew SEEK had to be measured against print and to beat it;
print was a deep pool to swim in and they were a long way behind
the leaders in that field. They focussed on market sectors still on
the brink of going online with their advertising, like health care.
They changed the sales force structure, paying commissions on
advertising volume — not revenue — in hard-to-crack markets, and
added differential pricing. Trying to hurt print gave them a different
mind-set. They began contacting purely print advertisers, luring
them to online trials. They took the battle up to the newspapers.

By early 2000 SEEK was considering a share market float.
They might be losing $1 million some months, but losses as a
percentage of sales were declining, the business was growing
and revenue was growing. They were a few days from signing a
prospectus led by Macquarie Bank for an initial public offering
(IPO) when the first big shockwaves from the dotcom crash were
felt. They dropped the float and buckled down. They had just
signed a new deal that guaranteed distribution for the SEEK
website. In April 2000, the big search company Yahoo had bought
10 per cent of SEEK for $6 million and it gave them a solid buffer.
Yahoo was important strategically, as SEEK had been replaced by
Monster on the ninemsn site. Now they were on Yahoo.

Fairfax, still sailing on the rivers of gold, was oblivious to the
drumbeat from the shore. SEEK was almost the market leader

online: sometimes they were ahead of Fairfax and News Limited, sometimes they slipped back; no-one yet knew who would be the ultimate winner.

'Once we came on the radar,' Andrew Bassat said later, 'I think their Plan A was that we would run out of money — and they didn't need a Plan B because Plan A would occur. Then they would be back in charge.'

In February 2002, SEEK finally made money. It had taken four years and four months from the very start, working out of Irvin's office. They had burned through close to $20 million in capital and they had 150 people in the company. They threw a profit party at the Port Melbourne Yacht Club and flew in staff from Sydney and Auckland. As they celebrated, Andrew Bassat said he wondered what Fairfax and News Limited were up to now that it was clear the internet was not going away. 'It was pretty obvious to us when we first did our sums at the very start that at least 50 per cent of the revenue and 100 per cent of profits at Fairfax came from classified advertising. So once the classifieds came under attack — well, the board should have worked all that out.'

By the start of 2003, problems at Fairfax were biting. Newspaper circulation was falling and advertising followed, particularly the big-money display advertising that had helped make Fairfax untouchable. Unlike the Murdoch newspapers, which could be supported in good times and bad by funnels of money from News Corp's diversified international media and film interests, Fairfax had a narrow base.

Back in September 1999, Fairfax had put its digital businesses into the subsidiary known as f2, backed by $100 million to spend over three years. f2 promptly launched CitySearch, a regional directories site for events, calendars, transport and weather information. Nigel Dews, Fairfax's digital chief, believed Fairfax's branded online classifieds would triumph naturally over outsiders. As far as investing big money in the web went, Dews' focus was on building up CitySearch, not acquiring one of the 'pure-plays', as digital companies like SEEK were known due to their focus on a single agenda. Dews would say later that he always had a close watch on SEEK and that at the start of 2003, he sought a meeting with SEEK's chairman Irvin Rockman. According to Dews he asked whether Rockman might sell a block of shares to Fairfax and a figure of $10 million was canvassed for roughly 20 per cent of the shares. Dews, who had no approval from the Fairfax board for these talks, said later that he discussed the $10 million figure with Hilmer. Rockman, however, promptly doubled the price and Hilmer lost interest. Whether Rockman was testing how far he could push Fairfax, or was just playing cat and mouse, was unclear; he was a man with a sense of humour.

It was an odd notion that Rockman, who remained chairman of SEEK until 2005, would be quietly negotiating the sale of his own shares in the company founded by his son and the Bassats, and would do so with no reference to anyone else. Paul Bassat later poured cold water on the notion that Rockman was doing anything other than playing. 'I would be sceptical that Irvin would ever engage in serious discussions with Fairfax about selling his shareholding.'

Unbeknownst to Fairfax at the time, the doors to SEEK were about to close for good as James Packer arrived. Fairfax took one last brief turn on the dance floor with the Bassat brothers following the appointment of Alan Revell as commercial director in April 2003.

Revell tried to prod Hilmer to focus on SEEK. The discussions at the Fairfax top table revolved around maintaining the company's print advertising dominance. It was a simple equation. If that didn't hold up, there was no dividend. There was a constant debate about the thrusting online classified pure-plays. Should Fairfax buy in or try to kill them? Should Fairfax invest more in its own sites — like MyCareer — or should they just admit the game was up and go after the pure-plays in jobs, real estate and cars?

'I think most directors thought that Fairfax was a big powerful beast and should be able to dominate,' Revell would say later. 'And none of the pure-plays wanted to be owned by someone who would crush them. If you sold 80 per cent of yourself to Fairfax, you wouldn't expect your growth to stay strong for long. The difficulty was that Fairfax made a lot of money out of classifieds.'

There were discussions at Fairfax about taking over SEEK and folding in the Fairfax MyCareer site. A new Fairfax-owned SEEK could be controlled; it would not be allowed to operate with an overriding mission to kill print. But the plan went nowhere, just as it had for the three preceding years. During that time SEEK had gone up in value tenfold. But at Fairfax, SEEK was never perceived as enough of a threat to warrant Fairfax's chief executive calling in the investment banks to work on an acquisition.

And while SEEK was growing, most of the top executives at Fairfax were caught up in classic big company turf wars. It was print versus digital, executive versus executive, newspaper versus newspaper and, for a fair amount of time, print versus the chief executive. There were fiefdoms everywhere. One Fairfax editorial executive in particular clashed with Hilmer. Greg Hywood had been editor-in-chief of three newspapers: *The Australian Financial*

Review, The Sydney Morning Herald, and then *The Age.* By the late 1990s he had a foot in both the commercial and editorial camps after Fairfax introduced a joint publisher-editor-in-chief model. Hywood and Hilmer could not have been more different. They had argued over the Fairfax strategy of investing in CitySearch. Hywood wanted Hilmer to invest heavily in the company's existing online sites, to spend money integrating the classified advertising with the online newspapers. But Dews controlled the digital strategy and his focus was CitySearch. And he had Hilmer's unwavering support.

After the dotcom crash in 2000 and 2001 the Fairfax board had pulled its horns in, insisting the digital division had to break even and going cold on pouring more money into the online classifieds, even though Fairfax sites like Domain, MyCareer and Drive had been competing strongly against digital-only companies like SEEK, realestate.com.au and carsales.com.au. For Fairfax, pulling back was a catastrophic mistake. The directories company had proved disastrous too. In May 2002, Fairfax sold CitySearch to Telstra for $20 million, admitting defeat. Ironically, Hywood and Dews would leave Fairfax on the same day in April 2003: after a restructure, Hywood was fired; Dews was offered a job in strategy and declined. Suddenly both were gone. In the 2003 annual report, Fairfax revealed the combined losses of f2 since its inception in 1999 were $120 million.

In early 2003, Hilmer was focussed on striking a deal to buy Independent Newspapers Ltd, a New Zealand publishing company 45 per cent owned by News Corp. On 20 March, the Fairfax board approved proceeding with the acquisition for $1.1 billion.

By then, James Packer was courting SEEK, refusing to take no for an answer, driving the Bassats back and forth, visiting John

Alexander at the Nine Network, setting up meetings with his father, and planning to dissolve the joint venture with the floundering Monster as quickly as he could. His priorities and those at Fairfax could not have been more different.

The Fairfax board had been under the chairmanship of Dean Wills — a former chairman of Coca-Cola Amatil — since the end of 2002, when Brian Powers had returned to the United States. In June 2003, amidst almost daily reports in newspapers and magazines about the amazing advance of the pure-play internet companies eating into the Fairfax business, the Fairfax board set its forward strategy to include strengthening its key advertising franchises. To this end, the board papers identified both SEEK and Monster as targets, with a value of $100 million on SEEK's head. The rationale, stated in the board papers, was to hold Fairfax's 'leadership in total employment', and to deal more effectively with the 'online threat to print'.

But Fred Hilmer would not call on the Bassats to seduce them with honeyed words. There would be no CEO-to-CEO outreach to the Bassats, to show respect and admiration for their achievements. Instead Hilmer instructed Alan Revell to open talks. Revell in turn went to Longreach, a boutique investment bank he knew, to help explore the disposition of the Bassats to a friendly Fairfax tie-up. At Longreach, one of the partners knew Irvin Rockman personally and through him, Matthew Rockman. Another partner, Barry Davies — an adviser to Mambo founder Dare Jennings — had set up a meeting way back in June 2001 with the Bassats to introduce Nigel Dews.

Now, in June 2003, Davies pushed hard, working with Revell to get Fairfax swiftly onto the Bassats' radar. It was clear to an experienced investment banker, even if not to the chief executive of Fairfax, that there was no time to lose as SEEK ran like a buzz saw through the Fairfax classifieds. Davies could see it would be a disaster if Fairfax failed to buy at least half of SEEK as soon as possible.

At 5 p.m. on 3 July 2003, a Longreach team led by Davies, together with Alan Revell, met the Bassat brothers at SEEK's Melbourne headquarters, not realising the Bassats were sitting on a secret. They were already betrothed to James Packer and were four weeks away from the public announcement of Packer's stake in SEEK.

Trying to gauge the Bassats' mindset, Revell suggested they put aside price and just assume a large cheque was in the other room, and consider what SEEK would look like under Fairfax. It was clear the Bassats would not be happy. They thought Fairfax would simply buy their business to kill it.

Barry Davies would say later that he felt thwarted by the lack of engagement from the top levels of Fairfax about an investment in SEEK. He knew the reservations the Bassats and the Rockmans harboured about Fairfax as an owner were real. It was possible that even had Hilmer mobilised heavily and deployed serious resources and charm, Fairfax might not have got off the ground. The real frustration was that there seemed to be little appetite or focus within Fairfax for a SEEK investment.

On 23 July 2003, Barry Davies emailed Revell. 'Did you get to talk to Fred on this subject yet?' he asked. Revell phoned Davies to say that he was trying to get Hilmer to a meeting with Longreach. Two days later, news reports carried the amazing speculation that James Packer was circling SEEK. Davies urgently emailed Revell.

I think we need to expedite our session with you and Fred given the Packer story. We have some views about the respective strengths and weaknesses of Fairfax and PBL but one way or another SEEK is now in play. I've left a message on your cellphone and will keep trying. In the meantime we're updating our contact details for the SEEK shareholder register.

Revell had left his mobile phone at home and missed the calls. But he picked up Davies' email and wrote back to say he had left a message for Paul Bassatt, who had not returned the call. 'Will talk with Fred next week,' Revell concluded. Later that day, Davies gave it another try, creating a document for Fairfax to canvass the options. He code-named SEEK as Sixpack. He cautioned that if talks were underway with PBL, then SEEK was 'in play', a potential takeover target. His analysis was blunt and should have sent loud alarm bells through the top of Fairfax. No-one had a stronger economic and strategic vested interest in the number one position in online classifieds than Fairfax, Davies warned. He urged the company to table an offer for SEEK immediately. Any investment by PBL would put James Packer at the table with Fairfax not even in the room. Davies warned in a perspicacious aside that not acting immediately could be construed by SEEK as Fairfax having no serious interest, despite the recent overtures by Revell. Davies recommended making an offer that ensured SEEK would continue to grow; it would be an incentive to the young management team to stay.

A week later, on 30 July, Davies emailed Revell again. No-one from Longreach had yet been able to meet Hilmer to discuss

SEEK. 'Alan, how did you go on this subject in your session yesterday? We've done some work on the shareholder register and have sent a draft appointment letter to Rob as requested. I'll call you to discuss arrangements for getting in front of Fred ... I'd like to have Fred meet all three of us.'

The next day, 31 July, PBL announced that it had dissolved its joint venture with Monster.

On Friday 1 August, a frustrated Barry Davies was still trying for a meeting with Hilmer. But the Fairfax chief executive seemed unhurried. In an email to Alan Revell, Davies again proposed he bring Jonathan Fennel and Jeff White, the other two principals of Longreach, to any meeting. He pointed out that White had a relationship with Fairfax director David Gonski going back to 1991, while Jonathan Fennel had had a long association with SEEK through its chairman, Irvin Rockman.

Revell's emailed reply on Saturday 2 August indicated just how low a priority SEEK was at Fairfax, even as rumours of Packer's ambitions were building in the market: 'Barry, spoke to Fred last night. He is going to New Zealand for their results etc. next week and won't be back in the office until the middle of the following week ... Let's pick it up on his/my return (if not at the City to Surf!).'

Fred Hilmer finally received the bad news during a Fairfax off-site meeting to discuss Fairfax's future. It was the end of the day and everyone was at dinner when Hilmer broke off to huddle with another executive. Then he told the rest of the table what he had just heard: James Packer had bought into SEEK for over $30 million. Hilmer described the price as ridiculous. PBL's investment had put a valuation of $132 million on SEEK, way beyond what Fairfax believed it was worth. But it was a sobering moment; SEEK had a very good business plan, they all agreed, and they were smart guys. Now they had a shareholder with very deep pockets. But Fairfax did not believe SEEK had become a gorilla with a war chest big enough to kill them. Not for a minute. That would be outright fantasy.

Soon after the PBL–SEEK tie was announced on 4 August, Hilmer publicly stated that he had considered buying a stake in SEEK, but believed that at $33 million, PBL had paid too much. It was not a sum Fairfax would have paid.

At Longreach, the news of Packer's play prompted a last round of effort to put Fairfax back in the game, if only they could get Hilmer to agree to an aggressive retaliation. Jeff White picked up the phone to call David Gonski. Longreach still had not had a meeting with Hilmer. White recalled later: 'We were not getting any traction. I said to Gonski, "Can you get us a meeting and tell Fred he should talk to us?" But coming in over the top never makes a CEO happy.'

Finally, on 7 August 2003, three days after the PBL–SEEK deal was announced, Fred Hilmer met with Longreach. Hilmer told the investment bankers he did not trust the Bassat brothers; Davies and his partners urged Hilmer and his executives to hit back fast if they were to have a chance of upsetting the Packer deal.

After the meeting, Jeff White emailed Hilmer.

Fred, thanks for the opportunity to meet with you, Nick, Mike and David today. To reiterate, in order to move things forward, we believe that Fairfax should undertake the following actions: arrange a meeting with Gresham CEA for you to understand directly their views on a competing offer and the PBL deal; access as much legal documentation on SEEK and the deal as possible and review that to assess the current legal position (e.g. need for shareholder approvals etc.) and hence options for Fairfax. Longreach would be pleased to organise both of these matters, which we believe could be undertaken quite quickly. Once this was done, Fairfax would then be in a much better position to determine an appropriate strategy regarding SEEK and the PBL/SEEK deal.

Regards, Jeff White

And there it ended. Hilmer was not disposed to put a proposition to the Fairfax board to buy SEEK. 'It would be management's role to put a proposal to the board and it didn't come to that,' Hilmer recalled later.

Andrew Bassat observed later that Hilmer would have found it difficult even if he had pursued them. SEEK simply did not trust Fairfax as a part-owner and felt that any support they provided would have been short term at best. 'Fred gets sometimes unfairly criticised for not doing the deal James did. But he would not have been able to get that deal. And that's because even if they had gotten behind us for six months, after that, we knew they would not have been behind us.'

The deal Fairfax had needed to protect one of its three massive revenue categories was lost. Allegations of complacency, arrogance and lack of foresight would and could be thrown at the company in years to come. The Fairfax board had not only failed to buy a stake in SEEK, but they had also failed to mount a takeover to protect an exposed flank. In the end, Fairfax was outwitted — not just by SEEK's brilliant young founders, but also by a lifelong foe from the heart of the old media world. For James Packer, buying into SEEK for $33 million was not just a great deal that would eventually turn into a massive $440 million when he sold, but it gave him the opportunity to turn the screws on hated enemies.

Two days before the deal between PBL and SEEK was announced in August 2003, Alan Revell — who had not given up hope himself — had phoned Paul Bassat. He told Bassat that Fairfax was hearing more rumours that SEEK was set to do a deal with James Packer. What was going on?

'I said, "I can't comment,"' Bassat recalled later. 'Alan said "Oh, those guys have probably wined and dined you and taken you on the *Arctic P* [the Packer's massive converted ice-breaker] and out to Ellerston [the family compound in the countryside]." I replied, "Well, we must be a cheap date because they haven't done any of that."'

The disappointed Revell had something else to say to the SEEK founder. 'Don't do it,' he warned. 'It'll be a disaster.'

'A disaster for you or for us?' Bassat asked.

Eight years later, on Wednesday 15 June 2011, Paul Bassat received an email from his brother Andrew to tell him that the market capitalisation of SEEK had just closed higher than Fairfax for the first time ever.

By late 2012, only eighteen months later, SEEK's market capitalisation was well over $2 billion. SEEK was twice the size of Fairfax.

CHAPTER TWO

A PROPERTY TOO GOOD
TO REFUSE

Lachlan Murdoch was 29 years old in 2000 and the deputy
chief of operations at News Corporation, the global media giant
controlled by his family. He was head of the company's newspapers
worldwide, and had been chairman and chief executive of the
Australian division News Limited for three years. He was a resident
of Sydney, where he cut a glamorous figure with his American
accent, his Princeton education and his supermodel wife Sarah on
his arm. He was sought for his professional connections, but his
personal network had flourished mostly through friends in the arts.
Sometimes the two were intertwined.

One afternoon in October 2000, Murdoch picked up the
phone in his office at Holt Street, Surry Hills, a gritty urban area
where the huge News Limited building stood amid narrow streets
and tiny downbeat shops. John McGrath, a celebrity Sydney real

estate agent and one of the Eastern suburbs 'in crowd', was on the line. The two young men had met on the board of the Museum of Contemporary Art Young Patrons group and they moved in similar social circles. But McGrath was not calling about art or dinner. He was a director of a small internet start-up called realestate.com.au that was going broke as fast as it could burn through cash, even after floating on the stock market a year before. It was all hands on deck and the auditors had been called in. The directors knew the company was not far from collapsing. 'I can call Lachlan,' McGrath had told his fellow board members as they cast for a lifeline during a special board meeting to canvass what final options they might have.

At 6 p.m. on 19 October, McGrath and Lachlan Murdoch met for a drink after work. It was a preliminary meeting for McGrath to outline the scope of the problem. Realestate.com.au had been founded in 1995 and floated in December 1999 by Macquarie Bank, a big investor with nearly 30 per cent of the shares. On the eve of the float ninemsn, the joint venture between the Packer family-controlled PBL and Microsoft, had also taken a 10 per cent stake in exchange for a cash injection and promotion on the ninemsn website. But in the year since the float, realestate.com.au had been acting like a company ten times its size, splashing out on Italian furniture for the boardroom and layers of executives. In late August 2000, Macquarie had stumped up more money in the form of a $2 million loan facility, after questions from the Australian Stock Exchange about whether there was enough cash to last six months. The dotcom bubble that had made tech stocks hot had burst and Macquarie now baulked at more loans. Realestate.com.au needed a wealthy investor.

Murdoch was interested in what McGrath had to say. News was in a never-ending battle with Fairfax for classified advertising. A strongly branded property website was something that could make strategic sense for News Limited to support, even if it was far from clear that it could become any kind of dominant player. The downside was that News, like Fairfax, would be wary of anything with the potential to cut into valuable print advertising carried in the newspapers. And it was not a good time to be making rash investments in the new-wave tech sector. After the heady days when major companies threw money at online firms just to be in the game, the crash of 2000 had changed everything. The internet had transmogrified from a precocious *enfant terrible* to a problem child in a few short months. News Limited's digital arm News Interactive had launched several small News-branded sites, but an external stand-alone investment in a listed dotcom would be right outside the usual company format. But Murdoch was sufficiently intrigued, and he offered McGrath an opportunity to take it further.

The following day, McGrath arrived at Holt Street for a formal meeting with Murdoch. He had with him Greg Duncan, who ran the boutique mergers and acquisitions advisory firm Silverstream and had advised McGrath on the structure of his own company. Duncan also had an interest in classic cars and by the late 1990s he was a partner in Trivett, a prestige car business for the luxury market. McGrath had invited Duncan to come in as an adviser to the board of realestate.com.au to work on a restructure of the company before it exhausted its available cash. Duncan had put together a proposal for McGrath to put in front of the young media heir with very deep pockets.

They took the lift to level five, a new floor on top of the building where Lachlan Murdoch had designed and built his office. Pale furnishings and bookshelves gave way to an urban rooftop view. Behind the desk a door led to a panelled meeting room that Murdoch called the war room, with sliding doors to conceal the whiteboard and separate access for visitors from the corridor. Waiting in the war room for McGrath were Murdoch and his digital media executives Patrice McAree and Warren Bright, as well as the new business development officer for News Interactive, Simon Baker. As they sipped tea and coffee, McGrath and Duncan put their business case, outlining the history of realestate.com.au and its funding crisis. The company was on its knees: it needed a cash injection of more than $7 million to pay the bills and keep going.

The meeting ran for an hour. McGrath and Duncan could see that News was interested but there was no clear way ahead. Murdoch sat back, with his chair away from the table, letting his managers lead the talks on how to develop a strategy. Greg Duncan would recall later:

> Lachlan Murdoch listened for an hour, allowing everyone
> an opportunity to explore the options, and then he pulled
> his chair forward to the table and said, 'This is how I think
> we should do it.' He talked about the various mastheads that
> News had and what they might put in as cash and what they
> could put in as advertising and branding and how this could
> be the lifeblood we needed. We were asking for cash, but
> Lachlan laid out a strategy that would put in a lot less cash
> than we wanted, but with other elements in kind. The deal

was not concluded in that room, but his strategy became the foundation for the document.

Murdoch was not prepared to invest $7 million. His counter-proposal was a little over $2 million in cash plus a range of contra advertising and marketing options, branding the dotcom in News Limited newspapers and committing News sales teams to sell realestate.com.au services. The contra equated to $8.5 million; together with cash of $2.25 million the deal would add up to $10.75 million. And News would assume responsibility for a loan facility provided to realestate.com.au by Macquarie Bank.

John McGrath could feel blood flowing through his veins again. There was a lot of handshaking, although the deal would remain conditional until the details were ironed out and the deal approved by News Corporation executives in the United States and the board of realestate.com.au. As they left Holt Street with a lighter step, Duncan turned to McGrath and remarked with some astonishment, 'I think Lachlan gets it. He moved very fast.'

Lachlan Murdoch phoned David DeVoe, News Corp's chief financial officer in New York, where the News Corp treasury division was based. He met with a slightly sceptical response as he outlined the proposal. After the dotcom crash, no-one was putting money into loss-making, cash-burning websites. A deal like this, even a small one, with the potential to eat into News' own classified advertising in Australia, did not make everyone happy. But it was peanuts and DeVoe ticked it.

'We thought it was pretty interesting and we cut a pretty sharp deal,' Lachlan Murdoch commented later. 'They needed cash, they were burning through cash, but the real deal for them was the contra.'

Realestate.com.au, a slip of a web company with not much but its name to recommend it, had been rescued virtually minutes from its dying breath. And oddly enough, by an heir to one of the world's biggest and most powerful traditional media conglomerates. It was a David and Goliath deal and while it seemed the investment might only nip at the heels of the Murdoch family's bitter foes at Fairfax — where Lachlan and his father Rupert were looked down on — Lachlan Murdoch had made up his mind to back it.

By involving the News Limited suburban sales forces to help push realestate.com.au, and by branding it all over News Limited papers, Lachlan could see a chance to build a significant position in online property. It would be an uphill battle in a newspaper-based empire where print was king. And it would give News Limited's own classified advertising managers headaches. Like Fairfax managers, they would want to protect their print revenue at all costs. But the world already had shifted beneath their feet. Realestate.com.au was a public company with its own agenda — which was to chomp into traditional classified print advertising. Lachlan Murdoch had introduced the piranhas into his pond, and he would protect them.

'We wanted REA [as realestate.com.au later became known] to grow,' Murdoch said later. 'I said to our people, "we're not going to tell REA to back off. You have to compete with them." If REA didn't eat our lunch, then someone else would. It wasn't that tough to hold the line on a sometimes unpopular directive because I was the boss. REA had to be allowed to be its own business. If we had tried to force it (to be subservient to the print business), that would have just opened the opportunity for other online-only players.'

Realestate.com.au had begun as so many internet companies did, sprouting from nothing, started in a garage by a couple of computer nerds. In 1995, just four years before the company was floated, Martin Howell and Karl Sabljak were working at the Royal Melbourne Institute of Technology (RMIT). Both were computer systems administrators. Howell looked after RMIT's big internal computer system and Sabljak looked after the PC Windows side of things. One day, Sabljak spotted a student surfing the web on a computer displaying what looked remarkably like a magazine. It was the *Playboy* website. If *Playboy* was now online, then everything could go online. Howell was transfixed by a different website — he had found one for ordering flowers. That got things going for him. And with that, the idea for an online company was born. If you were into computers you could see the future. You might not know just what you wanted to do, but you had to be part of it. The Mosaic web browser, created at the US National Center for Supercomputing Applications in 1992, was the game-changer, making the web easy to use for all, able to run on home PCs and crammed with graphics and easy to follow links. After Mosaic, anyone could surf the web. Martin Howell used it to browse every site he could find.

Howell and Sabljak set up a rudimentary office in the garage of Sabljak's home in the outer Melbourne suburb of Doncaster East on the edge of the old orchard district of Templestowe, which by then was a mixed suburb of 1960s brick veneer houses and nouveau-colonnaded mansions spilling around a massive cemetery. They called their first company Netwide Solutions, filled the garage with phone lines and began providing internet connections and computer services to fledgling clients. They built websites and sold computers; it was a little bit of everything. Some of it they did for nothing. As they tried to sign clients they struck the same question put to new businesses everywhere: 'What have you done before?'

But Howell and Sabljak had another idea as well. They had developed a relationship with Property Seeker, a software provider for real estate agents, which was going broke. They merged, and in the process acquired a plethora of agents and properties for a web portal. They acquired two new business partners in the merger: Gerrard Giummarra and Joel Tipping. They had something else too: a great name. Howell and Sabljak had scanned the Yellow Pages phone directory searching for inspiration, and then flicked open *The Age* newspaper. They stared at each other. Half of the newspaper was real estate advertising. They had raced to find out if realestate.com.au was available as a URL. They registered it at 10 a.m. on Tuesday 8 August 1995.

For the next few years Sabljak and Howell ran the business from the garage, often slogging away until 2 a.m. after working all day at RMIT. Howell was the technical guy with experience with Unix and other computer operating systems; Sabljak looked after sales and graphics and the creative side as well as becoming a one-man help desk. His wife Carmel did the accounting and administration, and his younger brother Steve helped when he could get out of his studies. Eventually Steve sold his interest in the company to his brother and Howell.

In March 1999, Fairfax launched the website drive.com. au for cars, then in October 1999, it launched domain.com.

au for property. Howell and Sabljak scanned domain.com.au. Realestate.com.au already had a big following. Was it possible this huge newspaper company could squash them? Howell was proud of the realestate.com.au site he had built. He decided domain.com.au had poor technology, it was fiddly and confusing to use, and its images were too small. Howell had a guiding rule for realestate.com.au: users should get to a property in no more than three clicks. He spent vast amounts of time 'optimising' to make the site as fast as possible. Realestate.com.au put up large images, and they could tell from the hits that customers loved it. It was just a better user experience. Howell and his business partners had a great URL and they had a great site — if they could just afford the costs of keeping it all going.

They were madly trying to grow the number of properties they had online. Where Fairfax and News Limited were constrained in dropping the price of online ads on their company websites in order to avoid cannibalising print, pure-plays like realestate.com.au and the jobs website SEEK, set up by the Bassats, could set prices where they wanted, and as low as they wanted.

Realestate.com.au was trying to grab market share by allowing property agents to put up as many ads as they liked for a fixed fee. This was the core of the dotcom philosophy: to give things away almost for free in pursuit of market share to build the number one brand name. Worrying about losses and charging for profit would come later — if they survived.

By early 1999, realestate.com.au was actively touting for new business, anything to get more eyeballs on their site. In May, it arrived at the doors of Macquarie Bank, one of the most powerful institutions on the Australian corporate scene, both feared and respected for its sky-rocketing share price and its impossible-to-understand pyrotechnics with leveraged finance.

Andrew Barnes was the executive director of banking services, where real estate formed the biggest single client division. When two salesmen from realestate.com.au made an appointment to see him, Barnes was more than happy to take the meeting. He was sitting on the top of a tree of real estate agents who generated a huge stream of income for the bank and he was interested in anything in that space. When the two salesmen arrived they asked Barnes the same simple question they put to anyone: would Macquarie like to advertise on their website?

Barnes looked at the site and listened to their pitch. Then he changed the course of history for online property in Australia with a quite different suggestion. 'I won't advertise,' he said. 'But I'd like to buy the company.' Barnes was no tech head, but he liked the realestate.com.au URL. His business was all about how to connect with customers; as far as Barnes was concerned, the internet was clunky, but this seemed far better than walking up and down the street looking at property on a hot day. He could see in his mind a virtual High Street, an online shop window. Barnes decided there was more to the little site than met the eye and he opened negotiations for Macquarie to buy a controlling stake of 51 per cent for just under $1 million on 7 June 1999. The price would never be so cheap again. But it was only the start.

'The theory I had was that this was like an arms race,' Barnes recalled later. 'Because it was all about traffic. I decided I had to be more involved. We had the name but how could we win the race with me running the banking division? We decided almost instantaneously to go to float, to raise cash, to try to generate a lot of newspaper headlines and hope that that would drive eyeballs.'

No sooner was the news out than Barnes' predictions proved right. Newspaper headlines proliferated about the coming float of a tiny dotcom by a star bank, and traffic to the site increased 45 per cent. Barnes paid to have the name of the website plastered on the sides of buses. He kept a close eye on Fairfax with its domain site. Only one could win, and he was convinced the media giants would remain hampered by their need to protect existing print classified revenue streams. Rupert Murdoch was rumoured to believe the internet could destroy his business. Fairfax was reluctant to take domain.com.au off the leash. Nobody wanted to damage what they had.

Macquarie, however, could afford to treat realestate.com.au exactly like the dotcom start-up it was. Barnes relinquished his responsibilities at Macquarie to work on the float. He decided he needed some strong real estate brand names to bring added credibility and he rang John McGrath, a client of Macquarie's real estate business, who had established his own agency 11 years before. McGrath, a slim, intense workaholic, had a highly respected fast-growing business. Recruiting him would send a strong signal. Barnes wanted to show this was not just a Macquarie company, but had the imprimatur of the industry it planned to flood. He told McGrath under a veil of secrecy that Macquarie had 'an internet thing', and asked him to become a director. He outlined a business case, telling him about the great URL, the planned float and the expectation of fast growth.

McGrath, who had his own website underway, told Barnes he would only be interested in exchange for equity in the business.

Barnes agreed and McGrath joined the board on 15 September 1999. Next Barnes called on Steve Vamos, the chief executive of the Packers' ninemsn. Vamos too, said, 'We're in.'

What followed was a frantic race to get the float started. The offer opened on 25 October 1999 and closed on 5 November. By a remarkable coincidence, Fairfax's domain.com.au went live with its first sale listing uploaded on 16 October 1999 and its first rental listing on 29 October. This was four years behind the launch of realestate.com.au. Domain had been a print product — a lifestyle liftout — since 1996. Fairfax had held onto its classifieds as a single entity in print for way too long. The sharp little competitor realestate.com.au already had a beachhead in the new world.

With Andrew Barnes as chairman, and 15 million shares issued at 50 cents, realestate.com.au was admitted to the Australian Stock Exchange on Monday 29 November 1999. They began trading on 1 December 1999. The shares soon ran up to $1.50, although they would come down just as sharply when public nervousness over the dotcoms overwhelmed the human desire for a quick profit out of nothing. On listing, Macquarie was the biggest shareholder with 29.7 per cent, followed by the founders Karl Sabljak and Martin Howell and their business partners with 6.63 per cent each. John McGrath had 4.79 per cent. The day after the float, they announced to the market that the Packers' ninemsn was on board too, with 10 per cent equity in exchange for a distribution deal and a fee of $200,000 in the first year and $400,000 in the second year. Now they had real estate agents, the best URL address and ninemsn to drive the traffic.

But if the float was intended to grow the company aggressively, it soon became evident that online businesses needed far more than good intentions. Six months later Andrew Barnes left Macquarie, signalling the end of his time with realestate.com.au as well. Macquarie's chief executive Allan Moss, a man with guru-like status in the investment community, approached John Niland to become an independent chairman of realestate.com.au. Niland, the vice chancellor and president of the University of New South Wales, was appointed in May 2000. Earlier that month realestate.com.au had announced a linkup with internet and media content supplier Horan Wall and Walker to provide editorial copy and online tools like financial calculators for consumers logging onto the site. Deals like this had helped the company build its online offering, but it had spent money on crazy ventures too, like sponsoring a tennis tournament. Niland discovered that realestate.com.au was going through cash like a fire in a forest.

Niland decided there were two serious possibilities for a new partner willing to put in more cash. He turned his mind to the big newspaper players, Fairfax and News Limited. Perhaps one of these giants might want to invest in the future, in an online advertising pure-play. At least he hoped so.

On 22 June 2000, Niland arrived at the Fairfax headquarters at 201 Sussex Street in Darling Harbour. The building was an odd site for a newspaper company that had once owned its own fortress-like premises on Broadway, complete with vast printing presses that roared late into the night as trucks idled outside, waiting to be loaded, and journalists stumbled out after late shifts. But the old building was long gone. Now, newspaper content was transmitted digitally to remote printing plants. The Sydney journalists and Fairfax management had moved to Sussex Street, taking the top nine floors of an office tower that looked as though it was intended for accountants and managers. Fairfax's own management, and chief executive Fred Hilmer, were quartered on Level 19, in a suite of offices, boardrooms and dining rooms strung along curved hallways, with spectacular views of Darling Harbour and the Imax theatre on one side and the Sydney Aquarium and cruise-ship docks on the other.

Niland had an appointment with Nigel Dews, head of Fairfax's digital arm f2, in the Fairfax boardroom. It was the first of a number of conversations, but Niland, who could hear the clock ticking back in his own boardroom, found that Fairfax was preoccupied with a different countdown: to the Sydney Olympics. His attempts to engage Fairfax fell to nothing. Everything went into abeyance in the months that followed and Niland was never invited to a discussion with Hilmer. On 10 October 2000, realestate.com.au announced to the ASX that discussions on a joint venture with Fairfax's domain.com.au had been abandoned.

Niland recalled later: 'My general sense is that Fairfax could have had it. They certainly were offered the first bite of the cherry. I have a very clear recollection of again trying to get an appointment with Fairfax at the time of the Sydney Olympics [in the second half of September 2000]. But I didn't sense any significant interest from Fairfax at all.'

Niland was also conducting talks with the wealthy Queensland property data firm RP Data. Realestate.com.au would eventually acquire the RP Data site property.com.au, and establish contracts covering years of data exchange between the two firms.

As the end of 2000 loomed, there was growing desperation in the realestate.com.au boardroom. Niland found himself waking in the night worrying about how to pay long service leave to employees. 'We were almost on the beach,' he said.

With Fairfax not interested, the directors turned anxious hopes to the prospect of getting News Limited on the hook. Was there any way that might get off the ground? Niland had met with the head of News Interactive, Patrice McAree, in June, but what they needed now was a turbo-charged introduction to the very top of the company. And they needed it straight away. 'I can call Lachlan,' John McGrath said. Niland, who had called in the board on 17 October 2000 to warn they were nearing insolvency, told him there was no time to waste.

Going to Lachlan Murdoch was a shot in the dark, but on the other hand, if there was anyone at News Limited who could save them, it was Murdoch. He was the ultimate boss. With his support a deal could get through. Without it, there was no point in even talking.

Murdoch's interest was piqued and he understood the urgency. He invited McGrath to a meeting and he gave some thought to how he could make it work. News Limited's chief financial officer Peter Macourt later recalled: 'I was not in the subsequent meeting but I remember Lachlan coming into my office beforehand and talking about what he wanted and how he might achieve it, and how to structure it by putting in marketing and branding as part of the offer.'

The deal was done and it was done quickly. On 30 November 2000, News Limited announced it had invested cash of $2.25 million in realestate.com.au, plus advertising, marketing and other contra for a total investment worth $10.75 million. News Limited would take a 44.2 per cent stake with an option to acquire a further 10 million shares over the next five years and it would have two directors on the board once the deal was cemented. Macquarie Bank would remain a shareholder but News would acquire the outstanding amount of Macquarie's loan facilities. Macquarie had lost faith in a company that had fallen over to trade between 15 and 20 cents.

On the same day the News deal was announced, Niland addressed the realestate.com.au annual general meeting. It was 12 months since listing. They had ventured into a business not tried before in Australia, Niland said, and they had had few reference points. Nevertheless user traffic was up fourfold and they had grabbed 25 per cent of agents in the market. This had to be set against the struggle to reduce cash burn. By cutting the deal with News, the future was more assured. Niland would say later: 'By the time News invested it was no more than weeks from going under. We had already been getting legal advice for some time on the elements that constitute an insolvency calculation.'

After the issue of shares to News Limited, the 10.7 per cent stake held by the PBL–Microsoft joint venture ninemsn was diluted, reducing its holding to 4.85 per cent. But it was a stake that had cost ninemsn only $600,000 in cash. The rest was a distribution deal. And this was a minnow among the many plays ninemsn was juggling. Who knew whether realestate.com.au would ever be *the one*? The internet space was crammed with online advertising from the tiddlers through to the aggressive newcomers like SEEK, and the internal company sites controlled by the giants, Telstra, Fairfax, News and PBL.

There was irritation in various commercial offices at News Limited after the deal was done. They were getting into bed with an internet pure-play, and one they had to carry. It was provocative for tabloid papers in the stable, like *The Courier-Mail* in Queensland and *The Adelaide Advertiser* in South Australia. They were forced to support a business dedicated to taking away their revenue and harming the papers. Realestate.com.au was listed and it had its own management structure, something that was equally confronting. Lachlan Murdoch ensured it stayed that way. It could not be dampened or slowed by News' other businesses.

Notwithstanding the hoopla surrounding News Limited's investment, realestate.com.au was still in dire straits. By the time News had closed the deal, the company had consumed a chief executive with the departure of Kevin Jamieson at the end of October 2000. His replacement Nigel Purves was gone too in less than a year. The $2.25 million in cash invested by News was soon disappearing as well. Just four weeks after News Limited directors joined the board, the half yearly report showed sales of $1.6 million and a net loss of $2.6 million.

But there were some encouraging moments that suggested the site had a foothold. In April 2001, the Ray White Group inked an agreement to allow Ray White agencies to link directly to realestate.com.au. It was a small step but it presaged what would come later with a massive investment in the website by this signature agency. The first green shoots broke the surface in May 2001 when Red Sheriff, a company which audited website traffic statistics, revealed realestate.com.au had shot past Fairfax's domain.com.au with 95,000 more visitors to its site. Horrifyingly for Fairfax, domain.com.au had fallen to second place. It was a moment in time when the new passed the old and the advertising world that had been comprehensively dominated by Fairfax showed its first cracks.

In August 2001, the board of realestate.com.au appointed Simon Baker as chief executive. Baker had been at News Limited for just two weeks when John McGrath first called on Lachlan Murdoch for help. He was an aggressive and talented former McKinsey & Co project manager, and he became an alternate director for News on the realestate.com.au board, then chief operating officer, and finally chief executive. He set about turning the company around.

A year after Baker's appointment, in August 2002, he announced that the number of agents subscribing to realestate.com. au had jumped from 1250 to over 2000, and that revenue for the year ending June 2002 had shot up 50 per cent to $5.7 million. The business was operationally cash positive at last. And there was more good news. Macquarie had sold a 15.8 per cent stake in realestate.com.au to the Ray White Group, bringing more 'name' kudos in a highly competitive and backbiting industry.

In June 2003, John Niland was invited to join the Macquarie board. He resigned as chairman of realestate.com.au and was replaced by John McGrath.

Niland's last address as chairman in November 2002 showed how far the fledgling dotcom had already travelled. He reported the company was the clear leader in the market, with its long-term viability secured. The share price, which had gone as low as five cents in 2001, was up by 68 per cent on the year to 18.5 cents. Visits to the site had increased 110 per cent to 2.1 million a month. Niland identified the key elements of the transformation: the consistent branding in over 90 News Limited suburban newspapers, the continued strong performance of the News Interactive network in driving traffic to realestate.com.au, and a

new wider distribution deal on the ninemsn site. The mess that
Lachlan Murdoch had taken a chance on now had both media and
real estate giants as major shareholders. It was a different company
in a different league.

At Fairfax, the board had responded to the dotcom crash by
warning Hilmer that the digital businesses had to break even. The
notion of forging ahead with a loss-leader was not acceptable. The
company had already sold its faltering CitySearch to Telstra for
$20 million. But the conservative stance clearly wasn't paying off:
domain.com.au had not been able to beat realestate.com.au.

Martin Howell, the co-founder of realestate.com.au, remained
surprised that Fairfax had failed to recognise the power of the site
in its earliest days. He could never fathom why Fairfax did not buy
it outright. 'Before we listed [in 1999] I was amazed that we didn't
get any offers from Fairfax to buy us. It was because of the fear of
cannibalisation and thinking the newspapers would be around for
100 years. I think they shot themselves in the foot. They did the
same with the online jobs and missed SEEK.'

By 2005, realestate.com.au was the number one site in its field. It
had purchased the number three site, property.com.au, turning the
field into a two-horse race against Fairfax's domain.com.au. The
business had begun to grow internationally with Baker pushing
aggressively.

But it would not be long before it was in a battle of a
different order altogether — a battle with its host, News Limited.
Realestate.com.au had simply become too attractive. News decided
to mount a takeover, seeking control and the highest economic

interest possible. It had no plans to take the company private, but it wanted to lay claim to the revenue.

In 2005, Lachlan Murdoch phoned James Packer to tell him that News Limited planned to launch a takeover bid for the portion of realestate.com.au that it didn't already own. Would Packer agree to sell him ninemsn's stake?

The pair had remained close through all the rugged days of 2001 after One.Tel crashed, exposing both to scarifying public humiliation. Packer had been rebuilding his life and he already had 25 per cent of his own favourite pure-play — the internet jobs site, SEEK.

He agreed to sell. Packer remained deeply grateful for the way the Murdochs had treated him after One.Tel. And he had a view that realestate.com.au was not making a lot of money. He would be forced to admit later that he had been wrong on the company's prospects. 'With the benefit of hindsight, Lachlan got the better of me on that one,' he conceded.

Ninemsn agreed to sell 3 per cent of its 4.85 per cent stake in realestate.com.au to News immediately. The balance of its holding, a further 1.85 per cent, would later be sold into the bid. On 1 August 2005, News Limited announced a takeover bid at $2.00 a share and revealed it had secured 3 per cent of the company that day from ninemsn.

Ten days later, a board sub-committee comprising directors John McGrath and Sam White from the Ray White Group hit back, declaring the offer hostile and uninvited. They recommended shareholders not accept and said they would refuse to sell their own shares. White's own view was that if the bid did not have the number 4 in front of it, there wasn't a deal.

Sam White was born and bred in the property business. He had watched closely how News Limited, a company with a reputation for tight control, had handled its relationship with realestate.com.au. He had been surprised to find that News looked for synergies but had not tried to break them. By contrast, he was convinced that Fairfax had never really given domain.com.au a mandate to grow into a major online business. The company was looking for a way to prop up and subsidise print, rather than letting domain.com.au be its own animal. News Limited had allowed realestate.com.au to stay outside the company and to develop its own personality, although not without internal tensions at News. White believed that Lachlan Murdoch's original strategy to brand realestate.com.au throughout News' suburban newspapers while keeping it outside as an aggressive, independent company, underpinned the success that came later. 'That was a critical move for realestate.com.au. That was probably the key move. The benefit over time was that it gave us the impetus of News without the control. So News couldn't stuff it up. Simon Baker, the CEO, fought very hard for that independence from print and Lachie backed him up.'

With News now the aggressor in a takeover, McGrath, as chairman of realestate.com.au, was not prepared to hand the company over cheaply. He called in an old friend and adviser to help. Warren Lee and John McGrath had met when Lee was a young lawyer straight out of university and working for Freehills in the late 1980s. Back then, McGrath was dating a librarian at the law firm and they had met socially. They knew each other too from their membership of the Young Presidents' Association. Later, Lee had been appointed a managing director of News Interactive, helping to set up News Limited's internal online advertising sites. Now he was an executive director at advisory firm Grant Samuel.

Lee advised the board that the News bid of $2.00 was way too low. It was hardly a big premium for delivering control to News of an online success that had hit its stride. The board recommended shareholders reject it, expecting News to come back with a higher offer, which it did, pitched at $2.50.

Lee advised McGrath to explore other options. News had already pounced on the Packer stake. Why shouldn't McGrath approach Fairfax to see if the big News Limited foe wanted to get in and play rough? Why not see if they could push the price up with a bit of competition? Lee contacted Ron Walker, the new chairman of Fairfax and the front man for any corporate swashbuckling at the media giant. Chief executive Fred Hilmer was a lame duck, having announced his resignation in May 2004; he would finally leave Fairfax in November 2005. The new chief executive David Kirk was about to start.

Walker, who loved a deal, found his interest piqued. He had been on the board of Fairfax since 2003 and chairman for a month. He flew to Sydney to meet McGrath and Lee in the Fairfax boardroom at Darling Harbour. Lee put it to him that Fairfax might like to buy into the number one real estate site that had left Fairfax's domain.com.au well behind. He was surprised by Walker's response. The chairman wanted to know what it would cost to buy out all shareholders, including News.

Lee was convinced that if News had pitched its takeover at $2.75 or $3.00 it might own all of realestate.com.au by now and he conveyed this to Walker. Lee could not have made it clearer: Walker would need to pay. Walker, after digesting this, said he would make some calls and left the room. Lee looked at McGrath and said in amazement, 'I think Fairfax is about to buy half. It'll be a first.'

But he had spoken too soon. When Walker returned he told them it would all be too hard. It would be a tough battle and News was unlikely to sell. Fairfax might be able to reach somewhere between 25 and 50 per cent, but Walker had no interest in holding a minority stake. Already Fairfax owned 11.6 per cent of the burgeoning auto site carsales.com, which it had acquired at the start of 2005. Now, six months later, Fairfax was finding it a frustrating experience. Unable to buy more shares in carsales.com, the Fairfax board was irritated with a stake in a fleet-of-foot online player it could not control. Realestate.com.au could end up being another one of these, and who could say if it would ever grow much further anyway.

Lee decided to sound out the larger shareholders like the Ray White Group and RP Data, trying to assess how big a stake Fairfax might get. Lee wanted to get an auction going, but he knew he also needed to give Walker some certainty that he would not wade in and then end up stuck with 8 per cent at the mercy of News. Everybody wanted a piece of this action. Realeastate.com.au had done so well it had suitors everywhere. As John McGrath was fond of saying, 'If you're not number one on the web then you're nowhere.'

Lee soon had bad news. He could not persuade enough shareholders to nail their colours to the mast, to assure Walker that if Fairfax put down at least $2.75 it might get to 25 per cent. Fairfax was not willing to start a fight with News that might run to $3.00 a share or more. Fairfax walked away.

Realestate.com.au recommended that shareholders reject News Limited's $2.50 offer and the bid eventually lapsed. But News had moved into a position of control anyway. With the shares sold into the takeover by smaller shareholders and the 4.85 per cent from ninemsn, sold by James Packer to Lachlan Murdoch under a mate's agreement, News Limited had reached 54.91 per cent. By 13 December 2005 it was up to 58.57 per cent after exercising the original options deal made in 2000 when News first bought in.

By 2008, after a series of rights issues, News Limited owned 60.7 per cent. The company's market capitalisation was over $500 million. On 1 December 2008, realestate.com.au changed its name to REA Group. The old days in the Doncaster garage were now just part of the legend.

Four years later, in November 2012, REA was worth an astounding $18 a share with a market capitalisation of $2.4 billion. News still had 60.7 per cent of the company, a stake worth $1.44 billion, listed in the News Corporation investments column along with BSkyB.

The stellar growth continued. Three months later in February 2013, REA was an arrow on a chart with a market capitalisation of $3.4 billion. Lachlan Murdoch's original investment of $2.25 million and $8 million in contra deals had turned into a brontosaurus worth $2 billion to News Corp. It was the deal of the decade in Australia's online space.

In 2000 Fairfax had had the chance to buy into what would eventually become the REA Group, but had turned up its nose at bailing out the fledgling company realestate.com.au when John Niland arrived in the Fairfax boardroom with a begging bowl that might take 20 cents a share to fill. By early 2013, REA was more than three times the size of Fairfax, with a share price of more than $26.00.

Twice Fairfax had missed out on taking control of some of the greatest online advertising companies in Australian history. They had missed SEEK and they had missed realestate.com.au. James Packer had bought into one and Lachlan Murdoch the other. Fairfax was standing on the sidelines.

CHAPTER THREE

DRIVE BABY DRIVE

Wal Pisciotta liked to ride his favourite horse, Carbon Color, known as CC, on the trails round his farm at Emerald in the Dandenong Ranges outside Melbourne. She was a Tennessee Walking Horse, a breed popular with long-ago plantation owners who spent long days in the saddle in the American South. Pisciotta had been importing and breeding Tennessee Walkers since 1998 and could expound happily on their attributes — a calm, sensible nature and an unusual 'running walk', with one hoof always on the ground.

Sometimes he would ride with a neighbour and they would talk about horses and business. Pisciotta ran a company that had started out selling computer systems to car dealers to manage their spare parts. In 1996 they had branched out audaciously, to lure classified advertising for the car market away from metropolitan newspapers and put it online. It might have seemed like a fool's errand given the grip the powerful media companies had on advertising. Both News Limited and Fairfax newspapers had spawned car sections that carried thousands of auto ads for new and used cars every Saturday. The Fairfax papers, *The Age* and *The Sydney Morning Herald*, were so physically huge on the weekends — stuffed with classifieds — that they had the capacity to damage a front door if thrown hard enough by the paperboy. The classifieds were not known as Rivers of Gold for nothing. This was the revenue that paid for the journalism, and Fairfax seemed impregnable. But Pisciotta's company had found a great name for a website and they had all the optimistic brio of the outsider and nothing to lose. They called it carsales.com.au.

Laughing about his shares in the company, Pisciotta would say to his riding partner: 'You know, one day these things could be worth a lot of money. Ten years from now, nobody will be reading newspapers.'

American-born Pisciotta was a dapper and opinionated self-starter with a sense of humour and the personal conviction that came from getting ahead the hard way. In the 1960s, straight from high school in St Louis, he had gone to California with a band to play saxophone and perform rock'n'roll and blues covers. It was an exciting experience but he could see that you had to be lucky to break into the big time. At the end of the summer Pisciotta decided to quit. He returned home to St Louis.

'I told the guys, "In music you have to be one in a million to make it. But in business, you have to be one in a hundred. And I think I can be one in a hundred."'

He enrolled in college, taking classes only at night, and got a job crating refrigerators by day. He switched jobs several times. At the end of his second year of study, he got a new job on the help desk of a US company that produced daily reports and auto spare parts data. It was called CARS, an acronym for Computerised Automated Reporting Service. By the time he graduated in 1973 with a Bachelor of Business from the University of Alabama, Pisciotta had spent four years at university, and four years full-time in the workforce — simultaneously. He wore a big gold college ring with a diamond and an engraved image of pencils, a graph and a ledger.

When CARS licensed its software to an Australian computer business, Pisciotta was offered a job selling and installing the system. He arrived in Australia in 1974 and by 1980 he was the chief executive. It was a period of tremendous competition. In 1983, Reynolds and Reynolds, a big American competitor to CARS, arrived in Australia too. These two multinational companies had computerised car dealers across the world, fighting street-by-street for customers. In Australia it was soon clear there was not enough turf to go around. By 1985, Reynolds (now known as Reynolds & Reynolds) had taken over the Australian division of CARS Pty Ltd, with the 35-year-old Pisciotta appointed CEO. In 1992, the US parent company sold most of its Australian stake in a management buy-out. Pisciotta emerged with 37 per cent, Reynolds retained 14 per cent, and seven other Australian executives split the rest.

One day in August 1997, Greg Roebuck raced into Pisciotta's Mount Waverley office in the outer Melbourne suburbs, which was decked out with horseracing photos and a large mirror etched with an early Mercedes Benz racing car. Roebuck was a computer specialist and the Reynolds business development manager. He was clutching Drive, the lift-out auto section of the Fairfax newspaper *The Age*. The front page depicted a car grille with the words 'www.carsales.com.au' superimposed on the grille. The accompanying feature story was about classified advertising moving online — 'An end to haggling as we know it?' Roebuck had been shown it during a meeting with a Fairfax middle manager, who had explained to him in a condescending way that the data Reynolds collected was worth a desultory few cents per car. But Roebuck's attention was focussed on something else altogether. The light bulb had switched on and he rushed to see Pisciotta.

'That URL is available. Do you think we should buy it?'

'Absolutely,' Pisciotta replied. 'It's a free kick. And it'll be a good investment until we come up with something better.'

It cost them $200 to register carsales.com.au at lunchtime on 12 August 1997.

Roebuck had joined the company as a 23-year-old in 1983. He was a computer programmer, a technical expert with a spiky haircut, an easy grin and a sharp and focussed brain. He understood the intricacies of the car trade and all of its products. He would build a system that put Reynolds at the head of the pack, linking dealers' computers into a network to trade spare parts amongst themselves. At first they could do a search in one minute. Then Roebuck got it down to two seconds; then to one second; finally to less than a second.

The next step was to use the technology to allow dealers to trade used cars among themselves. But the product failed when the dealers resisted. Reynolds had all the data, but dealers wanted to do things the old way, buying through car wholesalers they knew well.

By 1996, the internet craze had seized everyone and Roebuck had pressed Pisciotta to put the used car data they had onto the web. Pisciotta was attracted to the idea. He recalled later:

> We quickly realised we were doing all this work for the dealers and getting a few thousand dollars a month for computerising them. But the same dealers were spending $100,000 a month for Fairfax to run display advertising in *The Age* and *The Sydney Morning Herald* — and News Limited was doing the same in *The Daily Telegraph*. Fairfax had a lock on it, and Rupert [Murdoch] kept trying to crack it. But it was suddenly very clear to us that in ten years' time the internet could take all this advertising because the information was so rich.

In 1996 they set up a website, carz.com.au, and started putting classified advertising for cars online for free. Roebuck had tried to register cars.com.au, but he was stymied by a review underway of the registration of generic names. In the end he settled for carz as the next best thing. At first, they didn't charge. Like seek.com.au in recruitment and realestate.com.au in property, they just wanted to turn up the volume, to get themselves noticed and have something to fill the site. They operated along the same lines as other hungry classified start-ups — typing in data and ads themselves, often after car dealers faxed the material across. They polished and re-polished the listings, adding more and more car specifications. Then they added photos.

In 1997, Pisciotta and Roebuck turned carz.com.au into carsales.com.au, when Fairfax foolishly failed to register the name itself. Pisciotta and Roebuck now had the best name and they had joined a pioneer movement taking on the giants. Realestate.com.au, which would surge to number one in online property, had been founded in 1995. SEEK, the brainchild of the Bassats that eventually mowed Fairfax down in online recruitment, sprang to life in 1998. Fairfax was oblivious to the dynamism of these reedy start-ups. (It would issue an announcement to the Australian Stock Exchange about the launch of its own car website, drive.com.au, in March 1999.)

In mid-1998, Greg Roebuck struck a deal with Steve Vamos, the chief executive of ninemsn — the joint venture between PBL and Microsoft. Ninemsn had its own auto site, carpoint.com.au, which was a subsidiary of Microsoft in the US. Under the deal between Roebuck and Vamos, carsales would provide carpoint with listings for used cars and the search engine to find them. In return, carsales gained exposure to the largest online audience in Australia. It would be a relationship with a short life span, but wider prospects.

Pisciotta had started buying space on roadside billboards — anything to push the carsales brand name and get a buzz going. But he wanted to push it further still, into the land of the enemy. He booked newspaper advertisements, large display ads, in papers owned by News Limited, Fairfax and West Australian Newspapers (WAN). But he had not banked on the newspapers suddenly waking up to the interloper in their midst and shoving back.

Pisciotta and Roebuck were attending a convention on the Gold Coast run by the peak body for the car industry, the Australian Automobile Dealers Association, when they heard that both Fairfax and News Limited had knocked back the ads within hours of each other. Roebuck called the advertising agency, to be told that all hell had broken loose. Pisciotta recalled later:

> Within the same two to three hour period, each
> newspaper, from both Fairfax and News Limited and
> in every capital city, rang our ad agency and cancelled
> the running of the ads submitted previously. They had
> had them for a couple of days before they all cancelled,
> virtually simultaneously. Only WAN ran the ad. Actually,
> we realised later we were lucky they caught it and
> cancelled as it saved us wasting money.

But Pisciotta and Roebuck were fuming. They decided to use the incident to attract attention. They called their state manager in Brisbane and before long two large white cardboard signs were delivered, fresh from a sign-writer. Each placard featured identical words in big blue type: 'STOP & SEE The Internet Site That News Ltd and Fairfax Have Refused to Advertise!!!'

They used tape to join the placards back to back. They hung the sign from the ceiling above their booth at the convention and let it twirl in the breeze from the air conditioning. It was not long before members of the organising committee arrived. Pisciotta recalled: 'They said, "You have to take that sign down. Otherwise they'll take legal action against you."'

They refused. Finally, after several hours, they relented and took it down. They blacked out the words 'News' and 'Fairfax' and strung it up again.

They had made their point. But if the newspaper companies thought they had washed their hands of the problem, they had only created the impetus for a new stunt from carsales and its attention-seeking owners. Pisciotta, a born stirrer, had more antics up his sleeve. His next target was television and he decided to do something with real impact. He contacted their ad agency to create a TV spot and booked it to run during the 1999 AFL Grand Final, the biggest sporting event on the calendar. It was an idea borrowed from the US Super Bowl, an event rich with promotional opportunities. For the sum of $100,000, carsales booked two thirty-second ads to run on the Seven Network during the game. That night Pisciotta attended a birthday party where he struck up a conversation with someone who had watched the match on TV. He recalled later: 'I met an electrician at the party and he said to me, "I went on that site carsales today. I figured they must be serious if they were advertising in the Grand Final."'

Traffic to carsales.com.au spiked in the days afterwards. But there were other consequences too. A manager at ninemsn — where ninemsn's carpoint website was powered by carsales — was furious at carsales gingering up publicity. 'You're not supposed to be advertising, that's our job,' he said angrily. He pushed Pisciotta to shut down carsales. Pisciotta refused, pointing out that carsales was a supplier to ninemsn, not a partner. To ninemsn, it was both incomprehensible and outrageous that this pushy online runt had managed to get under everyone's guard. In the end — in a remarkable stroke of good luck — carsales was dumped. They had erred when setting up the contract with ninemsn, signing a deal with no provision to terminate the relationship themselves. Now they had been fired. They were free to go head-to-head.

By early 2000, carsales was facing the same pressures as other internet companies, burning through cash, with little revenue. Greg Roebuck had already made the acquaintance of the SEEK founders at an internet conference and begun what would be regular six-monthly lunches, where they shared their experiences and tall tales of the major media companies. They had talked over whether there might be any value in putting SEEK and carsales together. Sometimes Pisciotta came too. Unlike SEEK and realestate.com.au, which had sprung from nothing, carsales.com.au had emerged from a traditional company. But their challenges were all cut from the same cloth and taking on the big boys in the newspaper classifieds called for the same obsession. It was a club of like minds.

Pisciotta and his Reynolds & Reynolds partners resolved to raise capital through a trade sale to dealers, transforming carsales.com.au from a Reynolds website to an unlisted public company. They had recruited Sak Ryopponen, a car industry executive who had worked for BMW, Saab and General Motors, as managing director. They commenced a road show and booked meeting rooms. They put up screens to demonstrate classifieds on the internet, and they pointed out that advertising was one of the dealers' biggest costs. The classifieds had created billionaires at Fairfax and News Limited, they said. But eventually, they predicted, people would stop looking in the newspapers for cars. Some might be online now, but in another ten years everyone would be online. They proposed that the dealer networks buy 51 per cent of carsales for $15 million. It was roughly 20 cents a share. But the dealers were reluctant. It was March 2000 and the first shock waves from the tech wreck were just beginning. In the end they raised just $5 million.

Soon though, a major investor arrived in the shape of Yahoo, one of the biggest search engines in the world. Yahoo was cashed up, but it also had something far more significant than cash. It had a very big portal. Yahoo became a shareholder in December 2000, paying $3 million for 11.6 per cent of the company with a deal for carsales to pay $1 million immediately for its placement on the Yahoo website, followed by a further $1 million a year for three years. Pisciotta granted boardroom observer status to a Yahoo representative, to recognise the company's investment and to take advantage of Yahoo's vast experience on the web.

But cash-flow problems continued to bedevil carsales. They might have raised $5 million from dealers and got cash from Yahoo, but they had substantial debts and they had been losing hundreds of thousands of dollars a month. They had repaid some debt, yet carsales' new managing director was ramping up spending on advertising even as the board pushed him to cut back. The losses grew from $200,000 per month in January 2001 to over $400,000 per month in April. Eventually, with only two months' worth of cash left in the bank, Ryopponen left the company in May 2001. He was replaced on an interim basis by Grant Taylor, a member of the original management buyout team in the Reynolds & Reynolds business. Within a month, the losses were cut in half and within 12 months, Taylor had returned the company to virtually breakeven. In May 2002 Greg Roebuck, who had succeeded Pisciotta as chief executive of Reynolds & Reynolds in 2000, left Reynolds and was appointed managing director of

Carsales.com.au Limited. He would remain a partner and director of Reynolds. Pisciotta was chairman of both companies.

Carsales.com.au was still under the radar: an odd beast with American antecedents, tucked away in suburban Melbourne and full of car dealers. But Nigel Dews, the head of Fairfax's digital arm f2, had made it his business to call Wal Pisciotta every so often. He invited him to *The Age* building on Spencer Street. It was clear to Pisciotta that Fairfax might someday contemplate trying to acquire a stake in carsales, but there was nothing serious so far. And Pisciotta was hardly welcoming. He did not want a conflicted print company with all its muscle inside his small tent. One early proposal from Fairfax was for carsales to supply data to create print advertisements — to run in Fairfax papers. It was hardly an attractive proposition for an online company. In another discussion, Dews told Greg Roebuck that he could probably get Hilmer on the phone to talk to him. Roebuck recalled later: 'My memory is this was presented as a great privilege to be able to speak to Fred. And my memory is there were no words of wisdom. We never felt we might in any way be a jewel in the crown; more that they were doing us a favour.'

By late 2004, as carsales consolidated a position in the top three auto sites online, it began to attract attention. Everyone wanted to talk to them. They had Telstra calling, News Limited and Fairfax. James Packer's high-profile deal with SEEK the year before had started to focus people's minds on the pure-plays. Fairfax had never seemed to have much appetite, but suddenly it was stirring.

'I never had a good feeling about Fairfax,' Pisciotta would say later. 'They were the enemy. How could they embrace online when they were trying to protect their business? And News was the same. They tried to build a relationship with us, but the worst thing we could have done was to go under their management structure and be restrained by them.'

News Limited had its own buttress in one sector of the online classifieds market. Lachlan Murdoch's deal to back realestate.com.au at the end of 2000 was paying off. Fairfax, though, had failed to buy into SEEK or make a hostile takeover, arguing that the company was overpriced and didn't want to talk to Fairfax anyway. Instead James Packer had acquired a large, friendly stake. Online car advertising, the third critical sector of the classifieds, was now eating into Fairfax's base. Carsales.com.au was the most aggressive player.

In February 2005, Fairfax's commercial director Alan Revell called Wal Pisciotta. Revell said he had important and exciting news to share. Pisciotta was reluctant to meet Revell one-on-one, but Revell pressed. 'You'll be very interested,' he said.

Pisciotta told Revell there was a carsales board meeting coming up. If Revell had something to say, he could say it to the whole board. Revell agreed. On the morning of the meeting, Revell flew to Melbourne. When he arrived at the airport he phoned Pisciotta to tell him that Fairfax had just become carsales' second largest shareholder. It was a bombshell. The carsales board, which had already convened at the Victorian Automobile Chamber of Commerce in St Kilda, had half an hour to consider what to do next before Revell and another Fairfax manager arrived. When he walked into the room, Revell told the directors that Fairfax had concluded a 'broad commercial arrangement' with Yahoo the day before which would entail Yahoo distributing Fairfax classified websites on the Yahoo portal. As part of the deal done by Revell, Fairfax had acquired Yahoo's 15 million shares, or 11.6 per cent of carsales.com.au. Carsales had been unhorsed.

Revell insisted that Fairfax saw it as a friendly investment. He then raised a startling addendum to his news: Fairfax understood that boardroom observer rights were attached to the Yahoo stake. He tried to plant the seed that one day Fairfax might own or control carsales.com.au. Revell might as well have announced that he was a cannibal and hungry too.

Pisciotta thanked him for delivering the news and then told Revell bluntly that Fairfax would not be viewed as a friendly investor but as a competitor, and moreover, there were no observer or other special rights attached to the shareholding. Fairfax would be treated in the same way as any other shareholder, and they would receive company communications in the same way too. They would certainly not be attending board meetings.

Pressed to reveal what Fairfax had paid for the Yahoo stake, Revell declined to say, citing commercial confidentiality.

One of the carsales directors, Geoff Brady, leaned forward. 'What did you pay for those shares?' he asked Revell. 'I'll give you a $1 million profit on it right now.'

Revell refused, reiterating that Fairfax regarded this as both a strategic stake and a friendly investment. He told them that Fairfax would like to buy more of carsales.

'That would cost you north of a dollar a share,' said Pisciotta.

Revell scoffed and he left soon after. The placement deal with Yahoo had cost Fairfax just a few million dollars, with the accompanying stake in carsales — thrown in because Yahoo didn't want it — acquired for next to nothing. Pisciotta recalled later:

> I said, 'Thank you for coming and if you have anything else
> to say you know how to contact us.' We recognised then
> that we had a hostile competitor shareholder with a strategic
> stake in our business. We were disappointed that Yahoo
> had sold without telling us, and we realised we had made
> a mistake in not attaching conditions to the Yahoo stake
> requiring them to sell to us first.

Roebuck regarded the attempt by Fairfax to climb into the boardroom as arrogant and a way of signalling 'game over'. With Fairfax throwing its weight around, they would need some serious ballast to fend off attempts by Fairfax to pressure their business. The last thing they wanted was Fairfax getting to 19.9 per cent. Notwithstanding that Hilmer had resigned nine months before — although he was yet to depart — Pisciotta and Roebuck expected Fairfax to circle like a shark, angling for a way to lift its stake. A traditional media company demanding boardroom rights was as good as a declaration of war.

Pisciotta and Roebuck stewed for a while. Fairfax clearly wanted to get as much of a chokehold as it could to impede carsales' growth, but it was not willing to pay for the privilege with a takeover. Pisciotta and Roebuck needed to erect some defences. The next time they met the Bassat brothers for lunch, in mid-May, they raised their Fairfax problem. One thing the Bassats had often said was that James Packer would like to meet them. He had proved a great investor in the SEEK business, respectful, supportive but pushing them strategically. He had believed in them and backed them. And he hated Fairfax. Perhaps one day carsales might want to do business with him.

'I think it's probably time we had that meeting with James if he's still interested,' Pisciotta said.

Paul Bassat moved fast. The next day Packer's executive assistant Jacquie Murray was on the phone. James, she said, would like to set up a meeting. Would next Tuesday suit? Unlike Fairfax, which had played around the edges of carsales for eight years, James Packer did not hesitate.

On 17 May 2005, Paul Bassat accompanied Pisciotta and Roebuck to make the introductions. They all arrived at Packer's Crown offices in Melbourne just as the Bassats had done two years before. Packer walked in with his hand out and the same big smile. 'I'm James Packer,' he said. He sat down and turned on the charm.

'I just want to say that I've admired you guys and your business for some time now. My guys keep telling me they're going to bury you and they're going to win. And every year you get further away. If there's any way we can work together I'm very interested.'

Packer told them he had a lot of assets in the space. He would be interested in combining some of these assets with the carsales business.

'Have a look at them and see what you think,' he suggested.

For Pisciotta and Roebuck it was like being in a parallel universe. They had been disappointed with the Fairfax saga, but Packer soon sold them on the idea he was someone they could trust.

PBL set up a data room and Gregg Haythorpe, the head of classified strategy, walked them through the 'Trader' assets

Packer was proposing to merge with carsales. This trove of automotive, trucking, boating and bike magazines had been assembled by Kerry Packer in his magazine division, Australian Consolidated Press, over many years. Haythorpe had managed it since 1986. There were magazines on earth-moving equipment, farm machinery, four-wheel drives, and real estate. Most of the advertising was dealers or brokers selling to each other. The magazines had been hugely competitive, undercutting newspaper pricing, and Haythorpe had added more and more to the stable. But with the arrival of the internet, various executives from the Microsoft–PBL joint venture ninemsn had circled, warning Haythorpe that his business would be gone in two years as the classifieds moved online.

Haythorpe had worried about ninemsn. Under the joint venture, all of the content from ACP's magazines had to be fed through the ninemsn pipeline. But he found a way to sidestep the contract. Under the ninemsn agreement, magazine content that spoke directly to consumers was channelled online. Haythorpe argued that business-to-business magazines, which included most of what was in his stable, were not trapped by this definition. They were trade publications. Haythorpe was not opposed to the internet; he just wanted to run his own online division outside the hungry ninemsn site. Carving out the trade magazines was a first step.

—————

Haythorpe had a strong ally and a new boss. Former Fairfax executive John Alexander had been hired by James Packer in 1998 after he was abruptly fired by Fairfax's chief executive Bob Muscat, himself a former News Limited executive. Alexander was an unpredictable but stellar editor with a sixth sense for what worked. Aloof and with a black sense of humour, he was into everything from sports to arts and on a first name basis at every good restaurant in town. His penchant for defining A and B teams among his newspaper's staff had kept journalists on edge. No explanation was given for the sacking other than Muscat believed they could no longer work together. But it followed a deep schism in the company that had seen Alexander, then editor-in-chief and publisher of *The Sydney Morning Herald*, and Greg Hywood, the editor-in-chief and publisher of *The Australian Financial Review*, locking horns. In a company replete with political players, Alexander was regarded as the wiliest of all.

Early in Alexander's tenure as chief executive of ACP, Haythorpe had commenced building his online business using data from the Trader magazine groups. Then they added something else: ninemsn's carpoint.com.au was struggling and Alexander sought to resurrect it, eventually taking it over with a capped management licence agreement under Haythorpe's control. Haythorpe had developed a relationship with car dealers, and he had a big sales force on the ground. They began selling packages, offering print and online advertising for a set price.

By the time Wal Pisciotta and Greg Roebuck decided to seek the support of the Packers to fend off Fairfax, Haythorpe was in Sydney working on business development for Alexander, who had been appointed chief executive of PBL in 2004. Alexander had the top executive position in a company ruled with an iron rod by the controlling shareholders, and most specifically by the lion, Kerry Packer. The job of CEO had crushed others before him but Alexander maintained good relations with both Kerry and James.

At Kerry's insistence, Alexander joined him for lunch in the PBL dining room every Tuesday for five years. Yet he was as much a supporter of James. These relationships would be tested in the carsales deal.

With his background in auto magazines, Haythorpe already knew Greg Roebuck. When the call came through to say that the founders of carsales would be coming for a meeting in Melbourne, he understood immediately what might be at stake. Already PBL had its shareholding in SEEK, snatched while Fairfax dithered and a favourite investment of James Packer. Now the Bassat brothers were bringing the two notoriously independent carsales partners, Pisciotta and Roebuck, to the table for introductions. Haythorpe and Anthony Klok, the head of business development, flew with Packer to Melbourne.

———

Roebuck and Pisciotta carefully examined what was on offer. They spent weeks assessing the Trader magazines, ACP's other print assets and the websites. They identified a string of print and online titles where they felt they could construct a deal with Packer. But then just as suddenly, they changed their minds. The deeper they went, the more they realised that they simply did not understand print. They were about to merge assets in a structure which would give PBL a huge stake in carsales. Certainly it would give carsales value in kind — not just substantial websites that would be crucial to growing the business, but also a powerful relationship with PBL and the muscle to push back against Fairfax. But they would end up with a raft of things they felt ill-equipped to run. Pisciotta slammed on the brakes.

We were working on the basis that we were going
to acquire all these print and online assets. But we
decided we didn't want to get into print. We didn't know
anything about it and it was challenged. And I rang James
Packer one day and said, 'I don't think we can do a deal
with the print assets.' He was disappointed. It had been
going on for months; he said he thought maybe it was deal
fatigue.

Packer had his heart set on carsales and he asked Haythorpe to keep trying to close a deal. He liked internet investments and he loved anything that caused trouble for Fairfax. He was about to sell his 4.85 per cent stake in realestate.com.au to News after a personal request from Lachlan Murdoch. But Packer still had SEEK and he was determined to be in bed with carsales too.

Alan Revell was oblivious to the negotiations underway between Packer and carsales and he had not given up on increasing Fairfax's stake in the company. In July 2005, Fairfax had made a $38 million investment to buy the dating website RSVP. After this purchase, Revell was spurred on to have another crack at the carsales founders. He emailed Roebuck, inviting him and Pisciotta to lunch. He mentioned that Fred Hilmer was keen to 'get down to business'. Even though carsales' negotiations with Packer had hit a road block, Roebuck rebuffed the advance:

In regards lunch, I think it could be a challenge. As you
would have gathered from the last meeting, the (carsales)
board have a reasonably black and white view on the
discussions and I would suggest that their position is clear.

Much as I hate turning down a free lunch, it's probably appropriate in this instance.

Revell persisted, emailing Roebuck on 18 July, and in the process revealing that Fairfax now understood that deals by James Packer and Lachlan Murdoch to invest in SEEK and REA had recalibrated valuations in the online market — yet still implying that these valuations were too high given that Fairfax had bought RSVP at an advantageous price. He wrote:

> Fair enough — we had another idea we wanted to discuss
> though … you would have read what we paid for rsvp,
> a strong market leader with FY06e earnings of at least
> $4 million. We thought that was fair — but I am sure you
> will think 9.7 x FY06e was cheap! So, given that we are
> likely to be apart on valuation, the idea is this: we pay a
> 'very full' price (e.g. taking into account seek/rea multiples),
> to increase our shareholding. Worth discussing? Or do you
> think it is 100pc or nothing?
> Alan.

Roebuck and Pisciotta had no interest in bargaining with Fairfax. Roebuck said later, 'The "black and white" referred to was "you either buy it all or none at all".' The media giant would not be allowed to creep up its shareholding in order to sit in the boardroom and crush the life out of carsales from within. If Fairfax wanted to take control then it would have to do so in the proper way — through a full takeover. 'They didn't want to buy it all, so we didn't want another talk-fest,' Roebuck said.

As far as having lunch with Hilmer, Wal Pisciotta saw no point at all. Hilmer was finished at Fairfax. 'I said, "Why would I want to have lunch with Fred, because he has announced his resignation and he's leaving at the end of the year, so why would I have lunch? Because he can't back up anything he might say."

By August, things were back on track between PBL and carsales. Gregg Haythorpe had done as he was bid and had continued to push for a compromise. Eventually, after ACP's print assets were dropped from the deal, Pisciotta and Roebuck agreed. Subject to shareholder approval, carsales would acquire ACP's online classified Trader businesses, including carpoint, boatpoint, bikepoint, ihub and a research and statistics company, Equipment Research Group. They were businesses that had originally cost ACP probably a few hundred thousand dollars to create. In exchange, ACP Magazines Ltd would receive 41 per cent of carsales. Everyone in the deal liked everyone else. Packer had agreed to support carsales listing on the stock exchange in the future, at a time that suited the founding partners.

One senior figure at PBL was not happy, however. Kerry Packer regarded the deal as crazy. He was convinced that Fairfax would act in the same way as he would and move dramatically to take its 11.6 per cent stake in carsales to 19.9 per cent, and then bring down a huge foot to squash the PBL deal by rallying other shareholders to vote against it. He rounded on both James and John Alexander, shouting at them about their stupidity, mocking his son and warning them that Wal Pisciotta could just as easily dump the deal too. Then they would be dead on arrival. It was so easy to block and it would make PBL look ridiculous. Fairfax would never let them get away with it.

Kerry summoned Gregg Haythorpe and Anthony Klok to a meeting and warned his son and Alexander to stay out of the room. He wanted to scare Haythorpe and Klok into telling the truth as he saw it. He did not believe Pisciotta and Greg Roebuck would do the deal and he wanted confirmation that all the promises and handshakes were in James' head. He distrusted everything about the deal. Haythorpe recalled later:

> I thought John was coming to the meeting, and I said to Kerry, 'Do you want me to go and get John?' And Kerry said, 'I don't fucking want him. I want you two.' Then we went into a discussion about the deal, and he demanded to know if it was real. He wanted to know what was really going on and if it was all some kind of James and JA pipe dream. Anthony and I understood that if Kerry got angry, you stayed calm and talked to the facts. So we did that, and we talked about the potential outcome and what a great deal it could be. Anthony is very calm and considered and I think that meant Kerry could see there was no agenda of egos. But he pushed us and pushed us. And in the end he said, 'Alright, we'll see what you two guys can do.'

Kerry had cracked, but only with more scathing warnings. As pessimistic as ever about his son's investments, he was confident Fairfax would vote 'no' with its carsales stake. 'You're wasting your time,' he advised Alexander.

Pisciotta and Roebuck took the proposal to their board of directors. Later, when everyone was ready, the whole board came to Sydney to meet at PBL's headquarters on Park Street. When

James Packer arrived, they summarised the elements of the deal and then Packer and Pisciotta shook hands. It was an emotional moment for Pisciotta, who felt that it re-established the trust he had broken when he walked away from the agreement to take Packer's Trader print assets.

Fairfax found out not long before everyone else. Greg Roebuck was standing in the office of the Packer lawyers Arnold Bloch Liebler on a Friday afternoon when his phone rang. It was Alan Revell, phoning from the Whitsundays where he was on holidays. Revell said he had just had a call from Fairfax's chairman Ron Walker to say that carsales was about to cut a deal with PBL. Roebuck recalled later: 'Alan said to me on the phone: "Surely you're not? You would have told me." Alan said the news had ruined his holiday and he was shocked that I hadn't spoken to Fairfax first.'

On 3 October 2005, the deal between ACP and carsales was announced. It was approved by shareholders on 28 October 2005. Fairfax did not cast a vote. No negative votes were cast at all, and ACP acquired 91 million shares, or 41 per cent of carsales. Three executives from PBL would join the board: James Packer, John Alexander and Gregg Haythorpe. Wal Pisciotta would remain chairman.

It was a third lost opportunity for Fairfax. James Packer had already taken 25 per cent of SEEK; now he had a large piece of carsales too. The deal meant Fairfax's stake would be diluted to 7.6 per cent. Across the road, Lachlan Murdoch was in the process of wrapping up control of realestate.com.au. It was not just the pure-plays who had outflanked Fairfax in starting up online classifieds. The Packer and Murdoch dynasties had now snatched huge stakes in the pure-plays from under Fairfax's nose.

Fairfax still believed it had the three pillars of advertising well in hand. But Fred Hilmer's replacement, incoming chief executive David Kirk, sounded a note of caution in November 2005, telling the annual general meeting that further growth in the company's online classified advertising was crucial as newspapers everywhere suffered from a downturn in circulation. Advertising, Kirk said, accounted for 75 per cent of total Fairfax revenue.

The RSVP romance website was Fred Hilmer's last online acquisition before leaving Fairfax. Notwithstanding the strong financial forecasts for the site, the purchase had prompted considerable ridicule, and in some quarters, the jokes had a sharp edge. You might not be able to get a car or a job or a house online at Fairfax, they mocked, but you could always get a date.

Carsales, the pure-play spun from nothing by Greg Roebuck to suck the heart out of the auto classifieds, was bedding down its new relationship with PBL as 2005 closed.

Seven years later, by the end of 2012, the carsales share price had hit $7.80 with a market capitalisation of more than $1.8 billion. It kept climbing. Eight weeks on, at the end of February 2013, carsales' share price was $9 with a market capitalisation of $2.1 billion. SEEK was a little ahead at $9.70. Realestate.com.au had hit $25.80.

When Fairfax Media announced its half-year results on 2 February 2013, the share price closed at 53 cents.

CHAPTER FOUR

CHANNELLING FOXTEL

Rupert Murdoch's office on the seventh floor of 1211 Sixth Avenue between 47th and 48th Streets in New York City was a stone's throw from the diamond district and three blocks from the Algonquin Hotel, where the writer Dorothy Parker held court in the 1920s. It was adjacent to the skating rink at the Rockefeller Center and in sight of that slim art deco masterpiece, the GE building. For Murdoch, though, nowhere was as close as Australia, where he had inherited a small newspaper company from his father in 1952 and laid the foundations for a vast global media empire. Australia might be a day away by plane, but it was just a split second by phone, and Murdoch — the chairman and chief executive of News Corporation — followed developments in his homeland with a close eye.

In July 1995, Murdoch had flown to Australia to host an executive retreat on sunny Hayman Island for the top ranks of his News Corp managers from Australia, the US and the UK. He had British Labour Party leader Tony Blair and Australian Prime Minister Paul Keating as guests. Afterwards he would announce a stunning deal with the New South Wales Labor Government to establish 20th Century Fox studios in the heart of Sydney.

On the morning of 28 July, the day before he was due to return to New York, Murdoch opened his newspapers over breakfast. He was astonished to find a big story in a Fairfax paper reporting that Fairfax and the Australian Broadcasting Corporation were on the cusp of signing a deal to supply a 24-hour news channel to Foxtel — the pay TV operator owned 50/50 by his own News Corp and Telstra, the Australian phone giant.

Murdoch was incensed. Here was News' loathed competitor Fairfax, bragging as always and thinking it had a deal with his company. Ever vigilant to the advance of the enemy, he seized the phone and snapped off a command to one of his managers. In a nutshell, it was 'over my dead body'.

The instruction rippled swiftly through layers of News executives. Within minutes, Sam Chisholm had picked up the phone. Chisholm was the high-riding chief executive of BSkyB in London, a pay TV company 40 per cent owned by News; he oversaw the fledgling Foxtel, started the year before in Australia and yet to begin broadcasting. He had joined Murdoch and a phalanx of News Corp executives in Sydney for the gala announcement of the Fox Studios deal a week before.

Chisholm called Mark Booth, the chief executive of Foxtel in Sydney, and broke the bad news. Booth was to drop everything and under no circumstances to sign any deal with News' arch-competitors, those bastards at the ABC and Fairfax. It was not on.

Booth was stunned: he argued against the edict, only to be told it had come from Rupert himself. Booth was a Kansas-born American and a veteran of the US cable music channel MTV (Music Television). He had joined MTV in the US as national sales executive and by 1986 he was chief executive of MTV in Europe. Foxtel might be jointly owned with Telstra, but under the terms of their contract, News Corp managed the company and held the right to appoint the chief executive. Sam Chisholm, with a practised eye for talent, had recommended Booth to Murdoch to set up Foxtel in Australia. After a trip to meet the big man in New York, Booth landed the job.

For months Booth had been negotiating programming and channels to run on the new Foxtel service. He believed he had the authority to do the deals he was doing and he had shaken hands with people. When Chisholm called to veto the Fairfax–ABC deal, he could not believe his ears.

Booth planned that very day to sign a string of contracts with representatives from the ABC, Fairfax, and Cox Communications, the American cable TV provider. These three owned a company called Australian Information Media Pty Ltd (AIM), which was poised to create and sell a 24-hour news channel to Foxtel. AIM was owned 51 per cent by the ABC and 24.5 per cent each by Fairfax and Cox. The US companies Viacom (which owned children's programmer Nickelodeon) and CNN also had a stake in local Australian programming joint ventures with AIM.

The timing of the phone call from Chisholm could not have been worse. Directors of AIM and their lawyers were already waiting in the conference room at Booth's Foxtel offices at 155 George Street, Sydney. Booth had planned a party later in the day to celebrate the deals they were about to sign. He insisted to Chisholm that he wanted to speak to Murdoch himself. He recalled later: 'I had approved all this with Sam. And then I got a phone call from Sam to say it was all off at the last minute. I did speak to Rupert and it was three seconds, the shortest phone call I ever had with him.'

Murdoch was crystal clear. He had no intention of giving his foes a free kick. Murdoch played to win. Years later, his blocking move would prove to have delivered a strategic blow to Fairfax at a time when News held the dominant position in subscription television news, one of the growth sectors of the media industry as newspapers struggled. But in 1995, it was quite simply a club to the head of the national broadcaster and Murdoch's enemies at Fairfax.

While Booth tried to decide what to do next, Foxtel's legal adviser and former News Limited lawyer Richard Freudenstein, who had drawn up the contracts, went to meet the visitors who were waiting to sign, filled with anticipation.

'We've hit a snag,' Freudenstein told them.

They waited and waited. Freudenstein stalled and stalled. Finally Booth emerged and took the Fairfax representative, Doug Halley, and the Cox representative, Lindsay Gardner — both AIM directors — into his office. The lawyers waited outside.

Devastated, Booth said the deal was off. 'I'm sorry but we're not doing it.'

Doug Halley, who had been recruited to Fairfax from Goodman Fielder to work on corporate and business development as well as finance, was stunned. This was a fiasco, and the confusion over what had happened only grew when Booth indicated that Murdoch had crushed the deal, even as the contracts sat on the table. Eventually, the visitors left, leaving Booth and Freudenstein trying to fathom how to get out of the mess.

Lindsay Gardner from Cox was just as gob-smacked as Halley. His job at Cox was to negotiate with programmers and to put together joint venture deals just like this one with Fairfax and the ABC. He had been excited about the deal and had led the negotiations. On the way to the meeting he had been so confident about a good outcome, he had stopped his driver at a liquor store and bought four bottles of good champagne. At the Foxtel offices, he asked to keep them cold while the contracts were signed, and various lunches were moved around in the bar fridge to accommodate the celebratory bottles. He recalled later:

> Mark kept us waiting and it was about an hour, waiting in the conference room, and finally he came out and called myself and Doug. I was all bubbly and excited, and Mark said, 'I just got off the phone from Rupert and he doesn't want to do the deal.'
>
> And I said, 'Very funny,' thinking it was a joke.
>
> Mark said, 'Rupert's in the country and he's read about it and he doesn't want to do it.'
>
> I later learned that Rupert's reaction was: 'If there's going to be a news channel, it's bloody well not going to be Fairfax and the ABC, it's going to be us.'
>
> Doug was so angry. I asked Mark a bunch of questions to try to find a way to still do it. Mark deflected every entreaty and after ten minutes of getting nowhere we left.
>
> Later I said to Doug, 'Those fuckers have still got our champagne.'

The next day, 29 July, a news story published in *The Sydney Morning Herald* and written by Fairfax business journalist Sue Lecky reported that News Corp had vetoed the deal at the eleventh hour. Lecky reported AIM's new chief executive Julie Steiner as saying that the AIM shareholders had been told by Booth during a meeting the previous day that he had been instructed by Rupert Murdoch to halt discussions.

In the aftermath Doug Halley and Steiner, a former ABC executive, grappled with a crisis on many fronts — the credibility of their two organisations and the commitments they had made to others not the least of their problems. Fairfax had made some preparations for the new venture, establishing a video studio in the Fairfax building at Darling Park in Sydney for journalists to record audio and visual reports. This was easily abandoned. But Steiner had overseen the final stages of constructing a huge purpose-built studio and offices at the ABC's Gore Hill headquarters, commenced 18 months before. Over 100 staff had been recruited, some from the ABC but many externally, as the pay TV business was to be a stand-alone operation and had been independently financed. The studio sets were ready, TV anchors had been auditioned, and a host of enthusiastic youngsters was on site working.

When AIM was formed in late 1994, both Fairfax and the ABC had high hopes. Pay television was late arriving in Australia by contrast with America and the United Kingdom, where cable and satellite subscription broadcasting was well entrenched. But with the allocation of a second Australian telecommunications licence to Optus in 1991 to compete with the national carrier, Telecom (later known as Telstra), the die was cast. Subscription television was permitted from 1992 and with that the gates were open. The new licences and legislative changes — all opened up during the reformist Labor Governments of Prime Ministers Bob Hawke and Paul Keating — gave rise to a rush by the big players in every sector of media and telecommunications to secure for themselves the ringside seats. It was an era of unceasing jostling, political lobbying and brinkmanship, particularly between the take-no-prisoners dynasties, the Packers and Murdochs, with Telstra not far behind.

Kerry Packer, with his adored free-to-air Nine Network, was possibly the most antagonistic individual in Australia to the idea of pay TV and he would fight over it from inside and outside the tent for the rest of his life. Packer's son James, however, had no such one-eyed affection for traditional broadcast media as the old man. For the Murdochs, whose News Corp had sold the Ten Network to shopping centre mogul Frank Lowy in 1985, pay TV in Australia offered a chance to re-enter the broadcasting industry, but also to consolidate what had become a roaring financial success for News in the UK with its big stake in the subscription service BSkyB, overseen by Sam Chisholm. Telstra was angling for any way to throw roadblocks in front of Optus.

At the same time Fairfax, a one-time owner of the Seven Network, had just emerged from a four-year horror stretch that had started in 1987 with a privatisation bid by one member of the founding family, Warwick Fairfax Jr, and concluded when he lost control of the company altogether and it collapsed into receivership, emerging eventually wounded and in the hands of the Canadian media tycoon Conrad Black.

Fairfax no longer had any members of the Fairfax family on its board. Its days as a family dynasty were gone, although pride in the company's 150-year history remained rooted in the heart of its newspaper operations. The robust Fairfax corporate identity, expressed through its quality newspapers, was regarded by the Packer and Murdoch media dynasties as arrogant hubris.

Conrad Black had appointed South African media executive Stephen Mulholland as chief executive; he was widely expected to kick the company into shape and with it, kick some of the stuffing out of the famous Fairfax culture. Former News Limited executive Michael Hoy was appointed deputy chief executive and editorial director. In this role, Hoy embarked on a dizzying round of changes to the editors of the Fairfax newspapers, enveloping the company in political infighting and setting the scene for years of back-stabbing on executive row. The Packers and the Murdochs looked on with satisfaction.

The players in the pay TV industry were embroiled at the same time in their own merry-go-round of alliances — both at the level of the pay TV 'platform' operators, and amongst the many companies wanting to supply channels to run on these platforms. A joint venture between News Corp, the Packers' PBL and Telstra to acquire a satellite licence was formed and then collapsed. In the aftermath, News Corp and Telstra had formed Foxtel.

As the incipient pay television industry took shape, the three biggest pay TV platform operators were Foxtel, Optus Vision (a subsidiary of the licence holder Optus), and the satellite company Australis with its Galaxy service. Both PBL and the Seven Network took small stakes in Optus Vision.

The pay TV operators circled each other like wily cats, cutting a deal with Hollywood studios here, undercutting a deal with US cable suppliers there. There was a rush to create programming ventures and new channels. Everyone courted CNN, the revolutionary US 24-hour news network started by Ted Turner. In one of the more costly and crazy by-products of the government's plans for competition, Telstra and Optus Vision commenced building competing cable networks. To the astonishment of all, they planned to cable Australia twice. Sometimes their teams chased each other up and down the same streets. Finally, Optus stopped construction. So ferocious was the competition, no-one trusted anyone else.

At the ABC, the head of the corporation's pay TV development division, Kim Williams, had created an independently financed structure for a new content-supply company, AIM Pty Ltd, with a grant from the Commonwealth for the ABC's stake and a mix of investments from Fairfax and Cox. Williams had previously been the chief executive of organisations including the chamber music presenter Musica Viva, the independent television production house Southern Star Entertainment, and the Australian Film Commission before joining the ABC in December 1991. Between 1992 and 1994 he had forged the commercial partnerships to launch two subscription television channels — a children's channel and a 24-hour news channel — to offer the pay TV operators.

It was no secret that the AIM consortium was planning to develop and sell its two channels to as many pay TV operators as it could. Detailed news reports appeared in Fairfax newspapers as early as February 1995. *The Sydney Morning Herald* journalist Glenda Korporaal reported that the AIM channels were expected to become part of the basic programming of all three platform operators. The news channel would use footage from the ABC and CNN, with Fairfax journalists providing additional commentary. On 24 February 1995, Korporaal quoted Fairfax editorial director Michael Hoy describing the combination of Fairfax and the ABC to create pay TV news coverage as 'a powerhouse'. Fairfax would invest $20 million over five years, Hoy said, adding, 'Content is our strength. The future is in content.'

Williams was set to become chief executive of AIM, but in April 1995, he suddenly left the ABC. He had been offered a job too good to refuse, recruited by Rupert Murdoch to set up Fox Studios in Australia, a role that played to Williams' strengths in film and the arts, but this time inside a major corporation with deep pockets. When Williams quit, AIM was in negotiations to supply all three pay TV operators, Galaxy, Optus and Foxtel. In Williams' place, Julie Steiner was appointed chief executive of AIM. Steiner was the former head of ABC Enterprises, a division of the national broadcaster that handled the sale and distribution of ABC content and products.

By mid-1995, partnerships with big US program suppliers had broken and reformed in almost every sector of the Australian pay TV industry. Foxtel, seen as the lion, announced a deal with CNN's owner Turner International to take the American 24-hour news service. Optus Vision signed up for CNN as well. CNN was in the process of ring-fencing the globe with its news service, but this did not stop AIM continuing negotiations to sell its local Australian 24-hour news channel. Talks with Optus Vision and Galaxy went round in circles and by June, AIM had narrowed its negotiations to Foxtel and Galaxy.

On 20 July, the NSW Government announced that it had struck an agreement with Rupert Murdoch to lease the Sydney Showgrounds to establish an Australian base for 20th Century Fox. The deal for the showgrounds set off a wave of community protest and a campaign to attack the deal, noisily spearheaded by *The Sydney Morning Herald*. Murdoch and his executives, including News Limited chairman Ken Cowley and Sam Chisholm from BSkyB, were on hand for the Fox announcements, which closely followed the News Corp executive retreat on Hayman Island.

Then, on 27 July 1995, the first of a series of dominos started falling that within 24 hours would shatter the pay TV ambitions of both Fairfax and the ABC, crushing AIM's plans beneath Murdoch's foot.

Mark Furness, a sharp-nosed media reporter on *The Australian Financial Review* who had assiduously chased the pay TV developments and was known for his first-class contact book, picked up a tip that Fairfax and the ABC were about to do a deal with Foxtel. Furness rushed in to see his editor-in-chief, Greg Hywood, who liked a scoop and was keen to run the story. He told Furness to try to firm it up. Furness called Michael Hoy, hoping to hassle the Fairfax executive into confirming or denying. Hoy agreed to see him and told Furness to come to his office. When he arrived at the appointed time, Furness was startled to find two other Fairfax journalists waiting outside Hoy's mahogany row suite as well — Sue Lecky from *The Sydney Morning Herald*'s business desk, and Ben Potter, the Sydney correspondent for *The Age*. Lecky and Potter told Furness they had been called up by Hoy.

News stories by all three reporters appeared the following morning, 28 July, in the three main Fairfax newspapers. Under the headline 'ABC, Fairfax, Foxtel to form pay TV alliance', Furness had written a highly detailed report, describing the deal as in its final stage, with such nitty-gritty information as AIM readying to sign up exclusive agreements with Foxtel and Galaxy, but not Optus, and that a planned children's channel would be dropped in favour of a general entertainment channel in a separate joint venture with Foxtel. Furness quoted Julie Steiner saying cautiously that 'the ink had not hit the paper yet' and that she maintained open lines with Optus Vision.

'But unlike other negotiations relating to AIM, parties from all the camps expressed confidence to *The Australian Financial Review* that the deal would be completed,' Furness wrote.

Lecky's and Potter's news reports in *The Age* and *The SMH* covered similar territory, warning that the deal with Foxtel would be a blow to Optus Vision, which would have to source its local news from the Nine and Seven Networks. AIM planned to launch its news channel in mid-September, six weeks away. The headline on Lecky's story read: 'Pay TV venture close to signing a deal with Foxtel'. All in all it was a very good story and a scoop for Fairfax, getting the jump on a corporate breakthrough that should set the scene for both Fairfax and the ABC for years to come, putting them in pole position as content suppliers in the avalanche of pay television.

But unfortunately for Fairfax, the barrage of news reports in the company's newspapers caught Rupert Murdoch's attention almost before anyone else's — and before anything was signed.

28 July 1995 was a good day for Murdoch. US newspapers had just reported that Murdoch, who had become an American citizen in 1985 to meet US stipulations on foreign ownership of

television and radio, had just received a waiver from the US Federal Communications Commission enabling News Corp to retain control of a dozen television stations in his American Fox network.

Murdoch was justly proud of having built a phenomenal media empire and his was a company deeply imbued with the scrappy fighting spirit of its founder. There was nothing like bashing up the competition. It was company lore at News that Fairfax had a superiority complex and a sense of entitlement. Now Murdoch was reading a supposed scoop about his own company in the Fairfax press; Fairfax was crowing about a deal where nothing was signed. Foxtel was the prime mover in pay TV and Fairfax was just a hopeful supplier and a junior partner at that. Yet already Fairfax was beating its chest.

That was when Murdoch put his foot down; within hours, the deal was dead. Mark Booth, who had put so much effort into the negotiations with AIM, recalled later:

> We were ready to go. I thought it was a big coup for us.
> It was all very disappointing. Strategically though, it was
> a very smart thing for Rupert to do. Australia was only a
> small portion of Rupert's empire, but for Fairfax, Australia
> was the entire empire. This new technology was coming and
> Rupert was not going to cede any of the territory. This was
> all about long-term vision. And eventually they set up Sky
> in Australia — rather than hand over news and sports to
> the ABC and Fairfax. While it was uncomfortable for Sam
> to leave us hanging out there, he agreed with Rupert. I am
> sure he was flabbergasted, as were we really, that we had
> pulled off the deal [with AIM].

One Fairfax executive did not take the defeat lying down. After Booth had broken the news that the deal was off, a furious Doug Halley was determined to do what he could to resurrect it. He returned to his office at Darling Park and marched in to see the chief executive, Stephen Mulholland. Halley told Mulholland he was going to call Conrad Black, to ask Fairfax's controlling shareholder to use his heft as an international newspaper proprietor to pressure Murdoch to back off. Mulholland agreed and Halley phoned Black to argue for intervention at the mogul-level; then he sat and waited. Black called him a day later with depressing news. He had spoken to Murdoch and the News Corp boss would not relent. There would be no pay TV contracts for Fairfax — or for the ABC — with Foxtel. Halley recalled later:

> Conrad said he would make the call and he did make
> the call. He phoned me back the next day and said,
> 'Rupert's adamant that his decision is final and there is no
> opportunity for Fairfax on Foxtel.' Everybody had put in a
> lot of work. It was extremely surprising. We'd done the deal
> and had just been working on the documentation, so I don't
> think anybody was thinking we were still at risk of losing
> the deal. There was absolutely no thought in our minds that
> either Mark or Sam did not have the authority to do the
> deal. It was a complete renege.

It was several days before the first suspicions emerged that Fairfax had somehow seized defeat from the jaws of victory, jumping the gun by intimating the deal was a *fait accompli* before the contracts were signed. Media companies could be as susceptible as other companies to wanting to manage information about their own corporate interests. By fuelling a story picked up by a good reporter rather than giving him a 'no comment', Fairfax had unintentionally shot itself in the foot.

Just over a week later there was more bad news. On 9 August, Optus Vision issued a statement to say it had decided not to buy AIM's news service. Two days later, Julie Steiner insisted that she still expected AIM to secure a deal with a pay TV platform by its start date of 16 September. She told *The Sydney Morning Herald* that she was talking to Australis and to Optus — notwithstanding Optus Vision's announcement that it was not doing any deal because the AIM package was too expensive.

Fairfax newspapers continued to track the saga, reporting on 12 August that Steiner had defended the price of AIM's channels, saying they represented better value for viewers than other options. In the end though, AIM collapsed. Most of the staff working at the company's Gore Hill premises was retrenched. No pay TV operator was prepared to buy the AIM channels.

———

For Fairfax and the ABC it was a double blow. Not only did they lose the chance to get in on the ground floor of pay TV, neither organisation would have another opportunity to supply a paid-for service to an Australian pay TV operator. Fairfax would never manage to segue its vast journalistic resources from print to television, aside from talking heads on its newspaper websites and a deal with the Nine Network, 18 years later in 2013, for *The Australian Financial Review* to join forces on a Sunday morning business talk show. It would be 15 years after the AIM debacle that the ABC finally launched its own 24-hour news channel in 2010.

———

In 1999, four years after the AIM deal fell over, Lindsay Gardner was recruited from Cox in the US to News Corp as a top executive working on distribution deals for cable and networks. In the middle of that year, he was invited to dinner at the home of Rupert Murdoch at the top of Angelo Drive in Beverly Hills. Gardner had never met Murdoch before and when the media tycoon welcomed him at the front door and asked him about himself, Gardner could not resist raising an old ghost from the past.

> I said, 'Mr Murdoch, I was at Cox and we were one of the key partners in the AIM partnership. And I negotiated that deal with Mark Booth and you shut us down.' I just had to get this off my chest.
> And Rupert stood there in the foyer, and he took a beat, and then he said, 'That was an ill-conceived venture.'

———

For Foxtel, however, it was just the beginning. The service commenced broadcasting on 23 October 1995. Three months later on 19 February 1996, Sky News was launched to run on Foxtel. Sky was a 24-hour news channel with a former Network Ten journalist, Juanita Phillips, as the first newsreader. It was owned in equal thirds by BSkyB, the Nine Network and the Seven Network, bringing together content from the two leading Australian broadcasters and BSkyB's 24-hour UK service. The ownership structure behind Sky might have been confusing to outsiders riveted by the sniping between warring pay TV operators supported by either the Murdochs or the Packers. But Sky was a channel seeking the widest possible distribution.

Pay TV in Australia had become big business, attracting all the most powerful media players in the nation, but it was far from profitable. Millions of dollars drained from the wallets of the key investors. Access to vastly expensive Hollywood film deals became a tug of war between the operators. The Packers had tied up some Hollywood studios for Optus Vision. Australis had tied up others for Galaxy. Foxtel had cut into the action through a side-deal with Australis. In 1996 and again in 1997 Foxtel and Australis tried to merge, but were blocked on both occasions by the competition regulator. By mid-1997 the combined losses at these pay TV operators were almost $900 million. A year later, Australis Media collapsed. Mark Booth had left Foxtel in 1997 to help establish JSkyB in Japan, before taking over from Sam Chisholm as chief executive of BSkyB in London. Booth was replaced as chief executive of Foxtel by Tom Mockridge, a former journalist on *The Sydney Morning Herald*. He had been an adviser to Treasurer Paul Keating, and an executive at News Limited.

In 1997, a critical battle in the lifecycle of Foxtel was finally resolved. A campaign commenced by News Limited in 1994 to create Super League, modelled on Britain's highly lucrative Premier League soccer that ran on BSkyB, had transformed the ever-strained relationships between the two media dynasties into outright public war. It pitted mogul against mogul and tore apart the rugby code. Murdoch wanted Super League to beef up Foxtel. Packer fought to defend his free-to-air television rights and the opportunity to run the Australian Rugby League games on Optus Vision. Multi-million dollar skirmishes broke out, with poaching of players and massive contracts for rebels willing to cross from one side to the other. It was Packer v Murdoch. The top executives and directors of the companies (as well as the moguls themselves) were on the front line brawling. The sons and heirs, James and Lachlan, were up to their necks in the fight, stealing players back and forth across the line. James Packer recalled later: 'In a moment of bravery I said to my Dad, "The good news is News is losing five dollars for every dollar we're losing. The bad news is that means we go broke first." It didn't go down great with Dad.'

Once the inevitable litigation enveloped the battle, peace deals were explored but just as quickly fell over. Lachlan Murdoch was appointed chief executive of News Limited in 1997. 'When I became CEO, the number one priority was to get a peace deal,' he said later. A truce was finally struck, helped by negotiations between James and Lachlan involving many meetings, although hardly without trouble for this fight had been brought to boiling point. The Packer side pressed harder and harder for concessions and advantages. Only James Packer and Peter Barron, the Machiavellian one-time political strategist to Prime Minister Bob Hawke, and now Packer adviser, pushed for peace. Lachlan finally stormed out of a key meeting, threatening to sink the deal if PBL kept piling up demands, only to be followed by James, trying to turn him back. Ultimately the two younger men manoeuvred their fathers into position. PBL would hold onto its free-to-air TV rights in a ten-year deal and News Limited would take the pay TV rights for Foxtel for the next 25 years. The rugby firmament had been altered for good and the National Rugby League was born. It was the price of peace in the paddock.

After Super League, other aspects of business between these two dynasties could be looked at. A deal to give PBL a piece of Foxtel was stitched together and blessed during a heads-of-state meeting between Rupert Murdoch and Kerry Packer on board Murdoch's boat, *Morning Glory*, anchored in the Bay of Islands in New Zealand. PBL would be granted an option to buy half of News Corp's 50 per cent stake in Foxtel and half of its 100 per cent of Fox Sports but with News maintaining management control. Telstra still had the other 50 per cent of Foxtel. The deals stopped the bloodletting and freed everyone to move on. Foxtel at the time was a black hole with millions of dollars going down the drain and it seemed that News was not giving up much territory to settle the war.

In December 1998, at the urging of James Packer, PBL took up its option for 25 per cent of Foxtel for $157 million. (A year later, in October 1999, it took 50 per cent of Fox Sports for $69.5 million.) Kerry Packer agreed but not without a volley of shots. There were loud warnings to his executives and his son that pay TV would never grow to be as important or commercially successful as free-to-air and Nine. He regarded the Foxtel investment with considerable suspicion and no-one would be allowed to forget it.

Nine was the centre of Kerry's world. He kept a close watch on traditional media and when he was not watching his own Nine and the goings-on at News Limited, he was tracking developments at one other company in particular — Fairfax. In 1997, Packer had contrived to position PBL for a new tilt at the newspaper company. It was seven years since he had been forced to drop out of

Conrad Black's 1991 takeover consortium Tourang, after political controversy over whether Packer might use it to control Fairfax. Undeterred, and furious at being pushed out, Packer had kept his stake in Fairfax of 15 per cent.

With the election of John Howard's Liberal Government in 1996, Packer had anticipated changes to the laws preventing cross-holdings in newspapers and television, something Howard had publicly made it clear he was willing to consider. In 1997, Packer commenced a high-pressure public and private lobbying campaign. It would eventually collapse in the face of widespread political opposition in parliament. Howard was prepared to introduce new laws, but he was unable to garner the support, including in his own party, to push it through. He was caught, too, in the most uncomfortable of positions for a Prime Minister — between the demands of a media mogul controlling the leading television network with its influential nightly news, and another media mogul controlling the largest share of the national newspaper market, including the killer metropolitan tabloids. By assuaging the demands of one giant, Howard could fall victim to the fury of another. Rupert Murdoch's News Limited might benefit from a change that allowed it to buy into television, but it would still be restrained by the limits on foreign ownership. To allow everyone a piece of the pie, Howard would be forced to amend the foreign ownership laws too. By eventually dropping the planned reforms, Howard restored order in the jungle.

By 2000, there was relative harmony in pay TV. The Murdochs and the Packers had found an accommodation and had found, moreover, that peace was cheaper than war. James Packer had joined the board of Foxtel in 1998 after PBL became a shareholder; Lachlan Murdoch had been a director since July 1995.

Foxtel itself would soon have a new chief executive too, in the form of Kim Williams, the former ABC pay TV boss who had left the public broadcaster to run Fox Studios. In 2001, after six years at Fox, Williams decided it was time to move on. He phoned Lachlan Murdoch, then the chief executive of News Limited, whom he knew well, and they arranged to meet at Tre Scalini, a fashionable Italian lunch spot in Sydney's Surry Hills favoured by the media hierarchy. Williams told Murdoch of his plans to leave and Murdoch, startled, asked what it might take to change his mind.

Williams volunteered that he thought he could do a good job at Foxtel. Under the terms of its joint venture with Telstra, News still retained power to appoint the Foxtel chief executive and the current chief executive, Jim Blomfield, was leaving. Williams was not even on the short list, but it was Murdoch's call. Williams commenced as chief executive of Foxtel on 19 December 2001.

In 2002, Foxtel would cross swords bitterly again with Fairfax. Fred Hilmer had been chief executive since 1998 and had not played any part in the crushed AIM venture to produce a 24-hour news channel to run on Foxtel. But the distant echo of that debacle had endured in some offices along the executive corridors of the newspaper giant, and in any case it took little to raise hackles at Fairfax when the subject of News or PBL came up.

When Foxtel and Optus negotiated a deal in 2002 to share programming, Fairfax made sure that its protests were registered at the competition regulator. The rest of the media industry tried to smash the plan too, with Nick Falloon, chairman of the

Ten Network and a former chief executive of the Packers' PBL, lending his voice publicly in vehement opposition. At the time, subscription television had reached no more than 25 per cent of Australian homes and was still recovering from the catastrophic financial impact of the war over Super League and large outlays on Hollywood movies. But no-one was giving anyone else a free kick.

The chairman of the Australian Competition and Consumer Commission at the time, Professor Allan Fels, summed up the issue. Under the pact with Optus, Foxtel would gain control of Hollywood movies and even more sport, sharply reducing competition. It would make Foxtel a far more muscular operation, potentially enabling it to deploy that muscle to raise prices and pick off content suppliers.

The ACCC initially rejected the agreement between Foxtel and Optus in June 2002, but finally approved it in November 2002 with a stream of court enforceable undertakings and an access and pricing model for new channel suppliers who might find themselves unable to negotiate terms with Foxtel to their satisfaction in the future. The undertakings were designed to prevent anti-competitive behaviour, stopping Foxtel from squashing content suppliers. They specified, too, how many channels in the basic service belonged to Foxtel.

Through it all, Hilmer tried to stop the deal. Company representatives maintained that Fairfax wanted to produce its own channel to run on the Foxtel platform and expected to be blocked. Fairfax believed it would never be treated fairly and would end up in the last position on the remote control. Arguments were submitted about the dominance and aggregation of power in sports programming. But no Fairfax proposal for a channel was ever submitted.

Fairfax, it was assumed, was playing out an old grudge, settling scores for the embarrassment accorded by Rupert Murdoch to AIM seven years before. Outside all the arguments about competition there was no doubt that Fairfax wanted to cause trouble for News and Foxtel. Company executives regarded the Foxtel chief executive Kim Williams, with his forceful personality, as a target. They saw it as a satisfying collateral benefit if they could drive Williams into a fury. Fairfax's head of corporate affairs at the time, Bruce Wolpe, recalled later with some satisfaction: 'When we heard that Kim went nuclear over our filings with the ACCC we really enjoyed that moment.'

At PBL, where News and Telstra now had a partner in the Foxtel business, there remained a key troublemaker with the power to cause considerable angst for Williams if he chose. Kerry Packer would never give Foxtel the slightest break, much less a compliment, even as the subscriber base of the pay TV operator slowly began to lift. Packer still regarded subscription television as an unnecessary evil, a potential threat to his free-to-air business and, in a curmudgeonly backhander, a complete dud as well.

In 2003, when Foxtel announced it would invest $600 million converting to a digital platform and dramatically expand the number of channels and interactive services available, it met with nothing but criticism from Packer. He wanted no truck with the nonsense being spouted by Williams and promoted not just by Murdoch's son Lachlan, but his own son James as well. When Lachlan Murdoch told an industry conference that Foxtel carried 47 subscription channels owned by 39 different companies, a dozen of whom were Australian or Australian-based, it fell on deaf ears in Packer's office. Packer could not wait to start in sarcastically on Williams about Foxtel's profits, a favourite topic.

'You're like the airlines; they make no money but keep on flying,' he told Williams one day.

'Thanks for the insult, Kerry,' Williams replied.

Packer insisted that Foxtel independently finance its digital business; he wasn't throwing good money after bad. He made this a condition of Foxtel becoming a digital service, forcing Williams to secure a $550 million bank facility.

When Williams had first showed Packer plans for the digital recorder, Packer had become almost incandescent with rage. He was furious that it was possible to fast-forward through the advertisements and he gave Williams a full-throttle withering shakedown about this new advance. Williams would arrive at Foxtel's Sydney headquarters on one of the Pyrmont wharves for a demonstration in the boardroom. They would discuss the business framework and then they would move on to look at the technology. It was the thing Packer was most anxious about. He would become more and more worked up about the way the Foxtel IQ box could rewind and fast forward, essentially making the viewer the programmer. The technology might be cool, but Packer saw it as a threat to his beloved Nine. He would grow angrier and angrier, usually launching a spray of invective in Williams' direction, not sparing his son James, who sat through the tirades.

Packer eventually threw up what he hoped was a blocking action to protect his baby. He decreed that Nine would have first position on the digital guide and that there must be no thirty-second 'skip' button to allow viewers to fast forward through the advertisements.

Over the years, Williams and Packer formed a robust relationship.

Not one to step back from a fight, Williams had been known to describe his own style as aggressive–aggressive. But Packer unplugged was a challenge. He never stinted on providing feedback: once he got going it could run to six or seven hours, often with top PBL executives in the room. They were all used to it. Williams recalled later:

> One day Kerry phoned me and I quite politely said, 'Good morning, Kerry, how are you?'
>
> He replied, 'Stop being such a smart arse,' then proceeded to say, 'You're stealing my money.'
>
> I said to him, 'But, Kerry, it's your business as well.' I pointed out he was a shareholder in Foxtel.
>
> And he said, 'Well, I've only got 25 per cent of it.'

In early 2005, Packer invited Williams to address the PBL board on the subject of Foxtel's fortunes, how the business was going and, more to the point, where it was going. Williams could tell it wasn't going well when he glanced across and saw that Packer had three cigarettes going at the one time. After 20 minutes, Packer interrupted and commenced with some ferocity to share his views on everything related to Foxtel.

Packer knew that he needed a foot in pay TV. He might not have liked it, and he never warmed to it, but eventually, towards the end of his life, he accepted it. On Friday 23 December, three days before Packer's death, he and Williams spoke for an hour.

They discussed a bid for the AFL rights Packer had just signed which was intended to up the ante on the Seven Network, forcing it to bid more, as well as a range of other things. Then Packer turned the conversation to how Foxtel was going and Williams steeled himself for the outburst.

'They tell me you're going to break even,' Packer said.

Williams replied that he expected Foxtel to make a maiden profit of $4 million.

'Well done, son,' Packer said. 'You've kept at it.'

The unprecedented praise startled Williams more than any blast of rage had ever done. 'You moguls are pretty strange fellows,' Williams replied.

———

In October 2012, Consolidated Media Holdings — a listed company which held the Packers' 25 per cent stake in Foxtel and 50 per cent of Fox Sports — was sold to News Corporation for $2 billion. ConsMedia by then was owned 51 per cent by the Packers, 25 per cent by the West Australian media mogul Kerry Stokes (who controlled the Seven Network), and the rest by retail investors.

News Corp already owned 25 per cent of Foxtel and 50 per cent of Fox Sports. This implied the value of News' share in Australian subscription TV assets alone — 100 per cent of Fox Sports and 50 per cent of Foxtel — was not far short of $4 billion.

Fairfax was worth less than $1 billion.

CHAPTER FIVE

TURN OFF THE TV

Late on the evening of Monday 26 December 2005, Kerry Packer died at home in Bellevue Hill, losing a decades-long fight against ill health at the age of 68. It was a moment that transformed not just the lives of his family and friends, but the entire media landscape, as a dynasty turned on its axis. Packer had dominated television and stalked Fairfax for decades; he had maintained a tense, mutually suspicious, on-off detente with the Murdochs. He had been by turns scornful, terrifying and charming. Suddenly he was gone.

James Packer had arrived at his father's bedside just hours before, rushing from the Maldive Islands in the Indian Ocean. The next morning, a typically humid Sydney day, he wanted to be alone; he climbed into his dark blue Aston Martin to drive around for a while, listening to Elton John singing 'Rocket Man'. Then he phoned David Gonski, the high-profile corporate lawyer, adviser to the Packer family and former Fairfax director, to tell him that Kerry had died.

Gonski, who had first met Kerry Packer when he was a 27-year-old Freehills lawyer, was one of two executors of Kerry Packer's will, sharing the role with Kerry's closest friend, Melbourne property developer and horse racing king Lloyd Williams. Gonski could hear James' distress on the phone. He had lost his own father not long before and he said, 'Why don't you come round?'

When James Packer arrived weeping at the door they embraced, then sat with glasses of sparkling mineral water, talking about the loss of their fathers. And Gonski told Packer that his father's will had placed the empire in his hands.

Afterwards, Gonski drove from his Point Piper home to his office to collect the array of documents that formed Kerry Packer's last will and testament. Tuesday 27 December was a public holiday to make up for Christmas, which had fallen on a Sunday; even so, this was not a matter that could wait. This was no ordinary family: a vast and sprawling company had to be protected as news broke that one of the giants of the media and business world was gone. The wheels of the company must continue to roll smoothly forward.

The next day, 28 December, Gonski drove to the Packer family compound on Victoria Road, which by now was bristling with cameras and journalists. He phoned ahead and the gates swung open, then closed behind him. At 10 a.m. James Packer sat down with Gonski and Williams in his father's study, known as Kerry's card room, where the salient features of the will were outlined. Afterwards, they joined James' sister Gretel and his mother Ros in the sunroom, with its huge comfortable chairs favoured by Kerry. Gonski paid his respects and the will was read as they sipped tea. James had been given the keys to the kingdom, subject to various personal wishes. It was an inheritance with a net worth of more than $5 billion — over $6.5 billion in assets and roughly $1.5 billion in debt. It was a remarkable outcome given the years of battle between father and son and it revealed a significant reassessment by Packer of his son's business acumen and the mutual reconciliation that had played out as Packer faced the end of his life. Gonski said later: 'The will was based upon Kerry having enormous respect for James and his confidence in his business judgement, and the clauses were consistent with that, and the will was based on that. And the will entailed that he would look after the family.'

James Packer had arrived from the Maldives just in time to say goodbye but the real farewell between father and son had taken place in an hour-long phone call the week before. It had been a farewell carefully orchestrated by Kerry Packer without revealing to his son that the doctors had told him he had little time left. For years they had seemed like the old and the young bull charging in the same paddock. If declarations of love had not been easy in the past, they were made now. Kerry Packer would not leave loose ends behind. And while he had decided not to tell his son that he had only days to live, Packer had told his old friend Lloyd. 'Son, I'm off,' he said in his inimitable way, before insisting that Williams promise not to tell James. Williams kept his word, with one exception: he rang James, who was on the family's luxuriously converted ice-breaker, the *Arctic P* — known in the family as *Arctic* — to let him know that his father was once again very seriously ill. At least he would be prepared. Finally, Professor John Horvath, Kerry's personal physician and the Australian Government Chief Medical Officer, decided that James had to be told. As his father began to slip away, James rushed to board a plane.

It was exactly two weeks since James Packer had finished
giving evidence in the One.Tel civil case brought by the Australian
Securities and Investments Commission against One.Tel directors
Jodee Rich and Mark Silbermann. For ten days he was cross-
examined, concluding on 13 December. While James gave
evidence, his father was in Argentina visiting his estate and the
polo fields he loved. Kerry had considered staying in Australia
while his son was in court, but had decided in the end not to add
to the pressure. James' girlfriend Erica Baxter came to court every
day, and on some days his mother or his sister. It was a case replete
with highly damaging and contradictory evidence on all sides.
James was hammered by Rich's lawyers, who — among other
things — contended that James Packer had once told Rich that he
wanted his father to die. Newspaper headlines blazed with stories
about his relationship with his father. After it all, just one question
thumped through his brain: 'What's Dad going to say?' He found
out soon enough.

'Afterwards, Dad rang me from Argentina where he was on
what would be his last trip. He said, "They tell me you did well."
And then he told me to go to the boat and have a holiday.'

Kerry Packer had finally understood the shattering impact
One.Tel had had on his son. It had taken him a year in 2001 and
2002 to see that James had had a breakdown. Eventually, after
the intercession of friends, some fearing that James would take
his own life, Kerry had acknowledged that this was more than a
bitter financial lesson to be learned through public and private
humiliation and the court action that followed. The lifelong
'outside member' of the family, David Gyngell, had told Kerry that
his son was in a terrible way. After seeing James broken in spirit at

the end of 2001, the actor Tom Cruise, who had befriended him in better days during the filming of *Mission: Impossible II* in Sydney, had phoned Kerry to offer to take care of his son. Kerry Packer had agreed and he spoke to the actor regularly in the three months James was in his care. James Packer finally returned to Sydney on 1 October 2002 — bruised still, but alive. Later, when Fairfax newspaper reports of James becoming a Scientologist under Cruise's influence and tutelage reached their zenith, Kerry Packer had obtained a copy of the United Nations Human Rights charter and angrily sent it to the company's chief executive Fred Hilmer with a warning that he was violating the charter.

Now, after the One.Tel court hearings in 2005 and knowing he had only a short time left, Kerry Packer imposed no further punishments for the past on his son. James Packer left Sydney on a trip to the Maldives on 16 December 2005. Ten days later he returned to Sydney for his father's last hours, becoming head of the family at 38.

On 30 December, in a poignant moment freighted with irony, the black Mercedes hearse carrying Packer's coffin to Ellerston in the Hunter Valley slowed down on a country road as cattle crossed. The image, with the stillness of the countryside in the background and its metaphor of eternity, was snapped by a young photographer, Kitty Hill from the *Newcastle Herald*, owned by Fairfax, who happened upon the car and set off in pursuit.

Seven weeks later, on 17 February 2006, a formal state memorial service for Kerry Packer was held at the Sydney Opera House, with guests and mourners ranging from politicians, actors and cricketers to news hounds and old mates. During a moving eulogy to his father, James Packer told of their highs and lows, but then, three-quarters the way through, he raised a bitter reference to the old blood feud that coursed through his family. The Costigan Royal Commission of 1980 into the Federated Ship Painters and Dockers Union — an organisation rife with criminality — had tangentially implicated Kerry Packer in a string of allegations of murder, organised crime, tax evasion, drug running and pornography. When Fairfax's newspaper *The National Times* published sections of the report, Packer was given the codename 'Goanna'. Political foes such as then Prime Minister Bob Hawke and Deputy Opposition Leader John Howard later defended Packer and he was eventually cleared of the allegations. But the damage was done and the Packers had never forgotten. It was not just Costigan in James Packer's sights during his father's memorial service, but all the newspaper headlines that had accompanied the case. James was his father's son. Kerry had hated Fairfax for 'the Goanna'. James would never forgive the 'Goanna' headlines, but he hated Fairfax too for the coverage of One.Tel. He was convinced that the wall to wall reporting was because of the Packer and Murdoch names. With its television and magazines that looked into the underbelly of others' lives, media had made his family's fortune, but it had made him a target too.

———

James Packer's first deal after inheriting his father's media empire was in casinos. On 3 March 2006, ten weeks after Kerry's death, James boarded a Qantas flight with PBL's general counsel Guy Jalland and flew to Los Angeles and then on by private jet to Las Vegas. There, he struck a deal his father would never have agreed to: the purchase, with his partner Lawrence Ho, of the last remaining Macau casino licence from gaming and casino legend Steve Wynn for US $900 million.

James had opened negotiations with Wynn in January, just weeks after his father's death. This was his business now. He had pushed his father into buying Crown casino in Melbourne in 1999 from Lloyd Williams' company Hudson Conway, and he had fought with his father to take over Burswood casino in Western Australia — rolling him in the PBL boardroom in mid-2004 with the support of other directors in what was tantamount to an ambush. It was a battle that saw the chief executive of PBL, Peter Yates, fired by Kerry for his efforts. Yates was immediately replaced by one-time Fairfax editor John Alexander, who by then was running the Packers' TV and magazine divisions, Nine and ACP. If Kerry Packer had thought Alexander would help him to cripple the Burswood takeover, which had run into trouble, he was wrong: Alexander argued instead that it was the only way to go. Kerry had caved in, also agreeing to invest in a joint venture in Macau with Lawrence Ho, scion of the Ho family that dominated the territory's casino business — but he had agreed only to a capital-light $200 million. 'We've got to focus on Channel Nine,' Kerry would tell his son.

Now, eighteen months after the Burswood takeover and two weeks after his father's memorial service, James made an audacious, some said crazy, move: spending a vast portion of his inheritance and almost all of his liquidity on an over-priced new licence for an unbuilt casino in Macau. He signed the deal with Wynn to acquire Wynn Resorts' gaming sub-concession on 4 March 2006.

James had not taken his eyes off media, however. He loved new media and he had made a significant gamble on the internet with his investment in SEEK in 2003 in the comeback after One. Tel. He had followed this in 2005 with his large stake in carsales, achieved by merging the ACP Trader websites, stuffed with data, and the Carpoint website into carsales in exchange for equity. His biggest financial exposure to media, however, remained PBL's ownership of the Nine Network. This was the soul of the company but it was not a business that fanned the flames of obsession for James as it had for Kerry. James wanted to be ready to move in any direction when the Howard government's long-mooted changes to Australia's media laws came through.

Already he had begun moving pieces around in the 'old media' side of his business. After an approach soon after Kerry's death from Ron Walker, Fairfax's chairman and an old friend of the Packer family, to buy ACP's New Zealand print assets, John Alexander had slapped a huge price of $530 million on the table. But the deal quickly fell apart amidst considerable acrimony as Fairfax shifted its attention to winning a fight against Packer for the New Zealand auction house TradeMe. Two days after returning from Las Vegas where he signed the deal with Wynn, James lost the tussle with Fairfax for TradeMe. It rankled, not least because it reminded him of the 50 per cent of eBay Australia that had cost PBL $3 million in 1999 and that Kerry had sold for $120 million in August 2002 without consulting his son, a decision which still infuriated James.

On 14 March 2006, ten days after James Packer signed the deal with Wynn, John Howard's Communications Minister Helen Coonan announced that the Government would introduce sweeping changes, removing an array of controls on ownership of TV, radios and newspapers and scaling back controls on foreign ownership. James Packer had lobbied tirelessly for the laws to be relaxed, duchessing Howard, Coonan, and the Treasurer Peter Costello. Kerry Packer had always wanted the limits on cross-media ownership removed but he baulked at the removal of limits on foreign ownership, fearing this would favour Rupert Murdoch. But James Packer wanted both cross-media and foreign limits gone. He knew that changes to the laws that favoured the Packers could only obtain parliamentary support if they gave advantages to the Murdochs too. History had shown that politicians retreated when bull elephants fought to defend their patch. In any case, James was more than happy to support changes to the foreign rules; it meant he could sell Nine to a foreign company if he wanted to.

Coonan's announcement was the starter's whistle for a reorientation of the media world that would make it unrecognisable in a few short years. In particular, a light started flashing over Fairfax as speculation escalated in the markets and in media circles that the company would be prey in a takeover.

The last year of Kerry Packer's life, 2005, was the last year the Nine Network would comprehensively dominate the ratings for years to come. Kerry had fired his Nine chief executive David Leckie in 2002 and the network had endured constant ructions and executive firefights in the years since. Leckie was a loud and forceful character with TV instincts to match Packer's, something that had always riled the boss. Leckie had been close to James but in the aftermath of the One.Tel collapse, James had lost the power to defend him. After Leckie's departure, John Alexander was appointed head of Nine, while continuing as the boss of ACP. In June 2004, after Alexander became chief executive of PBL, his deputy David Gyngell took over Nine. Three months later, in a decision that sparked a chaotic interplay of competing executives, Kerry Packer brought back Sam Chisholm, placing him in the network in a position of power adjacent to Gyngell, a move followed by the return of other executives from Nine's heyday. The executive suite acquired a revolving door. If Gyngell had expected his long personal relationship with the Packers to provide protection, he soon found to the contrary, that his professional life was hell.

There was little James could do to break up the wars because this was his father's world. In any case, getting caught in the middle of it all was the last thing he wanted. There were brutal altercations between executives over costs, TV stars, management practices — pretty much anything. Finally, amidst all the arguments, David Gyngell quit abruptly in May 2005. Sam Chisholm took over on an interim basis while Kerry sought a permanent replacement. Three months before his death, Kerry tried to persuade his son to run Nine. But James could see that his relationship with his father would quickly become untenable if he took the job, and he refused.

Shortly after Kerry's death, James Packer signed off on the appointment of his friend Eddie McGuire, the host of Nine's *The Footy Show*, as the network's new boss. It was a decision to which Kerry had agreed but it was no less bizarre for that, and it opened the door to a new round of appalling publicity for Nine. It was followed by more shock waves — cost-cutting, redundancies, and the eye-watering saga of Mark Llewellyn, Nine's head of news, who was forced from his position then quit the company for a job at Seven. John Alexander was at the heart of much of the bloodshed, wielding the knife on costs with the ruthless pragmatism for which he was renowned. James Packer seethed under the inevitable attacks from Fairfax calling him a loser incapable of running a TV network — even though the tumultuous year before had actually been Kerry's last stand. Inside the organisation it may have felt like a series of turf wars, but in reality these were the early fracture lines as the tectonic plates shifted beneath the traditional media holdings of the Packer family.

James Packer's personal life reached a crossroads in March 2006 when he split up with Erica Baxter. He had missed buying TradeMe, his sale of ACP's New Zealand magazines to Fairfax had collapsed, Nine was in chaos and things were over with his girlfriend. He had, however, bought a new casino licence from Steve Wynn, a totemic deal signalling where he intended his business to go. The scene was now set for an extraordinary cascade of events in the heart of the media industry.

By late March, not three months after his father's death, James Packer had opened the door to conversations with investment bankers about selling Nine. He was thinking about his financial position and the scale of funding required for building casinos; already he had tried to sell ACP's New Zealand trade papers to Fairfax. Nicholas Moore, the head of investment banking at Macquarie Bank, had started the ball rolling by talking to Packer about merging Nine with Fairfax. That discussion had interested Packer in the bigger idea of selling Nine, or at least part of Nine.

Moore was one of a circle of investment bankers radiating around Packer, and Packer, briefly, was one of the biggest individual shareholders in Macquarie, the country's most aggressive merchant bank. At the same time, the head of investment banking at UBS, Matthew Grounds, was talking to Packer about selling half of Nine to a private equity firm: the American corporate raider Kohlberg

Kravis Roberts (known everywhere as simply KKR), whom Grounds was working with on a bid for the retail giant Coles Myer.

The silver-haired Moore with his patrician air and Grounds, the boyish-faced charmer, were two of the toughest investment bankers in the country and both close to Packer. Another, Chris Mackay, who had been chairman and chief executive of UBS, became a director of PBL as James reshaped his father's board with his own people. The fourth banker in James Packer's close circle, Ben Brazil, was an executive director of Macquarie who had worked directly for James at the Packer family's private company Consolidated Press Holdings in 2001. Slim enough to break in the breeze, he was known as 'Brains.'

On 31 March 2006 Matthew Grounds met with Packer to put forward arguments on behalf of KKR to consider a deal with private equity. Packer was not keen; he did not want half of Nine leveraged with debt and preferred a float on the stock market if anything. But Grounds had a card to play to keep the door open. One of the founders of KKR, George Roberts, had been in Australia working on the Coles deal. Before he left, and as his private plane readied for departure on 6 April, Grounds took Roberts to meet Packer at his Crown office. They had now met at least, and liked each other. From such simple beginnings, relationship deals could be built.

For the next three months James Packer would think about whether to sell out of media, debating the idea back and forth with his inner circle. He believed that Nine could be turned around if he had five years and he brought back David Gyngell as chief executive. But the risk was whether there would even be a viable business left in five years, given the surge of the internet and the increasing footprint of pay TV, where he was also a major shareholder. He remained convinced the internet would win.

After losing out on TradeMe, James had turned his attention to ramping up his existing holdings in a far more significant internet company, and one that cut to the heart of Fairfax. Eight months after taking a 41 per cent stake in carsales.com.au he was on the hunt for a bigger piece of this internet success. Packer's investment had already helped to ensure that Fairfax would never own carsales.

His interest in expanding his shareholding did not remain a secret long. In a news story published on 22 May 2006, *The Sydney Morning Herald* reported that PBL had approached Fairfax about buying the company's small stake in carsales, acquired by Fairfax in 2005 as part of a distribution deal with Yahoo. James Packer wanted those shares.

Fairfax sitting on seven per cent of the company annoyed him. James had joined the board of carsales and he raised the idea of trying to acquire Fairfax's 15 million shares, which now constituted 7.6 per cent of carsales after being diluted down when Packer bought in. It was 7.6 per cent too much for Packer's liking. The response of his fellow directors was the same. There was no love for Fairfax even though the dangers of a year before, when Fairfax had demanded boardroom rights, had passed. Packer quietly explored the issue with Fairfax's new chairman Ron Walker and he reported back to the carsales board that he had received a positive response.

Walker had known James Packer since James was a boy, and he had been a close friend of Kerry. As a founder of Hudson Conway with Lloyd Williams, Walker was a wealthy man. On the international board of the Grand Prix and a long-time federal treasurer of the Liberal Party, Walker had one of the best contact networks in business. He had been a director of Fairfax since 2003 and he had succeeded Dean Wills as chairman in October 2005.

Given the large holdings locked up by James Packer and the carsales founders, Walker knew that Fairfax could not increase its stake in carsales unless it mounted a hostile takeover, something Fairfax had no appetite for. Fairfax was locked out of the carsales boardroom with no way to curb the company's attack on Fairfax's core advertising business. But Packer wanted Fairfax out altogether, and he wanted to get to 50 per cent. He argued persuasively to Walker that it was a waste for Fairfax to sit on the register with no power. It was a lazy investment, tying up capital. They should just get out. Walker was interested in selling, but there were legal and regulatory hurdles that seemed insurmountable. Wal Pisciotta, the chairman of carsales, recalled later: 'In the following board meetings, we explored from time to time, ways the company might be able to acquire Fairfax's shareholding in carsales. But due to legal prohibition of preferential buybacks we were unable to develop such a strategy.'

Packer continued to think about it. Carsales was a remarkable business and it had, through dint of perseverance and a one-eyed focus on every scintilla of opportunity, smashed Fairfax's dominance in online car classifieds. Before many more months had gone by, he would find a way to unpick Fairfax from the share register altogether.

Packer's holdings in SEEK had proved a hugely successful investment for PBL too. SEEK was outflanking Fairfax, steadily cutting into online employment advertising. SEEK had floated the year before, in April 2005, and James Packer had become chairman upon listing. The float had made millionaires of its founders, the Bassat brothers and Matt Rockman, but it had also prompted an extraordinary attack from Fairfax, which suggested that — despite its aggressive public bravado — behind the scenes Fairfax was hurting.

Early in April 2005, with the SEEK float underway, an anonymous document titled 'The SEEK prospectus: Blue sky for who?' had made its way around journalists and financial institutions. There was no author listed to indicate its origins, but it was a savage denunciation of the pure-play online classified model. The document attacked SEEK head-on, asserting that the SEEK prospectus had failed to note the real story of online advertising, which was the success of hybrid print–online employment sites over dedicated pure-plays: 'If you relied solely on the SEEK prospectus, you would think that online employment classifieds growth was robust, with only blue sky ahead. And you would take a dim view of print employment classifieds,' the document sternly warned.

It attacked SEEK's bullish growth forecasts, describing key claims in the SEEK prospectus as gaffes. And it attacked SEEK's estimate that it was worth 33 per cent more than other companies in the media space. 'What we are hearing is that this is an argument which some professional investors are not buying.'

On 12 April 2005, this five-page document was emailed by a senior Fairfax business journalist to a banker at Macquarie Equity Capital Markets, which was handling the SEEK float. Thirty minutes later it was emailed from Macquarie to executives at PBL. Attached was a note from Macquarie to say that it had come from Fairfax and was being circulated to journalists and institutions.

Two days later, after the matter was raised with Fairfax by PBL lawyer Guy Jalland, Fairfax was forced to declare its hand, issuing a press statement acknowledging the document as its own and describing it as in-house analysis. It was a remarkable intervention by a top Australian company trying to damage the float of a minnow-sized competitor. But Fairfax had not finished. A Fairfax spokesman said in the statement, 'SEEK is acting like Chicken Little, saying the sky is falling, the sky is falling. But we wanted our troops to understand we have a good business with a good future.'

The SEEK float eventually closed at the end of April 2005 at $2.10, the upper end of the price range, valuing James Packer's 25 per cent, bought for $33 million 18 months before, at $150 million — and in a weak share market. Within a year, by May 2006, media speculation had grown that PBL would try to use its substantial holdings in both SEEK and carsales to push the two companies together, an idea soon publicly knocked on the head by the founders of SEEK.

On 23 June 2006, James Packer left for London to play polo, go to the tennis at Wimbledon and clear his head after the break-up with his girlfriend. He wanted time on his own to think and to leave behind the mess at Nine as his executives tore each other apart amidst rounds of staff sackings. But he failed utterly to anticipate the ferocity of the media coverage of his absence. Nine had attempted to suppress an affidavit that alleged — amongst other things — a brutal culture and the crudest of language used about a female star at the network. The affidavit formed part of a court action with Nine's former news chief Mark Llewellyn and there was uproar as the contents was splashed around.

Much as he wanted to escape it all, Packer had made a serious error of judgement by not delaying his trip. The chairman of News Corporation, Rupert Murdoch, had been selected as the most influential Australian of all time by *The Bulletin*, the flagship magazine owned by the Packers' Australian Consolidated Press. Murdoch was in Australia to attend the wedding of actress Nicole Kidman and the country music star Keith Urban, and he had agreed to attend *The Bulletin*'s gala lunch at Sydney's Machiavelli restaurant at which the list of the most influential people from all walks of life was to be announced.

On 26 June 2006 Murdoch was seated at the top table at Machiavelli with the chief executive of PBL, John Alexander, Treasurer Peter Costello and a host of business leaders. Reporting on the lunch later that day, the AAP wire service quoted the editor-in-chief of *The Bulletin*, Garry Linnell, describing Murdoch as 'close to being the most powerful unelected person on earth'. The chairman of Fairfax, Ron Walker, was on Murdoch's table but the chairman of PBL, James Packer, was not even in the country, having flown out three days earlier. Rupert might be the most important Australian in the world according to a Packer publication, but James had snubbed him to play polo. It was a lack of respect that Packer came to bitterly regret.

Four days later, the Murdoch-owned *The Daily Telegraph* in Sydney laid into James Packer with a string of blistering news stories and features that continued over two days. The unforgettable highlight, detailed in the racy, biting style that was the hallmark of this no-holds-barred tabloid, was the front-page headline on 30

June. 'He's just sacked 100 staff, his network is a mess, and he's in England for tennis and polo. HOME JAMES,' the paper roared.

The stories attacking Packer took out the whole front page, describing him as facing his biggest challenge since his father's death and mocking his spending spree on a new $100 million yacht and a $50 million refurbishment of his private jet. He was in London for schmoozing while the once impregnable Nine unravelled. He was the 'invisible man'. On and on it went. The spill of the story on page four was accompanied by a photo of Packer on a polo pony with another not-to-be-outdone headline: 'Packer has fun while Nine staff left fuming.' If that wasn't enough of a slapping, *The Tele* (as the paper was known) gave Packer more grief in a slashing editorial comment on page 28. This was a great story from any journalist's perspective: Nine was a legendary network and it was in more of a mess than anyone could have imagined. The reporting hit home.

The next day, Saturday 1 July, *The Tele* unleashed another incredible volley, with stories on pages 2, 27 and 28 eviscerating Packer's selection of Eddie McGuire as Nine CEO. It included a feature story illustrated with headshots of Packer and his executives titled 'Nine's ones to watch out for', a play on the Nine slogan 'Still the One.' Packer was named as 'the absent big boss'. Alexander was tagged a puppet-master and 'Prince of Darkness' whose fingerprints were everywhere.

As the tabloid onslaught continued, Packer was staying at the Metropolitan Hotel in London, perched between Mayfair and Knightsbridge, with its minimalist architecture and design, views across the Hyde Park treetops, and reputation as a hang-out for rock stars and models. Bankers — many of whom James knew well — came and went pitching deals. They were hunters in a world awash with private equity, and money growing on trees that most thought would flower in perpetuity. Asset values were rising and debt was cheap.

When Packer read *The Daily Telegraph* stories he was both furious and mortified. He was susceptible to ideas about how to hit back to defend himself. Some of the advisers and bankers surrounding him tossed around notions that might have seemed far-fetched to outsiders, but were entirely in keeping with the hothouse talk around Packer and the eyes-for-a-deal environment of investment banking. Among those ideas was the thought of buying another media organisation and using it to attack News Limited.

Nicholas Moore was in town, trying to buy the world. He had pushed Packer already to consider a tilt at Fairfax with Macquarie. There was no love lost in this group for the newspaper company and Moore thought it was time to move. Packer, raised from the cradle in media, was the perfect partner.

'Nick had said to me, "Let's buy Fairfax and we'll be able to punch back,"' Packer recalled later. In this financial environment with all of its 'Masters of the Universe' aggression and hubris, anything seemed possible.

Five years earlier, the Packers had sold their 14.9 per cent Fairfax stake held in a listed investment vehicle, CPH Investment Corporation, previously known as FXF Trust. That sale, at $4 a share on 19 July 2001, had been underwritten by UBS and had realised $436 million. It followed discussions between Kerry and James Packer with John Alexander, who had been recruited with one key objective. He could be warehoused for the future in case they mounted a takeover. Almost the first question they had asked him was what he thought about Fairfax. Alexander told them that if they wanted the company for emotional reasons he could see the benefit of owning a newspaper with influence. But he warned them against buying Fairfax, saying the business model was challenged and the classifieds were under threat.

James Packer wanted to be in casinos. He believed firmly that the internet was already beating Fairfax. He had spent years disparaging the company and investing in online classified pure-plays that had positioned themselves like vultures over Fairfax's business. To recant now would be a breathtaking step backwards.

Soon after the bombardment from *The Daily Telegraph*, Packer and Alexander, who had arrived in London for the tennis, called Nick Moore over for a meeting. Moore was staying at The Leonard, the designated London hotel for senior Macquarie management, known for its classic luxury and decor in the style of an exclusive gentleman's club.

Moore arrived as the afternoon sun streamed through the windows of Packer's suite. He talked Packer and Alexander through the bones of his ideas on Fairfax and the potential for a joint bid. For Macquarie to buy Fairfax, it would probably cost the share price, now floating around $3.40, plus 30 per cent. Moore said he was willing to pay up to $4.30 or $4.50 and he suggested that PBL could run Fairfax in exchange for a management fee.

John Alexander had strong views about his old stomping ground. He was opposed to getting into bed with a deal to buy the metropolitan papers, *The Age* and *The Sydney Morning Herald*. He was interested only in *The Australian Financial Review*. Alexander regarded *The AFR*, or *The Fin*, as it was known to insiders, as more stable and with the right type of clout. On his quick back-of-envelope calculation, the paper could be worth $500 million.

Buying it was not a new idea. Some six years before, James Packer had offered the then Fairfax CEO Fred Hilmer $500 million for 50 per cent of *The AFR* in a joint venture with Nine that could be morphed into business television, online business muscle for Nine, and potentially the creation of index funds branded with *AFR* logos. It was a lot of money for a newspaper but Hilmer had refused.

Packer and his various advisers held a week of informal talks in London about the Macquarie idea. Chris Mackay and Matthew Grounds argued that Packer should go the other way and sell Nine. Grounds had been consistently down on the idea of buying Fairfax. Ben Brazil, who had worked for Packer in the past and whose opinion James valued highly, played a critical role in the final decision. Playing devil's advocate, he pointed out the huge valuations of media companies, of Nine, ACP and Fairfax. The internet was slashing the business model and newspapers were already becoming known to some big investors as nothing but debt. But prices were high, ridiculously so. They talked for hours one night.

When he woke the next morning, Packer dumped the Fairfax idea. He wanted to get out of media, not further into it. He called Ben Brazil. 'At these prices I'm not a buyer, I'm a seller,' James told him. Then he called Matthew Grounds. 'Let's go the other way and sell.'

He said later, 'Nick Moore was desperate for me to buy Fairfax with him and Macquarie. He pushed me hard to look at it. I luckily dodged that bullet.'

Nick Moore recalled later: 'We did talk to James about a lot of things. For someone with a client like James it's our role to bring up ideas and we had a lot of "have you thought about it" conversations with him. James did have real interest in *The AFR* and he was actively debating the whole media space.'

James Packer might have made a rational business decision about media values, but he had made an emotional decision on another level. He was tired of the media battles and the vitriol. His father had excelled in this, and James was capable of throwing as much blood and gore as the next mogul, but he was sick of it. 'I saw traditional media as all fights and no reward; and I believed the internet was coming.'

In the end any further debate inside Macquarie over Fairfax was academic. Packer was not interested and the share price was rising in a market where investors anticipated takeovers if proposed new media laws were put in place. The Fairfax share price went past $4.50 within four months, past the level where Moore had any interest. Rather than buying Fairfax, Nine would be sold.

————

Macquarie put together a large team led by Jim Miller, head of the bank's infrastructure group, to create a proposal for an initial public offering (IPO) of PBL's media interests. It would be known as Project Oyster. James Packer returned from London on 25 July 2006 and within two weeks, presentations to PBL by Macquarie were underway, the first on 7 August, the next on 10 August.

But behind the scenes a dispute was soon brewing between Macquarie and UBS. James Packer had consulted Matthew Grounds, the head of UBS investment banking, keeping his options open with an array of advice. Grounds had already talked to Packer about a sale to private equity and he disagreed with the

Macquarie proposal for a leveraged IPO, which essentially meant raising huge debt to pay Packer for half of his company and then floating it to investors in the stock market.

Grounds wanted a doomsday scenario factored in to protect Packer. What if the stock market collapsed, or old media values plummeted? Packer would be stuck in a public company loaded with debt where he was the lead corporate investor while every small investor rode the share price down. It could look like One.Tel all over again, only worse.

Grounds reverted to his idea for Packer to sell to a private equity firm. That way he would have the proceeds from selling half of his company in his hands and that half would be owned by a private equity firm big enough to know what it was doing. There would be no small shareholders. It gave Packer the ability to sell the rest if and when he wanted, without the shackles of a public listing.

Grounds argued with Nick Moore, telling him he should not be pushing Packer into an IPO with leverage. It exposed the client to too much risk. Grounds decided to try to kill the Macquarie machine. He warned Moore that he would directly recommend that Packer not proceed with the Macquarie proposal. Moore was just as stubborn, arguing that the private equity structure Grounds was pushing would never work.

The Macquarie team was meeting with Nine's accountants, writing business plans and developing a prospectus. There was no doubt this could be a very significant and lucrative deal for Macquarie. Between the refinancing of Nine, the float itself, and other aspects, the fees could easily run to over a hundred million dollars. By the time Ben Brazil returned from London, Grounds was furious about the intensity of the Macquarie pressure. He phoned Brazil, saying, 'You've got to rein in your troops. They're animals.'

On the morning of Sunday 20 August 2006, Grounds sent Packer a long email with an assessment of four alternative scenarios for PBL:

1. spinning off the media assets to shareholders
2. an IPO with relatively low debt gearing
3. an IPO with high gearing (Macquarie's model)
4. selling 40 to 50 per cent of the media assets to private equity with the aim of a public listing in 2–4 years.

'There are risks in all 4,' Grounds wrote, 'but there are risks in everything.' But he warned Packer against the Macquarie model, arguing that Packer should not be exposed with a highly levered financial vehicle in the public equity markets for the next five to 10 years. He noted that even Macquarie's own media fund Macquarie Media was not saddled with the amount of debt Macquarie proposed for Packer. Grounds numbered the alternatives in order of preference: 4, 1, 2, 3 — putting the private equity deal as the best alternative, and advising Packer: 'This maximises the cash you take off the table at today's equity and debt prices.' He had placed the Macquarie proposal last.

On 22 August, the PBL board considered Macquarie's proposal. In the documents, PBL was code-named Pearl and Macquarie was Conch. The plan was for the 'releverage' and sale of MediaCo (as the proposed spin-off was tagged by Macquarie). It would include the Nine Network, ACP Magazines and the 50 per cent of ninemsn owned by PBL. By now the ACP magazine division was worth more than Kerry Packer's treasured Nine Network. ACP had made over $300 million in earnings in 2006, compared with around $80 million six years before. Since taking over in 1999, John Alexander had systematically cut costs, improved revenue and circulation and driven margins into record territory for magazines anywhere.

The PBL board rejected Project Oyster and resolved, as a matter of principle, to pursue a joint venture with a private equity firm instead. By now pushing the starter button on Project Y, they had endorsed the UBS strategy over Macquarie's. Packer appointed both banks to work on the project but he specified that he would personally deal only with Matthew Grounds and Ben Brazil on a daily basis. UBS would take the lion's share but Macquarie kept Project Oyster alive for another month in case the private equity deals fell through. It would receive a fee of close to $20 million for several meetings. Packer had wanted to look after Ben Brazil and Grounds had wanted to shut Nick Moore up. Giving Macquarie a slice of the action achieved both.

Packer became increasingly critical over time of the heavily leveraged IPO structure Macquarie had pushed and the risks for himself he believed it entailed. He said later, 'My reality as I look back is that Macquarie did not give me good advice. I just don't trust Macquarie. I believe they solve for themselves, not their clients.'

UBS was given the brief to negotiate directly with the private equity firms. A set number were invited to bid, with a non-negotiable fixed price set by Packer of $5.5 billion. This was made up of $4.5 billion in cash and $1 billion of equity for Packer in a new jointly-owned company which would later be called PBL Media. The companies invited to bid were KKR, CVC Asia Pacific,

Texas Pacific Group, and later two more — Providence Equity Partners and the Qatar Investment Authority. All they had to do was conduct due diligence, to examine the business. UBS agreed to underwrite the debt involved. There was no bidding war — at least, there was no bidding war on price. The auction was in the timing. Whoever got in first with a completed bid ready to sign would win. They had six weeks, which became seven by the end. The PE firms were asked to give a commitment that their investment committees had given approval. QIA, which was late to the race, asked for time to prepare its bid. Packer though, would not wait and QIA dropped out without ever starting. After an initial look, Providence said no. This left three strong contenders: KKR, CVC and TPG.

Given the foreign ownership limits governing media, there was still a question of control once the assets were sold. To get around this, a legal and financial structure was created to vest control with Packer. It would hold the deal together until the media laws changed, and it could be converted later to equity for a new owner.

———

Packer was convinced that he should include some serious internet assets alongside television and magazines, 'to sprinkle some internet dust,' as he put it. He would add ninemsn to the deal but he needed to sweeten it with another significant online stock as well. He had to decide between SEEK and carsales and in the end it came down to carsales, where he had a large controlling stake. As much as anything, he wanted to make sure that Fairfax could never get its hands on carsales, even though it was sitting on 7.6 per cent. Carsales was number one in the auto internet space. There had long been fights over that claim but since Packer had acquired his stake the year before, the arguments had died down. Packer knew Ron Walker was a seller, frustrated by the inability to move in any direction in the company, a blockade Packer himself had been instrumental in creating. On 22 September 2006, Packer's ACP Magazines signed a call option agreement with Fairfax to acquire part of Fairfax's carsales stake. On the same day, Packer boosted his holdings in SEEK, buying a further 2.4 per cent at a price of $5.04 cents per share. It was $35 million for just over two per cent of the company. Three years earlier, Packer had paid $33 million for 25 per cent. SEEK had been a phenomenal investment and it had hacked into the heart of the Fairfax business. But so had carsales, which had the added advantage of frustrating Fairfax, which had found itself stuck with one foot inside the door and the other outside.

Walker recalled later, 'I and the Fairfax board had the view that we didn't want to end up with a bunch of minority stakes in companies we couldn't control. We had tried and tried to buy more of carsales and there was no more available.'

On Saturday 23 September 2006 the chairman of carsales, Wal Pisciotta, was at his apartment on the Gold Coast when the phone rang. He picked it up to find James Packer on the line. Packer asked how he was. Pisciotta recalled later:

I said, 'Great,' as I was enjoying myself on holidays. James asked, 'Where are you?'

I said, 'At the coast,' and he apologised for wrecking my weekend. He had wanted to call earlier, but could not on legal advice. And then he apologised for creating a busier than expected weekend for me.

Packer was phoning to tell Pisciotta that on Monday morning, ACP would announce a full takeover bid for carsales and had already acquired from Fairfax the almost three per cent of stock allowed by law under the creep provisions of the Takeovers Act. He planned to make an offer for the rest of carsales at $1.21 per share. Pisciotta immediately understood that Packer, with a stake greater than 19.9 per cent, would have to extend the same offer to all shareholders.

Pisciotta began calling board members. They had a takeover hitting the deck on Monday and they needed expert advice as soon as possible. The price on the table was $1.21. Grant Samuel was contracted for an independent valuation. The board advised that the offer was fair and reasonable, but recommended against it. Carsales directors would not be selling into the takeover, except for one. Pisciotta offered to buy the stake of this director at the same price Packer had offered and they reached a deal.

Several days later, with some trepidation, Pisciotta decided to tell Packer that he had snapped up this stock himself.

I rang him and said, 'I just want to let you know I've just bought another four million shares from one of my large foundation shareholders.'

And James' reply to me was, 'All the good guys are buying them!'

I knew James mainly wanted to buy out Fairfax. It was not news to me that he wanted to get those Fairfax shares as he had already brought a proposal to the boardroom table.

Packer ended up with close to 51 per cent, including the Fairfax stake. Fairfax had sold its shares for $18 million. Carsales would go into the PBL Media deal with an imputed value of over $200 million dollars. With a price of $1.21 per share, carsales was proud of the inroads it had made against Fairfax, which had a share price of $4.50. This did not seem much for the newspaper giant and it was only on the back of a hot market for media stocks.

Packer had thought about trying to retain carsales in his own investment portfolio, but he knew something had to go: he had to add a good internet stock to the media assets for sale. He made an important commitment, however. He had always promised to support the carsales board when its directors decided it was time to float what remained an unlisted public company. Packer promised to ensure that any new owner understood this commitment was part of the deal.

Pisciotta said later: 'James said he would have liked to have held on to carsales but he couldn't. I looked across at him over the table and said, "Well, they had to have some growth assets." And he said, "Yes."'

Details of James Packer's plans to sell his media assets remained secret almost until the final deadline for the deal. On 16 October 2006, *The Sydney Morning Herald* reported the stunning news that PBL was considering the sale of Nine, ACP and ninemsn to private equity, with Newbridge Capital — part of TPG — tipped as a buyer. Packer would retain a shareholding in any new company. In the media industry you could have heard a pin drop — though the silence was soon followed by uproar. The idea of Packer selling Nine rather than buying Fairfax had arrived as a thunderclap, going against all public expectations. And then the speculation began again; the sale could mean only one thing. It must be a precursor to a cashed-up raid on Fairfax.

It was remarkable that the whole affair had stayed under wraps until the end. The deal was almost done, although it remained unclear which of the finalists — KKR or CVC — would finally make it across the line. The investment committee at TPG had ruled out an offer on the basis that the amount Packer wanted was too much.

There had been a last-minute drama for Packer when KKR's George Roberts insisted that PBL's pay television holdings, 25 per cent of Foxtel and 50 per cent of Fox Sports, should be included. He pressed Packer during a meeting in Packer's office. Roberts wanted to be completely aligned with Packer as a partner in his media interests but Packer had refused. He had an emotional attachment to the pay TV businesses. His father had had Nine; he had Foxtel. One thing became very clear from the meeting, though. For all that Packer liked him, Roberts was a seasoned corporate dealer and he might prove difficult in a business relationship if things got tough.

A dinner for the KKR team was held at the Packer compound in Bellevue Hill on the evening of Monday 16 October. A similar dinner had been held the previous week with CVC and its advisers at the home of David Gyngell, who was conveniently away. Amongst those on the guest list at Bellevue Hill were George Roberts, James Packer, John Alexander, Matthew Grounds, Chris Mackay, Ben Brazil and KKR's Australian boss, Justin Reizes. There was a handshake between Packer and Roberts, although no documents had been signed. When Roberts left later that night, he was confident the deal was his.

But soon after the guests from KKR had departed, Packer spent 15 minutes debating with his group of advisers whether to go the other way. In the end, CVC Asia Pacific and its Australian boss Adrian MacKenzie might be a more comfortable partner. Alexander then suggested they advise KKR and CVC that whoever signed first on the dotted line would win. Packer agreed; if CVC got there first, it won. Alexander placed a heads-up phone call to CVC and advised them not to dally.

Matthew Grounds had a race of his own as he had yet to receive approval for UBS to underwrite the debt on what would be the biggest such deal in Australia to date, although this approval would arrive overnight. Everyone was still sure KKR would get in first. KKR was prepared, it was huge, it had the profile and it was very determined.

Packer left for the airport. He was in the midst of a string of casino deals, including an attempt to list PBL Melco, his joint venture with Lawrence Ho, on the Nasdaq — a bid that by December would succeed — and a bid for a casino in Singapore.

Just before 6 a.m. the next morning, as Alexander was arriving at the Tattersall's Club to go to the gym, he answered his phone to hear exceptional news: CVC was prepared to submit documents. They were ready to sign. It was only Tuesday morning but the CVC investment committee meeting due on Wednesday to approve the transaction in the firm's London head office had been brought forward. Alexander abandoned the gym and rushed straight to the office. At 7 a.m., a PBL board sub-committee with Packer on the line from Singapore approved the deal and CVC was notified. There was a brief flurry as CVC asked for 48 hours to handle the mountain of paperwork, a request that was refused.

It was 17 October 2006 and by lunchtime James Packer had sold half of his media assets for the stupefying sum of $4.5 billion in cash, with an additional billion dollars of equity in the new company and $200 million in fees — a grand total of $5.7 billion. The deal would be the envy of an astonished investment community. By the end of the day Packer had decided to have framed for his office wall the email he had received from Matthew Grounds back on 22 August, advising him to choose a private equity sale and warning him against Macquarie's highly leveraged IPO.

Notwithstanding the excitement, there had been some difficult moments earlier in the day. Shortly after CVC received the go-ahead, George Roberts found out. He was in a car with Matthew Grounds driving to an early meeting when Packer called Grounds from Singapore to discuss the developments overnight. Grounds was caught between two clients, having introduced Roberts in the first place. 'You'd better speak to George,' he told Packer, then handed the phone to the founder of KKR.

Packer told Roberts that the deal had gone to CVC. Roberts was stunned. He did not hold back. He told Packer he was the worst thing he had ever heard of. Packer listened and waited for a break. He was ready for this. He reminded Roberts that KKR had done the same thing years before to Kerry Packer after agreeing to buy the Packers' Hoyts cinema business in the northeast of America in 2000. Roberts' partner Henry Kravis had shaken hands on the phone with Kerry, but KKR had broken the deal. It didn't matter. Roberts was incensed. Suddenly the line went dead in Packer's ear.

Grounds attempted to salvage the situation, suggesting a compromise to split the deal between KKR and CVC, but Roberts declined. He had no interest in doing business with Packer. Within weeks KKR would strike a mirror deal with Kerry Stokes, enabling Stokes to free up his own balance sheet and giving rise to endless debate in business circles over who had done better, Packer or Stokes. Later, Packer wrote to Roberts apologising but there was no reply.

PBL announced the deal on Wednesday 18 October 2006, several hours after the new media laws had cleared the House of Representatives. It was hard to say which development had more impact on the day. Packer had lobbied the government all year and he had lobbied the Family First Independent, Steve Fielding, heavily as well. A week before, on 12 October, it had been Fielding who had clinched the vote in the Senate. Now the whole package was through the parliament. For Packer it was an extraordinary double win.

Packer had also resolved a very significant issue in his personal life. He had reunited with Erica Baxter in August and he would propose to her in Melbourne on Christmas Day 2006. The following day, Boxing Day, marked the anniversary of his father's death.

This was the start of what would become a new generation and a new direction for the Packer dynasty. James had turned the compass irrevocably to casinos and resorts. He had not finished with his sell-down of the family media business yet — a business where Kerry had been so involved that he could talk about the content of an on-air promo for a new show for four hours with his feet on the desk — but James Packer was on his way out.

The changes in the media laws, Packer's sale to CVC, and the liquidity this raised had unleashed a waterfall of speculation that he planned a bid for Fairfax. But that door had closed. After all the years of watching the Packers through the barricades, Fairfax was safe enough. James Packer, though, could not resist a derogatory jibe. Speaking at PBL's annual general meeting on 26

October 2006, Packer said he could have bought a piece of Fairfax any time he chose. He said the Fairfax classifieds were under attack and under threat and he coolly mentioned his own role in that process, words which made little sense to most journalists at that time, but were heard clearly on the Fairfax executive floors.

'We have focussed our efforts on winning the classified categories Fairfax used to have a dominant position in,' Packer declared. 'I think we've done that to a significant extent.'

Another media mogul, however, remained suspicious of Packer's intentions. Rupert Murdoch had a sharp eye trained on Fairfax at any time. His interests were served by Fairfax remaining weak, and any prospect of a strong predator like Packer or Kerry Stokes moving on the newspaper group and shaking it up had his attention. With the media alight with the likelihood of a move on Fairfax, most likely by the cashed-up Packer, and rumours flying that Stokes had bought 2 per cent, Rupert put his own foot on some shares, buying 7.5 per cent of Fairfax. It was announced to the stock exchange on 20 October, two days after the announcement of the PBL Media spin-off. News and Fairfax described it as a 'friendly stake.' Murdoch's friendly stake could mean only one thing. He was there to be a troublemaker, to send a signal to Packer and Stokes. He could help defend Fairfax in order to keep it weak. Murdoch would sit on his competitor's share register for six months until the coast was clear, before selling the 75 million shares at $5.07. His presence, and the Packer deal, transformed Fairfax into a stock with some strength, a situation that would not last long.

Years later, Murdoch recalled the moment, and his unexpected manoeuvre to become a Fairfax shareholder, describing it as 'just a bit of mischief'.

CHAPTER SIX

RIVERS OF RED

The first glitter of headlights was suddenly visible as the Rolls Royce limousine swung onto the driveway leading into the Melbourne Cricket Ground. The low rumble of a motorcade filled the stadium; the crowd began to roar. The gleaming Rolls drew closer and the Prime Minister John Howard and the Chairman of the Commonwealth Games Organising Committee Ron Walker stood a little taller as they waited with the British Prime Minister, Tony Blair, to greet Queen Elizabeth II. She was dressed for the ceremonial opening of the Games in a lemon suit dusted with sparkling beads, matching black patent shoes and bag, a triple string of pearls, and a large diamond brooch perched upon her shoulder.

Ron Walker looked on at the approaching procession with particular satisfaction, as he had borrowed the Rolls Royce through the Prime Minister's department during the final stages of preparation for the Queen's visit. Suddenly Walker spied James

Packer in the VIP precinct and he resolved on the spur of the moment to invite Packer and his girlfriend Erica into the enclosed area with the possibility of perhaps meeting the Queen. He lifted the red tape to beckon them in.

But Packer had something else on his mind: he purposefully took the long way around the tape to Walker, and then put an arm around his neck, pulling him in tight and close in anger. Packer was completely furious. He berated the chairman of Fairfax for welching on a deal to buy ACP's magazine group in New Zealand, saying Walker would not have treated Kerry that way and that this act of bad faith would not be forgotten.

Startled at the sight of the chairman of the Games in what appeared to be a headlock, police moved towards them, shouting to Walker, 'Are you okay?'

A one-time Lord Mayor of Melbourne practised at smoothing out the ruffles in any drama, Walker disentangled himself and Packer, still angry, stepped back.

'It's just friends greeting each other,' Walker called jovially with a smile as Her Majesty's Rolls glided smoothly in.

It was 15 March 2006 and this brief altercation was the denouement of a fight that had its origins four months before, while Kerry Packer was still alive. In early November 2005 — not long after the appointment of Walker as Fairfax chairman and David Kirk, a former chief executive at the printing firm PMP, as Fairfax chief executive — the two had met with James Packer, PBL's chief executive John Alexander and other executives, at their Park Street offices to commence what Walker hoped would be a new era of peace in the media industry. Walker thought the time for war, with its cut-throat politics and double-crosses, had run its course and he was anxious to instigate a more gentlemanly way of doing business. He would argue privately in his own boardroom and in public that it was time to end the bile and hatred in the media industry. He planned to play a role in promoting this more co-operative environment, leading by example.

As part of the proposed new transparency, Kirk and Walker put their cards on the table, revealing they were interested in TradeMe, a New Zealand online auction house created in the classic start-up fashion in 1999 by a young man with a computer. It had grown to rival eBay in that country. Alexander and James Packer said they had no plans to buy TradeMe.

'It was all buddy, buddy, and how can we do things for the future, after our forefathers had been at war, and now we'll all work together,' Walker recalled.

Before 2005 was out, Kirk and Walker had also joined James Packer and Alexander for breakfast at Packer's Bondi apartment on the corner of Lamrock Avenue, taking in the wide sweep of the famous sandy curve with surfers bobbing on the waves. They tossed around ideas, some as outlandish as Fairfax buying into gambling products, others as predictable as PBL buying *The Australian Financial Review*, which Walker poured cold water on.

In November 2005, David Kirk and the founder of TradeMe, Sam Morgan, held their first meeting in a hotel in Wellington rather than in Morgan's office, where Kirk's presence might have set tongues wagging. As a former captain of the All Blacks, Kirk was a household name and a familiar face in New Zealand. His approach could not have been in starker contrast to that of his predecessor Fred Hilmer, who had always sent his managers to deal with the young guns building the websites to challenge

Fairfax classifieds. Kirk recognised the pride inherent in a successful start-up and he knew the only way to get what he wanted was to acknowledge TradeMe, chief executive to chief executive. What Kirk did not know, however, was that TradeMe had already blipped onto PBL's radar.

After his father died on 26 December 2005, James Packer moved swiftly to reorient the media empire he had inherited more heavily towards casinos. He had a substantial piece of SEEK and a major stake in the auto site carsales. Through Foxtel and Fox Sports he had a big slice of subscription TV. New media and pay TV and internet companies were his passions, by contrast with his waning interest in Nine and the huge portfolios of ACP magazines that had been his father's great obsessions.

On 1 February 2006, five weeks after his father's death, James Packer flew to New Zealand with a group of executives including Alexander to meet Sam Morgan himself. ACP managers in New Zealand had alerted Sydney to Morgan's thriving online business, planting the idea of investing in TradeMe months before, while Kerry Packer was still alive. They had approached Morgan through an investment bank without revealing to him who the client was.

Notwithstanding the peace talks with Walker, TradeMe had Packer's attention. It was causing serious damage in New Zealand to *Trade & Exchange*, a New Zealand version of the bartering bible the *Trading Post* in Australia; it was also hammering the Trader group of magazines owned by ACP.

Packer talked to Sam Morgan about the success of SEEK and he outlined a way he thought they could do business together. What Packer wanted was not a takeover but a large stake in

TradeMe, a facsimile of his investment in SEEK. Packer had other plans for major spending, and they revolved around casinos. He wanted TradeMe but he did not plan to spend the sort of serious money that could be better channelled into expanding his gaming interests. He could not buy all of TradeMe without taking on significant new debt; instead he proposed buying 25 per cent of the company, then floating the rest. Morgan pushed him to bid for more, but Packer was focussed on Macau. He was not going to splurge his liquidity on anything but casinos.

Sam Morgan now had two big predators on his hands; it was the first time anyone had acknowledged that TradeMe was making a lot of money and outstripping the print competition. Just as the founders of SEEK, carsales and realestate.com had wanted to be taken seriously by the big end of town, Morgan took great pride in the success of the company he had started as a small side project when he was a consultant at Deloitte. The business had been growing so fast he had barely paused to take stock.

Walker, meanwhile, had opened separate talks with James Packer about an entirely different New Zealand acquisition for Fairfax — ACP's New Zealand magazines and trade papers. No price was discussed. ACP was John Alexander's territory and Packer was preoccupied with his negotiations with Steve Wynn, carefully feeling his way around the likely cost of a Macau casino licence. He was busy too with the preparations for a memorial service for his father.

On 17 February 2006, the service for Kerry Packer was held at the Sydney Opera House with the harbour beyond sparkling in the sunlight. Walker attended the memorial for his old friend, and after it was over he bumped into John Alexander walking down to the Opera House steps. They stopped to talk and Walker asked Alexander what price he wanted for the New Zealand assets. Alexander nominated the huge sum of $530 million, reflecting the insane valuations for media at the time. Walker agreed to take it to his board and they shook hands. Walker phoned to tell Kirk.

The following day, 18 February, Walker flew to London on business for three days. As the chairman headed off, David Kirk considered the conundrum he faced over the ACP New Zealand assets with their hefty $530 million price tag. He was far from happy. Kirk's focus was TradeMe, which he anticipated would strip classified print ads from the New Zealand trade papers that Alexander seemed so keen to offload. It would all go to the internet. Kirk had other worries about the activities at Park Street, too. Sam Morgan had warned Kirk he had competition — without naming names — and Kirk was convinced it was Packer.

Kirk could visualise Fairfax paying James Packer over $500 million for his NZ publications and Packer then using the money for TradeMe. In effect, Fairfax would pay Packer to buy TradeMe. And now there had been a handshake on the steps of the Opera House between the Fairfax chairman and the chief executive of PBL. It might not be a binding deal and no due diligence had been done, but it was still a handshake and Kirk could not see how to get out of it.

Two days later, Ron Walker woke suddenly in the Berkeley Hotel on Wilton Place in Knightsbridge. It was the middle of a rainy London night and he could hear his phone ringing. He answered it to find a furious John Alexander on the other end. The conversation was so heated that the Fairfax chairman could barely get a word in. Eventually Walker understood the reason for the anger on the line from Sydney. Fairfax's Sunday paper, *The Sun-Herald*, had just published a gossip item by the tapped-in social writer Annette Sharp reporting tawdry details about women in Kerry Packer's life, which had distressed his widow Ros. Kerry had been dead for just five weeks and the memorial service had been two days ago, but here was Fairfax spreading mud. By the time Alexander had finished, Walker was under no illusions. No-one at PBL wanted to be doing business with Fairfax. All the happy talk was over. Fairfax was a disgrace.

Back in Sydney the phone line to David Kirk melted down as well. The new chief executive of Fairfax had been in the driver's seat for just four months, but he got an early taste of life in the fast lane when Alexander called. This call, like the call to Walker in London, concluded with a terse declaration that Fairfax could forget about a great new era doing business with PBL when it behaved like this.

It was music to Kirk's ears. If there was ever a moment when a news story had got a company off the hook, then this was such a moment for Fairfax. Kirk used it to pull out of the ACP deal. There might be unanticipated costs in terms of the infamous hate and bile, but after the shouting had stopped the promise to buy the ACP New Zealand assets was allowed to fall over. By early March Kirk was ready to close the deal that mattered to him, with Sam Morgan. He had had Walker's support from the start, although there was reluctance and anxiety amongst others on the Fairfax board. To some directors, TradeMe seemed to be not much more than Sam Morgan and a bunch of computers. It seemed to have no tangible assets, it was in a small market, it had high margins and prices could fall if a competitor came in. Kirk argued that TradeMe was a strong ecommerce business and a sound diversification away from newspapers and towards new revenue. Eventually the board accepted that while they might not all understand the business, they had to take some risks. And they had to back the new chief executive.

A special Fairfax board meeting at 4 p.m. on 1 March 2006, held in the MCG boardroom virtually on the eve of the Commonwealth Games, endorsed the acquisition. The board later shared a three-course meal of smoked salmon, roast lamb and cheese as they discussed what other acquisitions might be on the horizon. The ACP New Zealand deal, which would have cost Fairfax $500 million, had been vaporised.

Sam Morgan said later that other more subjective factors than price had played into his final decision about which way to go. Like Morgan, David Kirk was a New Zealander and he made Morgan feel at home in separating from his baby. The Packer entourage left Morgan with the sense that he was an item on a menu.

> I felt a lot more comfortable with Fairfax. With Packer's people, I felt a bit like I was someone in an episode of *The Sopranos*, someone who might not still be there in the next series. There were five or six of them coming over in their private plane and they were all in suits and I was just in my usual T-shirt.

On 6 March 2006, Kirk announced that Fairfax had brought TradeMe for NZ $700 million (AUD $625 million). Packer had thought he would sell his magazines and acquire TradeMe, but he had lost on both counts: Kirk had dodged the magazines and won

TradeMe. Ron Walker found that his hopes of peace in our time had evaporated, too, when an enraged James Packer confronted him nine days later at the opening of the Games as the Queen's motorcade rolled into view.

But Walker would have the last word. On 20 March 2006 he wrote to Packer, chastising him for his behaviour at the Games and outlining the events that culminated in the collapse of the agreement to buy the ACP magazines. He did not mince words.

Dear James,

I was saddened to be exposed to your uncharacteristic rudeness and physical aggression on the evening of the Opening Ceremony of the Commonwealth Games on Wednesday last ... let's deal in the facts: In late October or early November, John Alexander told me and David Kirk separately that TradeMe and the NBR [National Business Review] were two New Zealand assets that you were not interested in pursuing ...

To our dismay, when finalising the purchase of TradeMe, we were informed that you had visited Sam Morgan in New Zealand, and had tried to convince him to treat with you and not us, citing your success with Seek.

On 17 February, I briefly met with John Alexander and he told me he was prepared to sell your assets in NZ to Fairfax. On 19 February, whilst in London, I received a call from John saying that the deal was off, because of an article in the Sun-Herald that day ...

On Saturday 25 February, you called me to say we should go ahead with the deal with John subject to due diligence and a meeting with the New Zealand Commerce Commission. On Monday 27 February, our CFO Sankar Narayan called Geoff Kleeman [PBL's chief financial officer] to arrange a meeting, and was told that he was away. I received a call from John Alexander in London a few days later to say that [radio and newspaper group] APN were interested and were seeking permission from their board to make a bid, and that I should hurry up, giving me the clear impression — for the second time — that you did not feel committed to a sale to us.

Days later, the TradeMe deal was completed and your personal calls to Sam Morgan were revealed, trying to convince him to complete a deal with you rather than with Fairfax. When I was told this I felt betrayed because of the consistent undertakings given to us by both you and John that you were not interested in pursuing TradeMe. It is a sad start to something that I had hoped would be a long-term relationship, but I honestly hope that we can once again have another meeting and put things right.

I wish you well,

Ron

For David Kirk, a neophyte swimming in the deep and bitter pool of Australian media, the lessons of the ACP–*Sun-Herald*–TradeMe battle were capped off when he made a series of personal phone calls at Walker's behest to apologise to Kerry Packer's widow Ros and to Gretel and James Packer for the *Sun-Herald* item. Later, the Fairfax board grilled Kirk about how far the newspaper could go and where the boundary lay between good taste and bad taste, although no directions were given to the chief executive and the discussion ultimately petered out. Soon after, another apology was forthcoming, this time from James Packer, who wrote to Walker to apologise for his behaviour at the Games.

Packer recalled later: 'There's no doubt I was hoping that I could skin Ron and I probably did behave badly. Ron called me on it and I apologised to him, because I genuinely love Ron and we had been friends for a long time.'

Kirk regarded TradeMe as a significant achievement and it was consistent with his strategy to diversify revenue away from classified print advertising revenue in the metropolitan newspapers. But he had not counted on the scepticism in the market and many analysts bagged him. The outspoken founder of 452 Capital, Peter Morgan, declared that there were bigger issues for Kirk to deal with than internet purchases in New Zealand. The announcement of the TradeMe deal overshadowed the half-year results to 31 December 2005, announced by Kirk on the same day. A number of investors stood up in the meeting and asked him who he thought he was, going out and spending $600 million of the company's money when he had barely been there for five minutes. Kirk held his ground, retorting that you didn't have to be around for long to recognise a good business. Kirk's purchase of TradeMe in New Zealand was ridiculed too when compared to the AUD $552 million (US $580 million) paid in July 2005 by Rupert Murdoch's News Corp for MySpace, one of the hottest social networking sites in the world. (Later, MySpace would prove to have been a costly mistake: News sold it in 2011 for $35 million to a company backed by the singer Justin Timberlake.)

Kirk said he felt comfortable with TradeMe because he understood how it planned to make money for the next ten years. He knew too, that he had out-manoeuvred James Packer and delivered to Fairfax the first online deal that really mattered — ten years after the early green shoots that gave rise to the likes of SEEK, realestate.com and carsales.

David Kirk's appointment as chief executive of Fairfax bore more than a passing resemblance to a driver parachuting into the middle of a car race where the other competitors had been around the circuit several times and knew the treacherous bends and curves. But Hilmer had argued against recruiting a traditional newspaper executive, who would likely be beholden to the legacy print business, as his successor. After 18 months of assessing and interviewing a number of candidates — including a failed attempt to recruit former News Corp executive Doug Flynn, who went on to run the pest-control firm Rentokil — Kirk was hired. As Hilmer departed and Kirk entered, the Fairfax share price was $3.80. Hilmer had added $1 in the seven years since he started in October 1998.

Kirk arrived at Fairfax's headquarters in a modern and minimalist office tower at Darling Harbour in October 2005. The chief executive's suite at the end of a curving wood-panelled corridor had been home to four previous chief executives — Stephen Mulholland, Bob Mansfield, Bob Muscat and Hilmer — over the ten years that Fairfax had rented the top nine floors of the building. It was so far along the corridor that it had an isolated feel, as though chosen by someone who wanted no connection with the rowdy newspaper business that went on elsewhere in the building. The notion that this was a clubby world apart was enhanced by the large, dark timber desk, the heavy newspaper stand and odd accoutrements like a remote control door-opener that lay on the desk and operated in such a way that the office door always closed with a bang, as though it had been slammed shut. Kirk soon ordered this to be disconnected. Outside, Darling

Harbour shimmered in the sunshine as sightseers and commuters hurried by. There was nothing on the building's soaring exterior to indicate that one of the greatest media empires in the nation dwelled within, aside from the throngs of journalists drinking coffee and gossiping in the forecourt at the Brolga Terrace Café.

Kirk's name was synonymous with rugby union, where he was known for his fiercely competitive nature but also for his legendary stance as one of two players who had refused to join the rebel New Zealand team touring apartheid South Africa in 1986. In 1987 Kirk, as the 26-year-old captain of the All Blacks, had led his team to victory in the World Cup against France. He was famously photographed with his shock of rock-star hair and blood running from a cut over his eyebrow, triumphantly holding the golden Cup aloft. He quit rugby to take up a Rhodes scholarship at Oxford and later became a consultant at McKinsey.

As Kirk assessed his new empire in late 2005, he soon understood that Fairfax was facing potentially catastrophic structural challenges. Of greatest concern was the successful incursion of the pure-plays, the single-focus online advertising companies sending their root systems deep into Fairfax's monopoly on jobs, cars and property classifieds. Fairfax seemed to have developed little of its own entrepreneurial spirit, perhaps by dint of its position as a venerable institution with a storied history. It was not involved in any of the independent online classified players aside from a small stake in the auto market leader, carsales.

Kirk found he had a number of executives deeply concerned about how to defend the classifieds. They included Alan Revell, who had been burned by Fairfax's sluggish response to SEEK, but had overseen the acquisition from Yahoo of an 11.6 per cent stake in carsales, watered down months later to 7.6 per cent when the carsales founders joined forces with James Packer to defend themselves from Fairfax. Fairfax's 'new media' division was trying to make headway with the holiday homes website Stayz, and Kirk quickly decided to pounce on this property. He made his way onto the wavelength of the founder, Rob Hunt — a New Zealander himself, whose school had once played in competitions against Kirk's school. The tiny $12 million deal was agreed by December, just weeks after the new chief executive had started at Fairfax.

Kirk resolved to run corporate strategy himself, but he hired an American with a background in telecommunications in New Zealand to report to him directly on internet strategy. Jack Matthews was an outspoken take-no-prisoners operator and he wasted little time on the niceties of buttering up journalists and embedding himself in the Fairfax culture. Matthews wanted to go the other way, to dig up the culture and truck in new soil. Australia was in the midst of a jobs boom with advertising riding the wave, but Kirk was alarmed at how much revenue from the classifieds had been lost already. The prices charged for employment advertising were under pressure and Fairfax was losing volume. MyCareer, the Fairfax jobs site, was limping along at best. Property advertising was holding on with more certainty, but Kirk could see that the competition from the Murdoch-controlled realestate.com.au was growing exponentially.

The vertical classified advertising streams in the metropolitan newspapers might be disappearing but it remained a Fairfax mantra that the company could be a significant number two in the online classifieds market — and, moreover, that the pure-plays were not an existential threat. There was only one business in the past that had ever dominated print classifieds and that was Fairfax: and so it would be in the future. Yet circulation, too, was under pressure and falling at *The Sydney Morning Herald* and *The Age*. This played into the diminishing ad revenue as advertisers took note.

The biggest investment Fred Hilmer had made was the $1.1 billion purchase in 2003 of Independent Newspapers Ltd (INL), the New Zealand company then controlled by, and 45 per cent owned by, News Corp. INL had a dozen daily and weekly papers and dozens more free suburban papers filled with advertising. Hilmer was convinced that these publications would help to diversify Fairfax revenue as advertising was crimped by the attack of the internet on the Australian metro papers.

In March 2001 News had appointed Tom Mockridge to shake up INL and he had instigated a raft of cost savings and improved synergies. In early 2002, Hilmer and Mockridge had held a preliminary meeting to discuss a Fairfax bid for INL. Mockridge took it to the boss when he and Rupert Murdoch were in Milan in July 2002 for talks with Telecom Italia, which later led to the birth of Sky Italia. 'Rupert thought about it for a millisecond and said, "yes",' Mockridge recalled later.

INL's chairman was the veteran News Limited executive and director of News Corporation, Ken Cowley. Rupert and his son Lachlan, the head of the family's newspaper operations in Australia and the US, were more bearish on New Zealand than Fairfax executives. The Murdochs were more bearish too than Cowley, who had confidence in New Zealand and was reluctant to sell. But News was the Murdoch's company, so Cowley ramped up the price.

Fairfax initially offered $600 million, but that quickly mushroomed. Cowley pushed hard, forcing Fairfax to increase its offer three times. The numbers jumped sometimes by hundreds of millions of dollars.

Finally the Fairfax offer hit $1.1 billion, almost double the starting bid, and the Murdochs agreed. It was a spectacular deal for News. 'The Murdochs were over the moon about it,' Cowley recalled. 'We got a lot more for it than they ever expected because they didn't have any confidence in it business-wise or politically.'

Publicly, Cowley declared to the media that Fairfax had paid a significant premium on the book value: 'Although INL's directors were not actively seeking any expressions of interest in the publishing business at the time of the Fairfax offer, the offer was such that directors felt that the interests of the company and its shareholders would be best served by accepting it.'

The two-thirds of New Zealand's Sky TV owned by INL was excised from the sale. After the sale to Fairfax and the wind-up of INL, News retained 44 per cent of Sky. Lachlan Murdoch said later: 'Our long-term view of growth in New Zealand was negative. Fairfax came to us and we put a price on INL that was crazy, and we were almost shocked when they said yes. Tom's work at INL had not yet paid off, but in the next two years it did very well.'

The withering headline on a research paper published by CCZ Equities' Roger Colman on 23 May 2003, 'NZ: is this Fairfax's Vietnam?' summed up much of the market reaction to the very full price paid, as well as concerns of a future downturn in growth in New Zealand. Colman was a caustic critic of Fairfax but he produced the analysis to back his thesis; his view was that the competitor APN News & Media had the stronger newspapers, including *The New Zealand Herald*, which had the bulk of national advertising and thus premium earnings. He argued that Fairfax could hardly have paid a higher price and that real growth for New Zealand in 2004 was 'forecast to lie between 1.5 per cent–2.5 per cent, down from 4.4 per cent in 2002'.

Hilmer would not countenance the criticism and he pointed out that the NZ assets would account for 30 per cent of Fairfax revenue. He predicted it would add 20 per cent earnings per share in the following year, diversifying the business and making it less reliant on the Australian advertising cycle and the metros. He was cutting costs inside the business and adding revenue from new sources.

But it was not this unprecedented billion-dollar investment by Fairfax that sucked up the oxygen amongst analysts and journalists in the weeks to come. Just eight weeks after the INL deal, the news that bit hard into Fairfax was the stunning revelation that James Packer had bought into SEEK for what seemed like small change by comparison. Hilmer had paid $1.1 billion for INL and Packer had paid just $33 million for 25 per cent of SEEK. Hilmer described this figure as over-priced and not what Fairfax would have considered paying. But SEEK was hot property and Packer's tilt realigned the gulf between old and new media. The deal received wall-to-wall coverage, with profiles of SEEK's founders, beaming photos, 'insider' stories of how the deal was done, and general acclaim for Packer's perspicacity and the fact that Fairfax had been outwitted.

SEEK would change the dynamics in the way media companies were viewed. On 5 August 2003, the day after Packer's investment was announced, Macquarie Research's leading media analyst Alex Pollak issued a devastating paper on Fairfax titled 'SEEK: where the jobs are hiding'. It warned that with the professional employment market taking a turn for the worst, Fairfax's classified employment revenue growth was expected to be negative. SEEK would have a material impact on the valuation of Fairfax, with SEEK's online job ads growing at a phenomenal 20 per cent plus per year. In bold letters, the report summarised: 'In short, FXJ is now sharing with SEEK a market that it used to control as a virtual monopolist — it had 80 per cent of the employment jobs classified market in Sydney and Melbourne, worth around $200 million.'

If Fairfax was losing 2 per cent of its revenue from job ads annually, then given the high fixed costs of newspapers it would take only five years to halve the earnings. The blame, at least in part, according to Pollak, was to be laid at the feet of Fairfax's sortie into directories at the cost of defending its classified stranglehold in the early days of its online business.

> FXJ controlled 80 per cent of the jobs market through its
> newspaper 'gateway'. SEEK and the internet are an example
> of how technological change has turned this gateway into
> the high cost option. FXJ's only option would have been to
> dominate the online space from day 1, leveraging its very
> strong brand so aggressively that competition was unable to
> win even small amounts of traffic from advertisers or users.
> Instead, the company focussed its energy in the online space
> too broadly: CitySearch, Big Colour Pages etc.

The paper also referred to an earlier Macquarie research paper, 'Classified information: will online dry up FXJ rivers of gold?' published a year before on 13 August 2002. It had followed a visit to Fairfax by the Macquarie research team for a meeting with

Hilmer. Afterwards, they had cut the Fairfax share valuation by 77 cents.

One day after 'SEEK: where the jobs are hiding', Macquarie issued yet another paper looking at both Fairfax and PBL and titled: 'Still SEEKing classified'. It pointed out that PBL's investment gave SEEK access to capital, providing firepower to steal further market share from Fairfax. From PBL's perspective, it had gained 'a significant option on what we think is still an immature online employment market'. SEEK already had a clear lead and was expected to extend the 60 per cent share it had of the online jobs space. And that was just jobs, without looking at the damage being inflicted by the pure-plays on cars and property advertising.

If all of this had not stung the Fairfax board, more criticism was poured on Fairfax a year later. Publishing entrepreneur Eric Beecher had sold his company Text Media, with its suburban real estate advertising, to Fairfax for $65 million in early 2004. A one-time editor of *The Sydney Morning Herald*, Beecher had been something of a thorn in the side of Fairfax, with his successful forays into the smaller end of publishing and his 'insider' status as a commentator. Soon after selling Text to Fairfax, Beecher was commissioned by then Fairfax chairman Dean Wills to prepare an independent report on the threats facing the company.

Beecher delivered his 33-page report to the Fairfax board on 23 June 2004. Titled 'The state of the Fairfax business model', the report posed a devastating critique. In the opening pages Beecher stated that his motivation for agreeing to produce the report was concern for Fairfax's financial success, which in turn funded the company's journalism. Beecher was not a consultant, nor had he received a fee. He had had no access to confidential corporate information. 'My reason for acting now is that I believe there is a real likelihood of a Fairfax "catastrophe scenario" over the next few years,' he wrote. That catastrophe was Fairfax losing up to 40 per cent of its classified revenue within five years — an estimate that would turn out to be conservative.

Beecher argued that the board should focus on the risks inherent in the decline of advertising. If that risk was 10 or 15 per cent, they should be reinventing aspects of the business. He said the key to understanding the vulnerability of Fairfax was to accept that it was two businesses — a highly profitable classified business, and an unprofitable publishing business. The document included graphics and tables highlighting revenue for the past year in display advertising, classified line advertising and circulation, and then comparing this with the same categories at international publications like *The New York Times, The Boston Globe* and *The Philadelphia Inquirer,* as well as *The West Australian.*

Beecher's numbers showed that 56 per cent of Fairfax's revenue came from classifieds, 27 per cent from display advertising and 17 per cent from circulation (the cover price of the newspapers). At *The New York Times,* this was reversed, with 53 per cent of revenue from display ads, 18 per cent from classifieds and 29 per cent from circulation. The story at *The West Australian* was similar to the story at Fairfax. Beecher argued that international papers averaged around a 25 per cent reliance on classifieds — the sector most vulnerable to the insurgents of the internet. Fairfax therefore had greater exposure to attacks on the classifieds, and it had further to fall.

Beecher recommended that Fairfax consider establishing one or more small external companies, with seed capital of as little as $20 million, which would be owned by Fairfax but would be entirely outside the Fairfax culture, independent and free to compete as guerrillas in the vein of the classified advertising pure-plays.

Later, Beecher described his reception by the Fairfax board as mostly passive, with one notable exception. Others argued later that the board was put off by Beecher's tone and what they regarded as an unexpected harangue. In a 2012 report for the online media website *crikey*, which he owned, Beecher claimed that during his meeting with the board, Fairfax director Roger Corbett had picked up a weighty Saturday edition of *The Sydney Morning Herald*, and dropped it heavily on the table with the declaration that he did not want to hear again from someone suggesting that people would buy houses or search for jobs or cars without *'this'*. Corbett said later that he did not recall the incident.

> I have a vague memory of Beecher presenting at a board meeting. It was shortly after I joined the board. But if Beecher is inferring that we didn't understand what the potential impact was of the digital space on the written print classified ads of the future, then the answer is of course, yes and no. Yes, we were beginning to understand it had the potential to have a significant impact. But did we fully understand? No, along with most other newspaper companies in the world. The inference that I or the board was anti-digital is simply wrong.

Beecher was portrayed later by some Fairfax executives as a freelancing agent provocateur angling for a board seat. His report appeared destined for oblivion. Beecher said he was told it had been shredded. There was no doubt that he had struck a nerve.

Another review of the Fairfax business in 2004 was equally alarming but met with far less resistance. Sankar Narayan had joined Fairfax as chief financial officer in March 2004, just weeks before Hilmer announced his resignation, even though Hilmer would remain on deck for the 18 months it took to appoint his replacement. Narayan had a background as a CFO in companies as diverse as the internet start-up Shopfast, later sold to Coles, and Foxtel. He had a quirky sense of humour and an easy-going commitment to calling it as he saw it, and his frank advice was a breath of fresh air on executive row.

Soon after accepting the job, Narayan was asked by the board to spend three months reviewing the company. He returned with a chilling analysis: the classified business was seriously threatened. Fairfax, like so many other companies, had become complacent after the dotcom bubble burst, confident that the upstart pure-plays were done for. In Fairfax's case, where more than 80 per cent of revenue came from advertising in the metro newspapers, this blinkered approach had been a disaster. Narayan feared that hundreds of millions of dollars in revenue was under threat. He believed the company could hold on to its display advertising but that the line classifieds would wither in print and continue their wholesale migration online — and not to Fairfax sites.

For the Fairfax board, the messages from the outside world were becoming increasingly strident. Three months before Beecher's visit, *The Australian*'s Peter Nicholson had lampooned Fairfax with a cartoon published on 11 March 2004 that demonstrated the power of an image. Nicholson portrayed a wide green field with a huge golden river flowing through it, until it reached a cliff where the molten gold plunged over the edge. A signpost in the river, just before the cliff, read 'CLASSIFIEDS'. Further back on the river, two smiling businessmen rowed in a canoe named *Fairfax* as one declaimed, 'These Rivers of Gold flow for ever, don't they?'

Two years later, soon after Kirk's arrival and shortly after the TradeMe acquisition, Kirk and Narayan sat down to prepare a major strategy document on the state of Fairfax. It was 2006. Given the reports to the board by both Narayan and Beecher in the previous two years, and the pessimistic analysis of Fairfax's position by industry analysts going back to 2002, directors were hardly in the dark about the crisis. But what they needed was an updated report on the extent of the decline and how Kirk proposed to address it. Kirk's assessment was as clinical as Beecher's report had been passionate but the story was essentially the same.

The more they looked into the Fairfax classifieds, the famous three verticals, the clearer it became. The classifieds were gone or going. In preparation for a board meeting on 1 June 2006, Kirk and Narayan prepared a strategy pack designed to electrify. They analysed all sources of revenue in the company for the metropolitan newspapers and then broke it down into segments: the cover price (circulation), the display advertising, and the classified line ads with their subsets of jobs, property and cars — the rivers of gold. They produced a grid to show how vastly more profitable was classified line advertising over display advertising because of the volume and the margins achievable. There were few production costs associated with classifieds; these were small ads of a line or two, commanding very high prices. Display advertising was proportionately far less profitable, taking up more space on the page.

Then they asked, 'What's going to go?' Kirk and Narayan highlighted in red anything Kirk regarded as so comprehensively under threat that it would be lost — and lost quickly. This included all the classifieds. Jobs, property and cars were red, red, red.

They marked in yellow the sectors declining, but more slowly, including circulation and display advertising for real estate and classified display ads (line ads with pictures). In green they listed anything healthy. The primary display ads for jobs and cars were marked in green, although even this would soon prove far more optimistic than the reality.

'I don't remember much that was green,' Kirk said later. 'It was a sea of red ink and we presented this to the board. It was hundreds of millions of dollars that fell straight to the bottom line and profit, and it was vanishing.'

The preliminary estimates in the document concluded that $100 million of revenue was at risk in the next three to five years. This was equal to $75 million in earnings before interest and tax. Employment classifieds (lost mainly to SEEK) showed a very large decline and there was little hope that regional Fairfax publications could offset this revenue. The losses were almost entirely in the metropolitan newspapers. Real estate was just as bad. Fairfax car classifieds were a lost cause: 'Total lineage revenue (now only $8 million) to disappear in 3–5 years as private party car sales all migrate online.' This meant an ad that was simply a line or two, without even a photo of a Cortina, for example, was on the way out.

The document was a heat map revealing the stark collapse in the line classifieds that had always had the highest yields. In days gone by, the classifieds had been dripping in margins. It was probably the first time the Fairfax board had seen such a comprehensive breakdown of all of the advertising, sector by sector, to show what was at risk and over what time frame.

The board response was threefold. Firstly, Kirk was authorised to continue to diversify the revenue, as he had done with the TradeMe purchase, to minimise reliance on the metro papers. Secondly, he should cut the production costs of the metros; and thirdly, they would focus on building new online businesses internally.

The board began to discuss, as it had many times in years gone by, the potential for acquiring the Rural Press business of John B. Fairfax, secured out of the wreckage of Fairfax in the wake of Warwick Fairfax Jnr's privatisation bid in 1987. Rural Press papers were focussed on regional communities and such an acquisition, even with the debt burden it might entail, could offset the revenue decline of the metros. Regional papers might be below the radar as far as Fairfax's big-city culture went, but these papers were sturdy bastions of local ads and low-cost profit. In other words, they were money-spinners.

News Limited, with its own massive array of newspapers — some hugely profitable, others simply propped up — had the great benefit of a proprietor who had diversified his media and broadcasting assets around the world. Rupert Murdoch could stand behind any publications he wanted to, regardless of losses, profits or power.

Fairfax was ring-fenced by trouble. If the problems of sinking classifieds and thrusting online competitors were not enough, the Federal Government had signalled months earlier that the media laws would change and this meant just one thing to many media commentators: Fairfax was a target. It was doubly critical to increase the size of the company dramatically, both for revenue and market capitalisation. For Fairfax to defend itself it had to become much bigger.

One piece of the future, however, was about to slip through the company's fingers. After the dilution of Fairfax's carsales stake to 7.6 per cent in 2005, James Packer was back prowling, wanting to get his hands on the remaining shares held by Fairfax. Carsales had played a critical role of cutting into Fairfax's classified print advertising for cars. The founders, Wal Pisciotta and Greg Roebuck, now had a muscular partner in the shape of Packer, with his unbridled interest in anything that was bad for Fairfax and his willingness to prosecute war.

In May 2006, after the wash-up of the fight between Packer and Ron Walker over the ACP New Zealand assets, Packer approached Walker wanting to buy Fairfax's carsales stake. Walker was still hoping to repair relationships in the media industry and he wanted to mend fences with Packer. Carsales had made it clear that there was no easy road for Fairfax into its boardroom; the only option, which Fairfax had shown no appetite for, was a hostile takeover. Kirk was opposed to the sale of the carsales shares, but directors had agreed.

In September 2006, Fairfax signed a call option to sell 3 per cent of carsales to ACP for $8 million. Packer then launched a full takeover for carsales at $1.21 a share, the same price Fairfax had agreed to. Fairfax would sell its remaining 3.7 per cent of carsales into the takeover, reaping a total of $18 million for its entire stake. Packer was in the midst of a reorganisation of his business and the steps he took in the next month reframed the media industry, catapulting Fairfax into a new high-risk world that would ultimately reorient the company.

Packer and Walker had buried the hatchet after their months of fighting over TradeMe and the ACP magazines. The flurry of apologies earlier in the year had eased tensions on both sides and the promised sale of Fairfax's carsales stake to PBL had mollified Packer's fury over the lost ACP deal.

On Saturday 14 October 2006, Walker arranged to meet Packer at the Lamrock Café in Bondi, a popular and crowded haunt of Bondi locals, including plenty from the media industry. The meeting was calculated by Walker to attract attention, to hint that there might be some business underway. It did not fail. As they laughed demonstratively and chatted loudly, the pair was soon spied by eagle-eyes who phoned the newspapers. Afterwards, they ostentatiously climbed into Walker's bright red Mercedes Benz usually housed beneath his Elizabeth Bay apartment, to drive off along Campbell Parade. In the frenzied environment around media, with the Federal Government's new media laws expected soon, the sighting unleashed a blizzard of speculation on what the two were cooking up.

The Fairfax share price, $3.82 at the start of October 2006, had closed at $4.10 the day before Packer and Walker met. Two days later, on Monday 16 October, it opened at $4.16. By Friday it had climbed to $4.68. In those five days the media had turned on its head. James Packer had announced the sale of half of his media assets to CVC Asia Pacific on 18 October; the new media laws had passed on the same day. Also on that same day, *The Sydney Morning Herald*'s gossipy CBD column had reported James Packer's coffee in Bondi with Walker, illustrating the item with a cartoon of the pair zipping off in Walker's Mercedes. Within two days, Rupert Murdoch's News Limited had bought 7.5 per cent of Fairfax at

$5.20 a share. Rupert had taken a place at the table. The Fairfax share price had gone from $3.80 to $5.20 in three weeks. The business pages of the newspapers were soon full of conjecture that the great Fairfax company break-up was underway.

David Kirk was furious at all the loose talk. Three weeks later, at the Fairfax annual general meeting on 10 November, he described talk of the value that would be freed by a Fairfax carve-up — with all its imagery of the Packers and the Murdochs selecting bones from the carcass — as unadulterated rubbish. What Kirk did not say was that Fairfax had big plans of its own to deter the raiders and to secure the castle. And that these plans were well advanced.

Less than a month later, on Tuesday 5 December 2006, the AAP wire service reported the extraordinary news that Fairfax had yet another ruthless competitor sitting on its share register. Kerry Stokes' Seven Network had bought just under 3 per cent of the company back in mid-October, even before Rupert began circling. The latest frenzy drove Fairfax shares to $5.21 and then on to an astonishing $5.30. Journalists at the company's newspapers settled in for a bumpy ride.

CHAPTER SEVEN

A BIG FUTURE FOR NEWSPAPERS

The story hit the wire services and Bloomberg terminals like a crack of lightning. It was not quite as spectacular as a Packer selling out of Nine but it came close. Phones across the media industry ran hot. The Fairfax newspaper group had struck a $9 billion deal to merge with Rural Press, a publishing house known for hundreds of low-cost papers, titles specialising in horses and country matters, and *The Canberra Times*. Even in the cynical bastions of the Fairfax newsrooms, inured to endless years of corporate drama, there were gasps. It was Wednesday 6 December 2006, exactly 24 hours since news broke that the large shadow of Kerry Stokes had fallen across Fairfax as he joined Rupert Murdoch on the share register. With the arrival of Rural Press, a Fairfax was coming home to Fairfax.

John Brehmer Fairfax, known almost universally in the media industry as JB, carried in his DNA the lineage of the company —

to say nothing of the blood of its history. He had been a director of the old Fairfax from 1979 to 1987 and deputy chairman for the last two years of that time. After the wrecking ball of his second cousin Warwick Fairfax Jnr's ill-timed bid to take over the company in 1987, on the eve of a stock market crash that came to be known as Black Monday, JB and his own branch of the family had taken several assets in settlement, including Fairfax's then 48 per cent stake in Rural Press. They had moved to 51 per cent in 1989 and floated the company, gaining an adoring following of investors addicted to the profits that flowed. By the end of 2006 Rural Press was a powerhouse with a share price around $13.

The reconciliation of JB Fairfax with the company named after his family had officially commenced 11 weeks before, on 19 September 2006, a seasonably warm day with Sydney's Royal Botanic Gardens abloom in wisteria, tulips and pansies. Ron Walker and David Kirk, the chairman and chief executive of Fairfax, had arrived at JB's office overlooking the ferries zooming back and forth at Circular Quay. They made an odd couple: Walker a flamboyant and imposing figure at 198 centimetres tall, with a thatch of red hair and the ebullient confidence of a man on first-name terms in boardrooms around the country, and Kirk, with his small build, open smile and the focussed intensity of the winning rugby captain and Oxford scholar he had been. JB was waiting for them in his office on the 11th floor. A fastidious man with a penchant for charcoal suits or neat casual clothes that spoke of the country, he greeted them with a cup of tea.

This flirtation had got underway earlier in the year with an exchange of company results between JB and Walker, with little notes that said things like: 'Dear John, a good read,' and 'Dear Ron, an even better read.' It was an unprecedented time of bubbly stock markets and barbarians everywhere, as the private equity raiders scouring the world for deals were known. It had opened the eyes of even the sleepiest companies to new ways to expand, often predicated on significant debt, but this was the way business was done now. A failure to join the scramble for new partners could mean being left behind in the flotsam, once the aggressive leaders of the pack had selected their first choice. A company like Fairfax had one eye focussed on the rear vision mirror, waiting for opportunists to strike. But a bulky merger could make Fairfax relatively takeover-proof as well as providing fresh impetus to diversify the company's revenue.

How to price a deal between Fairfax and Rural Press was the most important question in the rules of engagement, given that the Fairfax share price had been settled at around $3.70 for some time and that Rural Press was close to $13. How to put two such disparate valuations into alignment in a way that satisfied one and did not break the bank for the other was the challenge.

But the remarkable reinvigoration of the Fairfax share price in October 2006 had dramatically shifted the balance. With media reports that Walker and the newly cashed-up James Packer had been out together for coffee, followed days later by the extraordinary news that Rupert Murdoch had bought a not-insignificant slice of Fairfax, the share price had shot over $5. In the highly charged media world, these two incidents together with the new media laws had established Fairfax as a takeover target. But it had also given it some heft. A merger with Rural Press funded by a mix of cash and shares became feasible. After years in the doldrums, Fairfax had a sufficiently high share price to take a seat in its own right in the media poker game.

There had been a long history of Fairfax dalliances with JB Fairfax since the family split in the 1980s. On one of those occasions, in September 2001, Fred Hilmer and JB had seriously discussed the prospects for a tie-up, although things had fallen apart later over differing versions of how much it would cost, and who had said what to whom. On 10 September 2001, JB had prepared a discussion note of points from a prior conversation with Hilmer, which he planned to raise in yet another meeting with Hilmer that day; in particular, what he understood Fairfax might pay for Rural Press: 'Price is determinant. $8 mentioned. Cash component of $300m capped,' JB wrote in his *aide-memoire*.

But JB's recollection, or his understanding of what Hilmer implied when he raised the number '8', soon became a point of disagreement between the two men. JB believed Hilmer had put a price per share on the table. Looking back years later, he recalled: 'Hilmer maintained that he never said $8. He said he could not possibly have said that because it was a dilutive exercise for the company. But I would not have said $8 unless I heard him say that number and I clearly wrote it down at the time. He maintained he was talking about a deal of between $800 million and $1 billion which would be capped with cash at $300 million.'

Hilmer was anxious to do business but only on his own terms and he was unable to pay the sort of premium for Rural Press JB was seeking. On 8 October 2001, JB pressed Hilmer regarding his change of heart over the $8. He wanted some clarity about what had gone wrong. 'I am appreciative of the open way our discussions progressed. I remain puzzled about the $8 and I must say I am a little confused about the way things have developed,' he wrote.

Another round of talks between a former chairman, Dean Wills, and JB commenced in 2005, although these too proved fruitless and after two or three sessions, JB lost interest. The next conversation was with Ron Walker immediately after Walker was appointed as chairman of Fairfax in August 2005 and had paid a round of visits to media proprietors.

Finally, in 2006, there was nothing uncertain or confusing about the approach to JB by Walker and Kirk. The media world was in the grip of febrile acquisition talk and the chairman and chief executive were both determined to enlarge Fairfax drastically, to defend it against unwelcome raiders lining up like a black storm on the horizon. Kirk was equally determined to use acquisitions to defend the company in the face of falling revenue from the Fairfax metropolitan papers. He wanted new revenue and he wanted to diversify as fast as he could, and he had the board behind him. It was the same strategy Hilmer had followed when buying the New Zealand newspapers assets from the Murdochs in 2003, although Hilmer had failed to grapple with a different company that mattered far more to Fairfax's long-time economic health, the online recruitment advertising site SEEK. Hilmer though, had bought an online oddity, the dating website RSVP — an investment that would perform very well over time, to the disbelief of journalists, but the relief of the board.

Kirk, a dealmaker by nature, already had brought a big internet player inside the Fairfax tent with TradeMe, and several small ones including Stayz. But Rural Press would rank as the biggest acquisition ever, rolling in earnings, firmly in the print space, but holding out hope that small communities would follow their favourite newspapers and weeklies online.

A Rural Press deal meant something else too: the cachet of the Fairfax name and the prestige that Rural Press's controlling shareholders could bring. It was a little like dressing Fairfax up as a dynasty again after 15 years of relentless boardroom turnover and the political machinations of major players like Conrad Black and Rodney Price — to say nothing of a stream of managing directors who included the receiver Des Nicholl, from Deloitte Ross Tohmatsu, appointed to run the company in 1990. Appointing a Fairfax to the board now as a major shareholder would be like applying a fresh coat of gilt to a faded picture frame.

———

During his tenure, Fred Hilmer had moved in more ways than one to strip away the imagery and history of the old Fairfax, trying to crack the romanticised notion that the company somehow had a position as a guardian of the jewels that was larger than the sum of its parts, and to plant it firmly in a more managerial present.

In 2002, in an act that seemed dismissive of a culture he had no time or respect for, Hilmer had given away to the National Portrait Gallery most of the historic Fairfax family portraits and marble busts that had featured in boardrooms and corridors. These works spoke to a company legacy in much the same way as any depiction of members of the Meyer and Graham families would to *The Washington Post*, the Ochs and Sulzberger families to *The New York Times*, and more latterly, the Murdochs to News Corp.

The National Portrait Gallery in Canberra had been delighted with the 13 historic works they had chosen, reflecting as they did the intersection of a family history and a company history reaching back to the 1850s. The works included a portrait of Sir

James Reading Fairfax painted in 1898 by Tom Roberts, the great Australian artist from the Heidelberg school. James Reading Fairfax was the son of John Fairfax who, together with a partner, had bought *The Sydney Morning Herald* in 1851 from its founders. James Reading became not just a major newspaper proprietor, but a businessman, a philanthropist and a social fixture. He was a founder of both the AMP and the Perpetual Trustee Company, where he could rightly claim one of the more unorthodox methods of becoming chairman. In 1885, on the occasion of their first board meeting in a temporary office in Pitt Street, the new directors of Perpetual faced a conundrum: how to choose the first chairman. After some discussion it was agreed that the heaviest gentleman should be elected chair. All directors were duly weighed and when the results of the competition were tabulated, James Reading Fairfax had won, a momentous event documented still in a display case in the company's Sydney offices.

During the first meeting between Ron Walker, David Kirk and John Fairfax, they sat around a small antique oak table in the Pitt Street offices of Marinya Media — a company owned by the JB wing of the Fairfaxes, which held a controlling 53 per cent of Rural Press. They agreed that the CEOs of the two businesses, Kirk from Fairfax and Brian McCarthy from Rural Press, should meet to discuss what a merger between the companies could look like. If there was scope at Fairfax to negotiate a financial structure to merge, then they had the blessing to see if the idea could fly in other ways.

They could also negotiate the framework of a more sensitive and potentially more treacherous aspect of a merger: their own future relationship and the details of their likely roles, and the ascendancy of one over the other. Both were strong characters accustomed to calling the shots. Kirk was not a newspaperman, but he had a strong entrepreneurial spirit and a strategy to redirect the fortunes of Fairfax to defend and strengthen it in the face of the internet. He had a managerial focus wrapped up in a very competitive temperament. His weakness, if anything, was that he was not a natural killer. McCarthy had a deeply personal commitment to Rural Press, having been at the company for 30 years and taking over as chief executive in 1994 when the market capitalisation was $416 million. It had now reached almost $3 billion, a testament to McCarthy's years of careful attention to cost control, something that had made him the darling of analysts and a constant feature of speculation over the years on potential Fairfax CEOs. Rural Press, though, had reached a plateau in terms of its expansion and development. The idea of a Fairfax merger offered new opportunities for both, and in a wider context, for the Rural Press managers and board as well.

By October 2006, just as James Packer was finalising the details of selling half of his own media assets and Stokes and Murdoch were climbing into the Fairfax register in readiness for a media play-off, things warmed up at Fairfax. McCarthy and Kirk met often at the Rural Press headquarters in St Leonards, a suburb on Sydney's north shore easily accessible by the main arterial road, the Pacific Highway. Kirk's might be a face that could not hide in Auckland or Wellington, but he could come and go with reasonable anonymity in St Leonards — and certainly without the stickybeak scrutiny that meetings at 'Fairfax central' in Darling Harbour would have sparked.

The talks were exploratory at first. Rural Press had a massive spread of newspapers and radio stations and a beachhead in the

US. By bringing together the metropolitan newspaper company, Fairfax, and the non-metro company, Rural Press, both chief executives were confident they could achieve a nationwide spread of the market, beneficial to each other. McCarthy felt that Fairfax's online real estate business domain.com.au could easily expand and strengthen the Rural Press country footprint. Similarly, but to a lesser degree, the online auto and jobs markets could be extended. Using the franchise of the internet classifieds was one of the attractions of the deal for Rural Press. Kirk made it crystal clear that the high-yield line classifieds at Fairfax were under pressure, but he believed that paid circulation in the newspapers had stabilised and that losses in display classifieds could be rebuilt.

McCarthy said later:

> The argument put to us was that the classifieds were nearly gone anyway. We sat across the table and we wanted to see the evidence that it was gone. We wanted to see the downside of our risk. Kirk said there was not much to lose. They had done a lot of work on this. So our thinking was that by offering total market coverage Australia-wide, we could grow the classifieds.

Kirk's primary motivation was the prospect of a new revenue pipe coming in. 'One of the reasons we did Rural Press was because regional papers had local ads and local cost structures and that was going to be ballast to provide cash to manage the transition for us from the loss of the classifieds.'

Initially, the negotiations were cautious but positive as Kirk and McCarthy and their chief financial officers combed through to identify synergies. But on 24 November 2006, things began to come unstuck. As they came closer to the point where final decisions would be made, tension over the price emerged. It had the capacity to make everyone step back to reconsider. But there was also another sticking point and it was something that had to be resolved squarely between McCarthy and Kirk. Brian McCarthy was not certain that he wanted to come to Fairfax, and he was considering quitting instead. Kirk had made it clear that he himself would be chief executive of the new company and that he wanted McCarthy as his deputy. Now McCarthy refused.

Kirk was scheduled that night to participate in a debate over the future of media at the Westin Hotel in the CBD. He arrived exhausted and downcast. He was due onstage to join a panel that included chief executive of the ABC Mark Scott, chief executive of Foxtel Kim Williams, and PBL boss James Packer. Feeling rung out after the long afternoon session in St Leonards, Kirk searched for Ron Walker, who was seated in the audience. Kirk explained to the chairman that Rural Press was baulking on price and that McCarthy was resisting joining the new company. Walker, knowing the positive view of McCarthy in the markets and amongst media analysts, and the damage that his refusal might inflict on the deal, told Kirk he would have to tell McCarthy that if he refused to come, the deal was off. Price was one thing, but this merger was also about bringing the feted Rural Press iron-fist management style on board, and McCarthy was the linchpin to this.

'I said, "Well, you can go back and say that we have to have management as well or we won't do the deal",' Walker recalled later.

McCarthy, though, had his mind set on finding a new challenge. To go from being chief executive to deputy chief executive, to play second fiddle after years as the boss, would not come easily to this highly competitive and aggressively single-minded executive.

> I didn't want to come. I was 56 and I thought I'd like to do something else. Kirk said that he would have to tell the Fairfax board. He rang back later and said, 'If you don't come, the deal's off.' I discussed it all with John [JB] and then I told Kirk that I would agree to come for 12 months. I knew I would be the deputy, and I said to David, 'I think I know a little more about newspapers than you do and I'll give you twelve months.'

The final two weeks, predictably in a deal this size, became a series of dramas and sensitive decisions. Marinya's shareholders — JB, his brother Tim and his two sisters Sally and Ruth — all had to be happy with the arrangement. Between them, they would have less than 15 per cent of the new company, by contrast with their majority holdings in Rural Press. At Fairfax, they would have no control and only two directors.

At the last minute there were less than subtle tensions over the chairman's position, but Walker made it clear he was not ceding ground and that Fairfax was the senior company in the deal. Marinya wanted three directors, but Fairfax refused; JB asked for an alternate director should either he or his son Nicholas be unable to attend board meetings and this was agreed.

David Kirk now had the ink drying on a huge deal of his own. It would not be long before he had blown all the speculation about Packer and Murdoch takeovers into the wind with the electrifying news that another dynasty, the Fairfaxes, had returned from exile.

On 6 December 2006 the deal was announced, and everyone was flushed with backslapping good spirits. Marinya would own 14 per cent of Fairfax, becoming the biggest shareholder in the company. JB and his executives organised champagne in their boardroom, and Kirk turned his planned Christmas drinks party into a celebration for the Fairfax side at his home in Hunter's Hill. It would be four months before the deal was finalised, in April 2007, and much remained to be settled. But as far as most people were concerned, it had been consummated already.

JB told journalists at the first press conference that while he might not aspire to be chairman, he would consider it if Ron Walker fell under a bus. It was a comment that would prove to have a long tail, although it was laughingly downplayed by all on the day.

Soon after, in a well-informed interview on 10 December, business columnist Alan Kohler asked Kirk about the appointment of Brian McCarthy, and how vital he was to the arrangement. Kirk replied truthfully, but few could have known how close to the bone his comments were or how close to collapse the deal had been just weeks before as McCarthy weighed up his future. He chose his words carefully.

'I would go so far to say that I don't think we would have got the deal done if Brian hadn't been prepared to commit to manage not only what he is managing today in Rural Press, but also all of our Australian publishing business.'

Kohler pushed harder: 'You mean you wouldn't have wanted to do it, or the deal wouldn't have got done from their side?'

'I don't think I would have wanted to do it. I think we need a manager of his calibre and his quality to come across and run those assets.'

Asked by Kohler about other planned investments and acquisitions, Kirk ruled out a number of things, including metropolitan radio networks and a lunge for Channel Ten, all the subject of speculation in the press at the time. 'I think it's a pretty tough business and it will probably get a little bit tougher. In metropolitan radio, music radio, not a lot of synergies with what we do, so probably not something we would be interested in.'

Seven months later these words rang strangely hollow when Kirk announced that Fairfax was buying back into radio after an absence of 20 years. In a joint deal with Macquarie Media Group, Southern Cross Broadcasting would be carved up with Fairfax paying $480 million in cash for the metropolitan radio stations and an array of assets including a TV production house, Southern Star. The deal was part of a strategy, driven from the very top by Fairfax's chairman, to return the company to its grand days of old — when it had interests in radio and television as well as newspapers.

———

While Fairfax was working on restoring members of the Fairfax family to the citadel, James Packer's plans for a dynastic unwinding of his own companies were well advanced. After striking the deal to sell half of his media properties to CVC, Packer was adding the finishing touches. The sale was an extraordinary move, upending decades of history, but after an initial blast of publicity, the hype about generations and first families had died down. He still had half of the company and this was perceived as meeting some of the emotional obligations to the past. In reality, Packer was divorcing media to focus on casinos and he could not have been happier to remove the shackles.

On 7 February 2007, PBL Media was created as a joint venture between PBL and CVC Asia Pacific, holding as its assets the Nine Network (including its one-third interest in Sky News), ACP Magazines, 50 per cent of ninemsn and 50.6 per cent of carsales.com. au. This new spin-off company owned the TV and magazine empire founded by James Packer's great-grandfather Robert Clyde Packer — a journalist turned newspaper owner — and then expanded by his grandfather Sir Frank into magazines and television, then expanded further again by his own father, Kerry. For all the mythology around Kerry's fanatical absorption in Nine, it had not stopped him selling the network when the price was high, then buying it back when the price was low. James Packer had no plans to buy anything back. The only real question in his mind was how quickly he could sell more of Nine and escape altogether from the public gaze.

Fairfax went the other way. Ten weeks later, on 20 April 2007, shareholders voted overwhelmingly in favour of a merger between Fairfax and Rural Press. Nineteen years after young Warwick had broken the family's hold, JB was returning to the company that bore his name. Everyone spoke of new beginnings. The AAP wire service, however, reported a shot across the bows from one cautious but powerful observer drawing attention to the $700 million in new debt created for the merger — which added to the $625 million in debt to fund the 2006 purchase of TradeMe. Standard & Poor's ratings agency had cut its long-term rating for Fairfax from BBB to BBB-minus. An S&P spokesman told AAP that while Rural Press enabled Fairfax to diversify, 'the rating downgrade reflects the added debt burden that this merger brings to the group and management's demonstrated appetite for higher leverage than prescribed by its past financial policies.'

On 23 April, the same day the Rural Press merger with Fairfax was legally concluded, it emerged that Kerry Stokes had sold his small stake in Fairfax. Two weeks later, News Limited announced that it too had sold out of Fairfax. Takeover fever had carried Fairfax from $3.80 to $5.20 a share and a merger with Rural Press. With a strange symmetry, the combination of Murdoch, Packer and Stokes had brought a Fairfax back to Fairfax.

———

Brian McCarthy started at Fairfax in June 2007. From the very start it was clear that he and David Kirk made an uncomfortable fit. After years as top dog, McCarthy made no secret of the fact that he regarded Kirk as a novice. But with McCarthy in charge of the giant metropolitan papers, it was his background of running small newspapers that fuelled misgivings in the commercial divisions and newsrooms. How would he grasp the complexity of papers like *The Sydney Morning Herald* and *The Age* after overseeing publications often run on a shoestring? As waves of Rural Press managers moved into top positions they were known pejoratively as 'the cardigans'.

Tensions quickly reached all corners, creating a sense of 'them' and 'us' that divided the company, leaving no quarter secure. Kirk's TradeMe deal was already completed but it was a deal that had impressed neither McCarthy nor JB. Both regarded TradeMe as expensive, and while they came later to see it as a good business, both felt it went against the grain for Fairfax. Their opinions and deep interest in closely analysing every development of the company's direction and strategic plans — McCarthy as deputy CEO and JB as a director — would come to be a thorn in the executive suites as well as the Fairfax boardroom.

Southern Cross Broadcasting was the deal that became a step too far for Marinya, although the plans for this acquisition had been underway for some months preceding the finalisation of the Rural Press merger. After joining the Fairfax board in April, JB made it clear that he felt rushed and uncomfortable with Southern Cross, a position that was loudly heard, but had not derailed the deal.

By November 2007, Fairfax had finalised the takeover of Southern Cross with its big-rating city radio stations, 3AW in Melbourne and 2UE in Sydney, as well as Southern Star. On 11 December 2007, Marinya's investment director Patrick Joyce was formally appointed as an alternative director on the Fairfax board. It was a signal that JB intended to maintain eyes and ears in the boardroom at all times. And it was an early signpost to the war which would soon splash blood all over the Fairfax boardroom, and which would not stop until all sides had been vanquished. Within days, speculation in the markets focussed on concern about Fairfax debt, and on 19 December 2007, the company issued a statement describing as incorrect, information in an analyst report from Citi that queried Fairfax's potential risks in refinancing the debt.

Before long Marinya, as a 14 per cent shareholder, was forcefully making its views known. The relationships at the top of the company and in the boardroom became steadily — and rapidly — more uncomfortable and confrontational. The issue causing most concern at Marinya was the prospect of more acquisitions. JB wanted to put a stop to the train. He recalled later:

> At the start, things were harmonious. But maybe with
> hindsight it was foolish to do a deal where we had only
> 14 per cent of the company. I think Brian McCarthy had

achieved everything possible at Rural Press and was looking for something new. He was fully aware of the difficulties of merging these two companies. And we were wrong in not insisting that McCarthy take over as CEO straight away, and also wrong in not insisting on a third board seat. It wouldn't have affected our control position, but with three directors it would have given us more influence.

The second and crucial stage of Kirk's plans to diversify earnings from radio on the back of the Southern Cross investment fell victim to a dispute in the boardroom. On 20 February 2008, Kirk took to the board a proposal to merge Southern Cross with the entrepreneur John Singleton's Macquarie Radio Network. He faced open revolt from JB and Nicholas Fairfax. Kirk's objective was for the company to establish a monopoly position in Sydney by merging the two commercial talk stations in the city on the back of the powerful talkback hosts in Macquarie's pay, including the controversial and top-ranking Alan Jones.

Already Fairfax had a monopoly in Melbourne, Perth and Brisbane. A merger would create a powerhouse Sydney commercial talkback presence and a national network that advertisers could not ignore. Kirk's financial modelling indicated that Fairfax could substantially improve earnings from its radio investments from around $30 million a year to more than $60 million a year with this expansion. It was the deal Kirk needed, but he was overruled by the board for the first time, with JB and Nicholas leading the revolt. They argued that the Southern Cross business had just been bought and needed to settle in. There was a political aspect to the resistance in the boardroom too. JB and other directors expressed their personal reluctance for buying a business with Alan Jones on the payroll. JB recalled later: 'I said it was ridiculous and we shouldn't go anywhere near metropolitan radio, and all the trouble that brings with the big name prima donnas. They'd paid a lot for Rural Press and they had paid a lot for Southern Cross.'

As well as flexing his muscle in the Fairfax boardroom, JB would also spend a considerable sum of money privately in 2008. Once the Rural Press sale was agreed, JB had turned his attention to estate planning. His family's big shareholdings in Rural Press had always been held through two family companies: Cambooya — owned by JB, his brother Tim and his sisters, Ruth and Sally — and Marinya Media, the private equity company owned by Cambooya. Marinya in turn had held, prior to the merger, 53 per cent of Rural Press as well as other investments.

Marinya and Cambooya were names steeped in the family history of John B. Fairfax and his siblings. Their father Sir Vincent Fairfax was born in 1909 at Cambooya in southeast Queensland, at the graceful Marinya homestead with its wide verandas and pretty gardens. The house later burned down, an event that found its echo many years later in 1989 as the company, then known as John Fairfax Holdings, frantically negotiated with a string of banks to avert collapse in the wake of young Warwick Fairfax's privatisation. On the night the refinancing deal was finally reached, an old church on Jersey Road in Sydney's Woollahra — where the foundation stone had been laid by John Fairfax, the founder of the company — burned down.

208

Realestate.com.au founder Karl Sabljak did the sales and graphics, his wife
Carmel did the accounting, 1996. They cut into Fairfax's market by letting
estate agents put as many ads online as they liked for a cheap fixed fee.
(Courtesy Karl Sabljak)

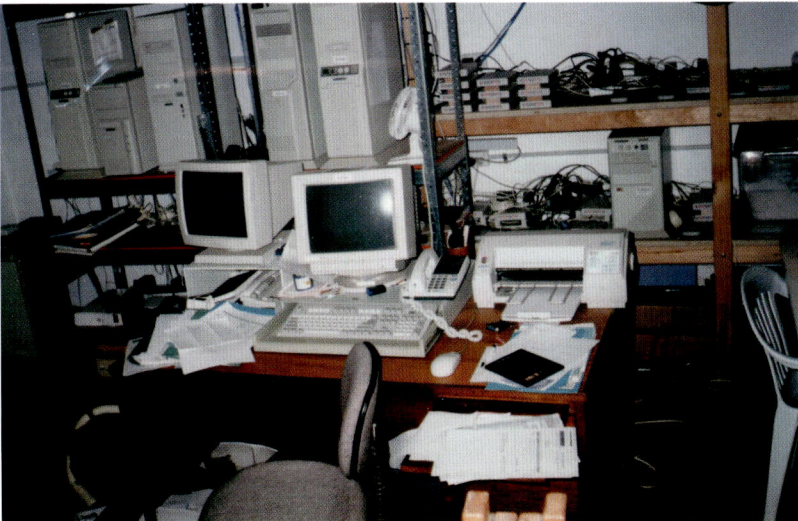

Taking on Fairfax, from Martin Howell's desk. When Howell and Sabljak
saw that half of *The Age* was real estate advertising, they raced out to register
realestate.com.au in 1995. (Courtesy Karl Sabljak)

Starting a website in the garage: realestate.com.au's first home at 9 St Clems Road in Doncaster East belied its big ambitions. By 2013 the company was worth $3.9 billion. (Courtesy Karl Sabljak)

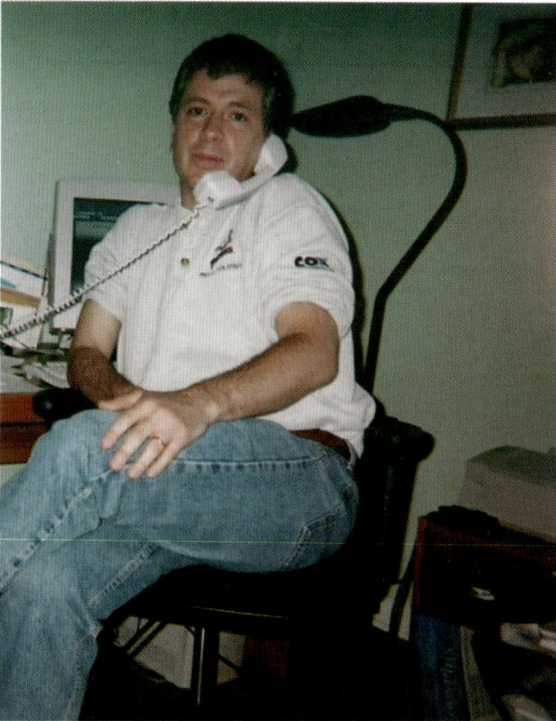

'Those fuckers kept our champagne': Lindsay Gardner from Cox Communications in 1996. He was furious when Fairfax's bid for a 24-hour pay TV news channel was squashed by Rupert Murdoch at the eleventh hour. (Courtesy Lindsay Gardner)

'Over my dead body': there was no place for Fairfax in Foxtel. Rupert Murdoch and Kerry Packer, just warming up. (Courtesy Ward O'Neill)

Fairfax had named their site for them: carsales.com.au on the cover of Drive, 1 August 1997. (Courtesy Fairfax Media)

Carsales' founders were furious when Fairfax and News blocked their ads, so they decided to do something about it. They hung this sign from the ceiling and let it twirl in the breeze at the 1998 car dealers' conference on the Gold Coast. (Courtesy Steve Kloss)

The troublemakers from carsales.com.au in 2000: chairman Wal Pisciotta at far left, chief executive Greg Roebuck front left in blue tie. (Photo www. davidisrael.com.au)

Lachlan Murdoch was not prepared to invest $7 million in realestate.com.au. Instead he proposed $2.25 million and some contra. (Sebastian Costanzo / Fairfax Syndication)

John McGrath takes gold in the 1999 Australasian Real Estate Institutes' Auctioneering Championships. McGrath called Lachlan Murdoch in 2000: if they didn't get help now, realestate.com.au would sink within weeks. (Courtesy John McGrath)

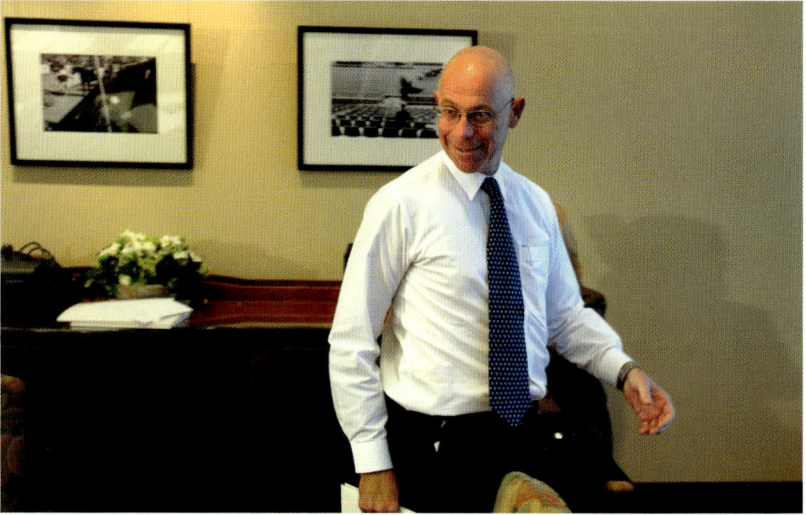

His eye on the main game: Fred Hilmer had spent $1.1 billion in 2003 buying newspapers in New Zealand from Rupert Murdoch. He told Paul Bassat that Murdoch had once advised him to remember two things: media grew faster than GDP and it always fragmented. (Peter Morris / Fairfax Syndication)

The SEEK founders had a young man's view of risk and they were hungry. Advertisers would fax their ads for the Saturday newspapers to SEEK on Friday night, then the Bassats and Matt Rockman would sit up late typing them onto the site. In June 2011, the market capitalisation of SEEK was $2.25 billion, bigger than Fairfax. Celebrating the listing of SEEK on the ASX in 2005, from left: Paul Bassat, Matthew Rockman, Andrew Bassat. (Courtesy Paul Bassat)

The messages from the outside world were becoming increasingly strident; even the cartoonists were having a go. By 2004 it was clear that the classifieds could wither on the vine. (Cartoon by Nicholson from *The Australian* www.nicholsoncartoons.com.au)

Ron Walker, chairman of the Commonwealth Games, greets Her Majesty in 2006. Minutes before the Queen arrived, James Packer marched over to Walker and pulled him in tight, berating him for welching on the deal to buy his magazines. (Courtesy Commonwealth Games Federation)

David Kirk had captained the All Blacks to victory in the 1987 World Cup, but nothing had prepared him for the rough and tumble at Fairfax. (John Selkirk / Fairfax Media)

On the eve of the Commonwealth Games, the Fairfax board met in Melbourne to sign off the TradeMe deal. They did not expect James Packer to be a good sport about losing. From left: Julia King, David Evans, Peter Young, Ron Walker, Mark Burrows, Roger Corbett, David Kirk. (Courtesy Shaney Balcombe)

With the media takeover frenzy, there had to be a way to get the Fairfax share price up. Sometimes it's just who you know: James Packer and Ron Walker riding in the red Merc at Bondi after coffee in 2006. (Courtesy John Shakespeare)

Sam Morgan suddenly had two big predators on his hands. It was the first time anyone had acknowledged that TradeMe was making a lot of money, and outstripping the competition. Sam Morgan in the TradeMe limo, 2006. (Courtesy Sam Morgan)

It became a war over power marked by frustration: David Kirk and Brian McCarthy were both strong characters accustomed to calling the shots. David Kirk (left) had his eyes on the digital space. 'I think I know a little bit more about newspapers than you do,' McCarthy (right) told him. (Nic Walker / Fairfax Syndication)

John Alexander was warehoused by the Packers in case they decided to buy Fairfax. 'Don't buy this company,' he told Kerry. 'The internet is going to take away its business.' (Andrew Quilty / Fairfax Syndication)

Kerry Stokes always had his eye on the competition, and in 2009 he could see that James Packer was in financial trouble. 'I think he's vulnerable,' he said. Stokes liked diving with whale sharks in the Solomons in his spare time. (Ryan Stokes)

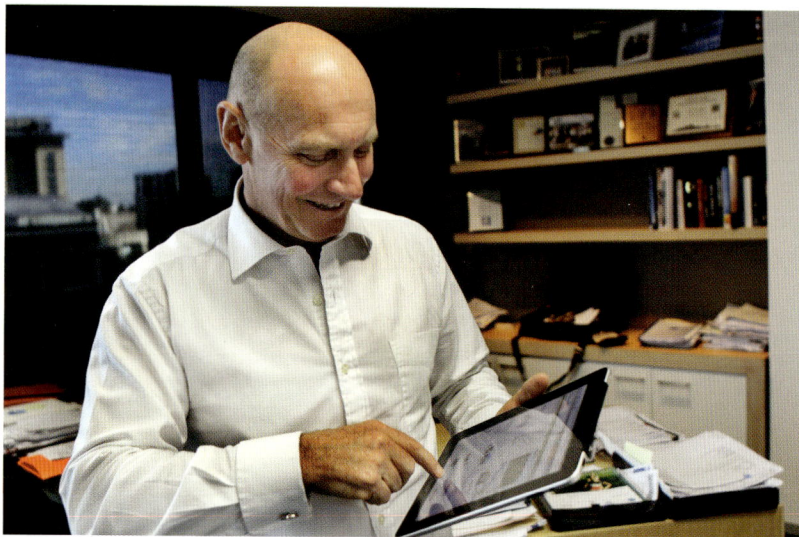

Brian McCarthy was used to running the show and his cost-cutting prowess had made him the darling of the analysts. But he came to blows with the Fairfax board over a strategy for the future. (Brendan Esposito / Fairfax Syndication)

It had started with the best of intentions: bringing a Fairfax back to Fairfax could bring new revenue and put some polish on the product. But by the end, John B. Fairfax and the Fairfax directors were swinging punches at each other. (Brendan Esposito / Fairfax Syndication)

Fairfax chairman Roger Corbett, right, put a new chief executive in the job, one-time *Financial Review* reporter Greg Hywood. It could be a new beginning after the stalemate of the McCarthy years. At least they could speak to each other. (Louie Douvis / Fairfax Syndication)

The first deal James Packer did after Kerry died was to buy a new casino licence. He flew with his lawyer Guy Jalland to Las Vegas to sign a deal with the gaming legend Steve Wynn for $900 million. (Photographer: Greg Allen-Waters)

By the time the deal was done, ConsMedia would be no more and Packer
had quit media. News Limited had bought his pay TV company with its big
Foxtel stake. Making nice together: Kim Williams, left, with James Packer
and Kerry Stokes in 2012. (Dan Himbrechts / Newspix)

After selling his boat and plane in the lockdown after the financial crisis,
James Packer was in an expansive mood. His new boat, *Seahorse*, sailed
through the Sydney Heads in November 2012 and parked in Rose Bay.
(Photo: Pamela Williams)

Lachlan and Sarah Murdoch arrive at the Press Club Hall of Fame dinner in Melbourne in 2012. Realestate.com.au had become News Corp's best pure-play digital business and it would go into the 'new News' with the newspapers. (Michael Clayton-Jones / Fairfax Syndication)

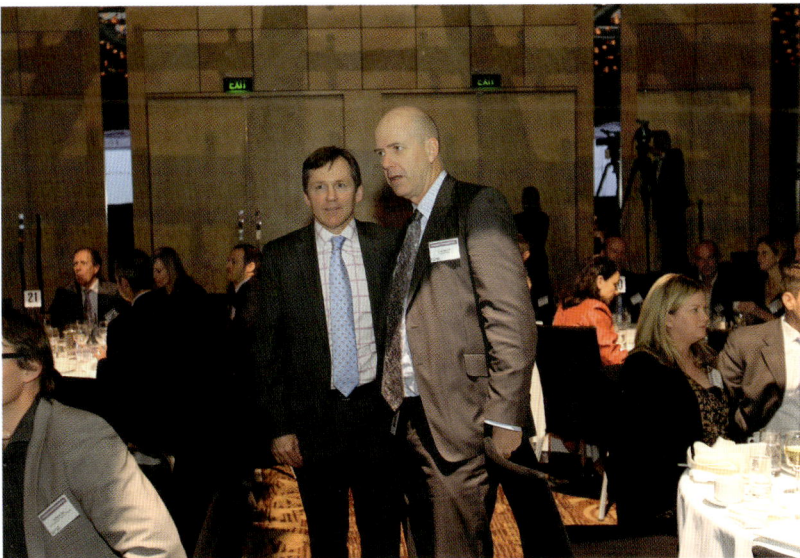

There are some things that have to be a secret between CEOs. David Kirk had discovered the classifieds were almost gone by 2006; in 2011 Greg Hywood had to work out what to do next. (Nic Walker / Fairfax Syndication)

The Fairfax boardroom had laid down its weapons, exhausted after four years of battle that culminated in the loss of two chief executives and a chairman. To save the company they would have to sack thousands. And then Gina Rinehart arrived. (Brendan Esposito / Fairfax Syndication)

As new generations of the Fairfax family grew in different directions, much of the old sentimentality of those days had evaporated. With the Fairfax–Rural Press merger on track, JB and his siblings began negotiations on a deal in mid-2007 to restructure their family company. JB would buy out the 62 per cent of shares in Marinya Media held by his brother and his two sisters. He would take over Marinya entirely, which would make Marinya the biggest shareholder in Fairfax Media with 14 per cent.

The siblings met in the modest southwest-facing Cambooya office at 19 Pitt Street, Sydney, a building owned by the much wider Fairfax clan including different arms of the family, and known as Fairfax House. The deal between the four siblings was negotiated with the assistance of a Cambooya executive, but with no outside advice.

The deal was concluded by February 2008. JB paid his siblings $4.50 a share, giving him control of Marinya's stake in Fairfax. At the time, the Fairfax share price was just over $4, making this a more than comfortable deal for the siblings. For JB, the return to Fairfax had now been concluded in a way that created great optimism. He had resolved the intergenerational interests with his family, giving him the ability to focus on his Fairfax investment without carrying the responsibility of his sisters' and brother's inheritance; he and his son Nick were Fairfax directors; and finally, they had Brian McCarthy, the trusted and admired chief executive who had kept Rural Press on the straight and narrow churning out dividends for many years and who was now running the whole Fairfax newspaper division. This boded well for the future, because if there was anyone the stock market and the media analysts trusted to run a newspaper company, it was Brian McCarthy.

At the end of December 2007, Fairfax moved into yet another new home, this time in Pyrmont. It had abandoned its massive old Broadway headquarters, with the presses and the composing rooms in the basement, after the disaster of young Warwick. Now it was leaving its cushy premises at Darling Harbour, moving out of the city centre to an area that was not as austere as Wapping in the UK, where big newspaper companies had relocated in the 1980s, but less extravagant than Darling Harbour, with its proximity to restaurants and department stores as well as the law courts and headquarters of Australia's biggest companies and banks.

The new Fairfax building was a bunker of darkened glass penned between old wharves, a casino, and Kerry Stokes' Seven Network headquarters, which filled a vast warehouse adjacent to the Pyrmont waterway. Fairfax had a new name too and it was proudly emblazoned across the top of the five-storey building: Fairfax Media. This was a new Fairfax: it had a big merger to bulk up against raiders and bring new income; it had bought into radio; it had a sparkling internet growth stock in TradeMe and it was ready to trumpet the new era. The classifieds might have run away, but there was every reason for optimism.

CHAPTER EIGHT

PARTY LIKE THERE'S NO TOMORROW

The first shock waves of the financial tsunami seemed so far away as to be irrelevant to Australia. In July 2007, when the siren sounded in America, it was too soon for any but the most plugged-in insiders to understand that this was not an undersea tremor but an earthquake. Two hedge funds owned by the big US investment bank Bear Stearns had gone broke after high-risk mortgage assets they held became worthless on the back of a downturn in demand. In less than a year, the share price of the mighty Bear Stearns plunged: from $150 in June 2007 to $30 eight months later. By March 2008, when Bear Stearns was sold to another Wall Street colossus, JP Morgan, for $2 a share, the tsunami was in the process of smashing the global financial system.

The bubble in the American housing market had started to burst in 2006, and as it did it unhinged a set of toxic financial instruments in the US banking system. These arrangements, known as asset-backed securities, mortgage-backed securities, and collateralised debt obligations (CDOs), had enabled the financial wizards of some of the world's most respected institutions to slice and dice assets — especially mortgages for borrowers who were unable to service them. Vast numbers of these mortgages had been issued with no requirement for proper documentation or credit checks. Such risky home loans were then packaged into blocks of assets by top banks and sold to investors. The mortgages were known as sub-prime loans and in time, they became the sub-prime crisis. The structure of this business was so arcane that it had remained beneath the radar of the American public. It was not a secret, however, to the financial wheelers and dealers packaging assets into CDOs, the big banks selling them, the regulators and ratings agencies watching over them, and the government mortgage bureaucracies like Freddie Mac and Fannie Mae where the quality controls failed. In other words, it was only the customers who knew nothing.

The sub-prime crisis would wreak such havoc that it would bring comparisons to the Great Depression. Companies that had confidently thrown themselves into debt-fuelled binges in the high times were crushed or struggled to survive as credit and liquidity dried up and values collapsed. Within a year, panic set in. In Australia, the impact was not head-on, but the outer waves battered the economy and with it the media industry, sensitive to any tiny shift in consumer spending and advertising. If the internet had already laid waste a business model reliant on plump advertising dollars while readers headed to the web for free newspapers, then the financial crisis would slash at what was left, leaving media companies around the world stuck with high labour and production costs and dwindling revenue.

Still, the end of 2007 remained a heady time for media as the overweening confidence of big companies that they could survive the new industrial revolution intersected with the *fin de siècle* debt-binge of the private equity barbarians. Australian media millionaires and billionaires were no exception. By the close of 2007, John B. Fairfax had finalised the series of transactions that made him the biggest shareholder in the listed Fairfax newspaper company and he was buying out his private family company at a frothy price. In December 2007, Rupert Murdoch's News Corp completed its $5 billion acquisition of Dow Jones, bringing into the stable *The Wall Street Journal* — a newspaper coveted by Murdoch for years — at a price that shocked analysts and provoked an avalanche of criticism, though most should have been accustomed by then to Murdoch's single-mindedness.

———

In June 2007, James Packer had created his own secondary shock wave with the announcement that he had divested himself of another slab of his remaining interests in traditional media. In a statement to the Australian Stock Exchange, PBL revealed that it had sold a further 25 per cent share of the joint venture, PBL Media, to its partner in the joint venture, CVC Asia Pacific, for $515 million. It had also sold to PBL Media its interest in Ticketek and Acer Arena for $210 million. CVC now owned 75 per cent of PBL Media and Packer just 25 per cent. He was heading for the exit. Given Packer's conviction that the internet was eating into media on every front, he believed there was a real chance that PBL Media would go broke. He had no interest personally in trying to turn around its main asset, the flailing Nine Network, and he certainly had no desire to be there if it crashed; he would undoubtedly be blamed. This was CVC's business now. Packer had a shopping list and it did not include media.

Packer then went berserk buying casinos. The initial $4.5 billion, plus the next $515 million, all in cold hard cash from CVC, burned a hole in his pocket and by late 2007 he had spent a very substantial sum — in Las Vegas. In June 2007, he had taken a 19.6 per cent stake in Fontainebleau Resorts, where the casino was yet to be built, for US $250 million; he had committed US $220 million for a 4.9 per cent stake in Station Casinos. He had taken an option on land to create Crown Las Vegas, a development that was not much more than a twinkle on the horizon, but would soak up a modest US $20 million in payments to keep the option alive. In conjunction with Macquarie Bank he took a 50 per cent stake in the Canadian Gateway Casino Group — a $US 1.5 billion deal struck in November 2007; they would have equity of close to US $400 million and the rest was debt.

Some of these investments were made with the biggest names in private equity, others with the biggest names in gaming. In late 2007, Packer had approached David Bonderman, a founder of the private equity firm Texas Pacific Group, after TPG and another renowned leveraged buyout firm, Apollo Global Management, announced their plans to buy Harrah's Entertainment Inc. Among other iconic gambling properties, Harrah's owned the luxury hotel and casino Caesars Palace, on the Las Vegas strip in Paradise, Nevada. Packer had met Bonderman in earlier years and he had renewed the friendship in 2006 when TPG ran a ruler over Packer's media assets. Before the year was out and with credit markets tightening, Packer had committed US $150 million for 2.5 per cent of Harrah's.

On 11 December 2007, Packer inked Crown's biggest casino deal: a commitment to acquire 100 per cent of Cannery Casino Resorts for US $1.75 billion plus US $50 million in costs from its owners, Millennium Gaming and Oaktree Capital Management. The deal was subject to regulatory approvals in Nevada and Pennsylvania, where the Cannery casinos were located. With the Australian dollar trading at close to 90 cents against the US dollar, Packer's commitment was worth $2 billion Australian dollars. He didn't stop there. In Macau, where he had a joint venture with Lawrence Ho, he invested a total of $750 million.

As he cast his acquisitive eye over the US casino world, the only Australian media assets Packer had any interest in still holding were in pay television and the internet. He had split PBL in 2007 into two companies: Crown for his casinos, and Consolidated Media Holdings — known as ConsMedia — for the handful of media assets he wished to keep. These were: 25 per cent of Foxtel, 50 per cent of Fox Sports (then known as Premier Media) and 27 per cent of SEEK. ConsMedia also owned Packer's remaining 25 per cent shareholding in the joint venture with CVC, PBL Media.

Suddenly, in January 2008, in what could only be described as exquisitely bad timing, Packer and his old friend Lachlan Murdoch announced a joint bid to privatise ConsMedia — with the exception of Packer's stake in SEEK, which would be excluded as it was listed on the stock market; his 27 per cent of SEEK did not give him control.

Murdoch had returned from New York in 2005 after several years running News Corp's US television and newspaper operations. He had walked away after a long-running and ultimately losing battle with some of his father's most hard-headed lieutenants. Back in Sydney, he began searching for investments in small media businesses, planting his feet in the ground far from the cut-throat executive ranks of his father's empire. But one business that Lachlan still had an affinity for was pay television. He had spent years on the board of Foxtel in Australia after playing a formative role in the establishment of the company. James Packer had joined the board after the peace deal that followed Super League and they had worked as partners to develop the business with Telstra, the third hand in the Foxtel partnership.

Packer owned 38 per cent of ConsMedia and with an offer of $4.80 a share the bid valued this company at $3.3 billion. It was a brave call given the churning share markets but it was a solid company with well-run assets. Lachlan Murdoch and James Packer understood it as well as anyone, given their early days with Foxtel. And with Packer's remaining 25 per cent of Nine still housed inside ConsMedia, analysts who were yet to grasp the impact the financial crisis would have on advertising revenue pointed to the wide mix of pay TV, free-to-air television and magazines that could pose a challenge to rivals across the media industry if the deal went ahead.

Two and a half months later, however, it just as dramatically fell over after wrangling on price between Packer and Providence Equity Partners, Murdoch's financial backers. Murdoch himself had become sceptical about the valuation assigned to ConsMedia's remaining 25 per cent of PBL Media, which was in line with the $515 million Packer had received for selling a third 25 per cent of PBL Media to CVC in June 2007. But the meltdown in global debt markets was also worsening by the day and questions were growing about PBL Media's capacity to pay interest on its debts.

To the surprise of many, Murdoch and Packer remained close after the deal collapsed, even though it had put them under the public microscope again. But the bonds forged during the eviscerating One.Tel experience appeared sufficiently solid to survive the dumped plan. For Murdoch, losing a deal that had been conjured at the end of the good times proved a stroke of luck as stock markets continued their wintry descent. Media was an industry openly exposed to the vicissitudes of consumer pessimism, and it was not a time for financial risk — except for the truly hyper-wealthy and the truly foolhardy, and those who were a mix of both.

In June 2008, at possibly the worst time given the roiling markets, Fairfax and the Fairfax family suddenly burst back into the business pages after the publication of what seemed at first blush a minor story in *The Australian*. The newspaper reported on a private business transaction made by John B. Fairfax that involved a $170 million margin loan secured against more than 60 per cent of his 211 million Fairfax shares. This loan had been used to buy out his siblings' shares in Marinya Media — which owned 14 per cent of Fairfax — in February that year. But the news was accompanied by speculation that the loan could be subject to a margin call by the lender, CommSec, after whetting the appetite of speculators and short sellers trading in Fairfax shares in an attempt to force JB into a vulnerable position.

Short sellers were circling the market like vultures, sniffing for companies where shareholders had big margin loans secured against stock. If they could work to force down the share prices of such companies, then the resulting margin calls on borrowers — after the value of shares offered as security fell below the value of a loan — could force them to sell cheaply, an opportunity for easy profits. If the Fairfax share price fell far enough, CommSec might execute a margin call and a large block of JB's shares might hit the market, or so the theory went. A margin loan secured against a borrower's share portfolio was common practice, but with this borrower on the board of directors and with his position as Fairfax's biggest shareholder, his personal financial arrangements were vulnerable to exposure.

Within days, Marinya's investment boss Patrick Joyce conceded publicly the margin loan had been established, but he denied that it was under any pressure. In interviews with Nick Tabakoff, the journalist behind the story, Joyce fiercely defended JB's financial security, calling the loan a short-term facility. He acknowledged however, that Fairfax shares had been used as collateral. 'As part of our capital management, we have a very conservative amount of debt, in the form of a loan secured against Fairfax stock. We have not been margin called, and speculation that we have been is completely unfounded.'

Joyce described Fairfax as a long-term investment for Marinya, and said he was confident about the long-term prospects for the company. He took the opportunity as well to scotch one other resilient rumour: that JB or forces on his behalf had begun agitating for him to take over as chairman from Ron Walker. It was just over a year since Marinya had become Fairfax's biggest shareholder and this rumour — in many incarnations — had been afloat almost from day one. Joyce dismissed it, stating clearly that Marinya fully supported the board and management.

One corollary of the revelations about JB's margin loan was to train an unwelcome spotlight on the Fairfax share price, which like the rest of the market had taken a sickening plunge. JB had bought out his three siblings at $4.50 a share in February 2008 — an extravagant premium of 45 cents per share on the $4.05 Fairfax traded at; by the end of June, four months later, Fairfax shares had dropped to $2.90.

Within a week of the reports in *The Australian*, JB's margin loan had been rearranged. But any privacy regarding his financial stake in Fairfax was swept away. As the financial crisis hacked into media stocks, the impact on JB's wealth became an object of fascination for newspaper reports. It was a high price to pay for a man whose business acumen had been unchallenged, reigning as he had over the hugely successful Rural Press for almost 20 years. Suddenly, he appeared to have walked beneath the Fairfax curse. Even more remarkably, for those with an interest in the Shakespearean dimensions of Fairfax mythology, JB had used debt and a high price to buy out the entire shareholdings of his family in the company on the eve of a market crash — a transaction that could not fail to trigger memories of the moment in 1987 when his cousin Warwick had done the same.

The first signs of disturbance in the Fairfax boardroom came with a story in *The Sydney Morning Herald* on 27 June that the margin loan had been canvassed by directors in a meeting that week. Ron Walker, tackled by reporters, refused to say if it had been discussed. Most soon forgot about it, and it would be a full year before the matter of the loan became ammunition for a shoot-out in the Fairfax boardroom. When that happened, it contributed to a hail of accusations, levelled from inside the boardroom, of calumny and deceit that made Fairfax yet again the poster child for corporate dysfunction. In the short term, though, it was just another damaging sideshow, attracting the interest of short sellers and Fairfax's rivals at News Limited, always delighted to find a fresh opportunity to report on bad blood at the competition.

———

On 15 September 2008 — if any further evidence was needed that a global tail-spin into financial Armageddon could not be halted — the behemoth, Lehman Brothers, collapsed. The fourth biggest financial institution in America, founded by cotton traders from Bavaria in 1850, Lehman became the largest bankruptcy recorded in American history. Just the day before, another securities firm, Merrill Lynch, had sold itself to Bank of America for US $50 billion, just half of what it was worth a year before. Others teetered on the brink.

James Packer, who had invested willy-nilly in casinos at the end of 2007, was now staring straight into the headwinds. The big call of selling out of media had seen him labelled a genius of market judgement 18 months before. Now, as the US gaming industry crashed with the economy, his investment strategy threatened to wipe out his business. If Packer had thought getting rid of his television and magazine empire would halt the relentless scrutiny he so hated, he would find out soon enough that he had nowhere to hide, and that a media tycoon of any stripe making a transition to gaming was fascinating news. Moreover, that bad news with a sprinkling of comeuppance could always find a home. Journalists loved a train crash.

The plunge in the Australian dollar in the second half of 2008 threatened to completely derail Packer. In December 2007, the deal he had struck for Cannery totalled US $1.8 billion, including costs, with the dollar trading at close to 90 cents. But by October 2008, the Australian dollar had plunged to 60 cents. Suddenly, a commitment valued at $2 billion Australian dollars had ballooned to $3 billion Australian dollars, a number with the potential to mow through the Packer family's wealth — and that was before the impact of his other US casino investments.

Packer was terrified. He had sold to private equity at the high point before the financial crisis, but he had bought from private equity soon after, with the market still foaming. And like all the other lemmings, he had gone over the cliff.

In the second half of 2008, the debacle for Packer was laid bare. Almost as swiftly as deals were finalised for Crown's casino investments across the El Dorado of US gaming — the famous Nevada strip — the whole twirling eco-system of gambling and casinos had begun to hit the wall. Many businesses saw their revenue crash by 30 per cent or more. Planned construction projects were ditched, left to a netherworld. The crisis went on and on, enveloping private equity, the construction industry, the casinos themselves and the jobs and housing markets that revolved around them, right down to the smallest nail salons and sequin shops in Vegas.

Packer started selling assets and he moved swiftly to cut his final ties with the media empire created by three generations of Packer men. On 27 October 2008, Packer and John Alexander dramatically quit the board of PBL Media. They would refuse to put any more funding into the massive debt vehicle that now owned the Nine Network. After all the billions of dollars he had made selling off his media companies to private equity, Packer wrote down the value of his last 25 per cent to zero. Forced to find sources of cash to survive, CVC Asia Pacific refinanced the debt itself with a cash injection that diluted Packer's interest to less than 1 per cent.

James Packer was now free of traditional media, although he was hardly out of its sights. His only media holding was 38 per cent of ConsMedia with its stake in SEEK, Foxtel and Fox Sports. ConsMedia had looked rosy in January at $4.80, but by October it was trading at $2. Share markets were down almost 40 per cent on the year and Packer's wealth was in free fall after the plunge in the US. He was exposed heavily in an industry that was hypersensitive to consumers pulling back.

As the mocking reports that he was in financial trouble began to appear late in 2008, Packer's old fury towards Fairfax, sublimated in the good days, re-emerged. He had no doubt that the company's journalists, with their do-good ethos and holier-than-thou attitude towards not just a Packer, but gaming as well, would soon see him on the end of a pike. Insofar as his bad times made for tantalising copy, Packer was not wrong, but it would certainly not be Fairfax alone that would find him an irresistible target. Before long, James Packer would run the gauntlet with reports on his gaming investments, his smoking, his weight and his depression running hot — not just at Fairfax, but everywhere from the ABC and the Seven Network to News Limited.

Fairfax had plenty of its own problems, of course, and by the end of October 2008 the share price had slid to a mind-numbing $1.81. For JB Fairfax — who had been a director of the company way back in 1987 when young Warwick had opened the debt vaults, just weeks before the great stock market crash — the collapse of the Bear Stearns hedge funds in 2007 should have rung an early bell. But JB, like so many others, had missed the signs. Now he was the owner of 14 per cent of a company standing on the edge of a yawning chasm. Already the print classifieds had come under attack in a decade-long fight as the pure-plays morphed from start-ups to giants controlling the gateway to internet advertising. The internet had plundered readers as well, attacking the second line of defence for media companies who raised revenue from cover prices: selling papers. With the financial crisis compounding these challenges, no-one could predict how deeply it would cut, nor what would be left behind when it was all over.

The Fairfax share price continued its downward spiral, reaching lows not seen in well over a decade. It kept the focus on the falling wealth of JB Fairfax, but it also helped to fuel a row that was brewing in the Fairfax boardroom. There remained real ill will towards JB over the margin loan earlier in the year and that ill will was returned in kind. Disclosure of the loan became a proxy in a growing power play for control of the company. JB had made it clear months before that his debt financing was not vulnerable to an attack by speculators, and he regarded his loans as his own business. Yet the divisions in the boardroom became more entrenched. As far as other directors were concerned, JB had recklessly exposed the company to risk, contributing to pressure on the share price with his margin loan. Even after the announcement that it had been refinanced away from Fairfax shares, many did not believe him. In the markets, big calls were still being made by short sellers in Fairfax stock. But from where JB sat, the problems lay in another direction entirely: Fairfax had gone on a binge of asset buying that had left it carrying too much debt.

The rivalry between David Kirk and Brian McCarthy had grown exponentially too. Rumours abounded that McCarthy had assured his Rural Press troops they would soon be running the company; when these rumours permeated the newsrooms, they seemed like a self-fulfilling prophecy. Rural Press had infiltrated every part of Fairfax, but somehow the two sides of this merger had never found common ground. Mistrust and a lack of respect characterised relationships throughout the building. McCarthy had flexed his muscle using the traditional power that rode alongside the metropolitan papers. Because these big papers were the heart of the business, with all their political influence and their capacity to campaign on issues, whoever ran them was in a position of considerable power in the company. McCarthy had never seen himself as subordinate to Kirk and there was a fundamental disagreement between the two about the direction Fairfax should take. It became a war over power and ego, marked by frustration. With McCarthy second-guessing Kirk and making no secret of his derisory view of the non-newspaperman, the executive floors were a tinderbox. The Fairfax merger with Rural Press had become a reverse takeover.

In late 2008, several large Fairfax shareholders met with Marinya executives to share concerns about the direction in which Kirk was taking the company. Picking up on this dissatisfaction and frustrated in their efforts to obtain Ron Walker's express agreement that acquisitions must stop, two key members of Marinya's inner circle spearheaded more talks with a broad range of other Fairfax shareholders. Patrick Joyce and Mark Johnson — the former Macquarie Bank director, corporate adviser and member of Marinya's investment committee — sounded out investment managers at companies like Maple Brown-Abbott, Lazard and Perpetual: Kirk was not doing enough to rein in debt, they suggested; McCarthy, who made it his business to rein in costs and was famed for it, had done a great job at Rural Press. Marinya disagreed with Kirk's fundamental strategy of acquisitions and diversification; by gearing Fairfax up with assets that might have better long-term prospects for structural growth than the city newspapers, he was also loading interest payments onto a company with high costs in labour and production — journalists and paper and presses. These concerns over the strategy eventually were put in writing to the Fairfax board.

Joyce said later:

There were strong signals that the global financial crisis was coming. And Kirk was showing zero signs of reducing debt, which was very worrying to us and most other shareholders to whom we spoke. We were concerned about the combination of high financial gearing with the high operational leverage inherent in the newspaper business model. We all wanted to stop acquiring assets and batten

down the hatches. All John, Nick and I wanted was a CEO
who faced up to the cyclical and structural reality we faced.
To achieve this we had to get rid of Kirk.

In August 2008, Kirk had announced 600 retrenchments, trying to
satisfy the appetite for cost cutting. The earnings from TradeMe,
$26 million in March 2006 when Fairfax bought it, had reached
almost $70 million. The Rural Press businesses had increased
their earnings. But the fight over debt and new assets continued:
$625 million for TradeMe, $250 million for Southern Cross
(the rest of the Southern Cross deal had been paid for in equity
through the Dividend Reinvestment Plan), and $700 million to
fund the cash element of Rural Press. The debt from these three
new businesses was initially $1.57 billion. New earnings since the
businesses were purchased totalled close to $350 million and this
had been used to reduce the debt to $1.2 billion. Kirk expected
the earnings to grow, to protect the future against the significant
decline in the metros. But it was already too late for this argument.
With the financial crisis and Marinya on the war path, the debt
was a political football.

Marinya produced its own modelling, which was discussed
with other shareholders, suggesting that Fairfax revenue need
not fall far for the company to be in danger of breaching debt
covenants that were a legacy of the acquisitions.

On the eve of the Fairfax annual meeting on 13 November
2008, the Fairfax share price closed at $1.60. The share market
was down by 50 per cent in the year but the fall at Fairfax was
closer to 70 per cent. The argument over how much blame
attached to the financial crisis, how much to the structural damage

wrought by the web, how much to debt and how much to short sellers seeking leverage through rumours about John B. Fairfax's financial situation, would rage for years. JB, uninterested in any arguments or debate about his margin loan, resolved to take aim at the man he regarded as the real culprit.

Kirk's speech at the annual meeting showed his own confidence that the diversification of the company would see it through the worst of the downturn. He had dug his heels in. 'Fairfax is better positioned today than at any time in its recent history to face these challenging times,' he assured the audience of large and small investors. He conceded, however, that business and consumer confidence, together with volatility in financial markets, had made it difficult to plot the path ahead. Profit, he said, was below the same point it had been at a year before, down by numbers he described as 'mid-teens'.

The share price continued downwards along with other media stocks. For all the diversification, Fairfax was still a high-cost newspaper company with a catastrophic collapse in its basic business model of advertising. It was still trying to publish the same spread of newspapers but getting less and less in return. Consumers and advertisers were sitting on their hands. Fairfax's debt load was manageable, but after the annual meeting, the focus of media analysts narrowed and their tone became more strident, expressing alarmist fears that Fairfax earnings could fall low enough to test the debt covenants. If the company could not repay its debts, how would it remain solvent? A new fight ensued over whether Fairfax should slash its dividend and steer the money to pay off debt. Walker said he saw no reason to amend the existing dividend policy, analysts were split in their opinions, and JB's position seemed opaque as newspaper reports suggested he depended on the dividends to service his own debts. Three weeks later, however, Nicholas Fairfax publicly supported the move, confirming the family position.

After the annual meeting Ron Walker received a letter from a major institutional shareholder asking for Kirk to be dismissed. The letter had been sent earlier in the day but had not been delivered in time for the board meeting preceding the annual meeting. It was an early sortie and the rest of the battalion was soon on its way.

Kirk had wholly underestimated the determination of Marinya as the biggest shareholder. By this point, JB's paper losses on his Fairfax investment were approaching $500 million and still the share price fell.

For some big institutional shareholders, both bemused and anxious, the war inside Fairfax came to resemble a circus. Patrick Joyce and Mark Johnson would arrive one week with their points of discussion; the following week Ron Walker would arrive with his own posse, directors Roger Corbett and Peter Young. In the end, the external pressure was enough to spook the Fairfax board. It was clear the undermining of Kirk would not stop.

By the first week of December 2008, the die was cast. The share price had hit $1.25 and the board had had enough of informal reports emanating from other managers in the company that Kirk and McCarthy had not spoken for weeks. The chief executive and the operational manager of the business were estranged, the board was under siege from investors, and the bottom had fallen out of advertising in the financial crisis. Walker and Corbett agreed to speak to Kirk. No decision had been made to terminate his contract but the board was wobbly.

On Thursday 4 December, the three men met. Walker and Corbett told Kirk that investors were unhappy and that those same investors were concerned McCarthy — the pin-up boy — might leave. The conversation finished inconclusively, but for Kirk the writing was on the wall. He was shaken by the talks and he sought out the chief financial officer, Sankar Narayan, for a discussion on what to do next. Narayan's opinion, frankly expressed, was that there was little Kirk could do with the power of an angry 14 per cent shareholder, with two board seats, ranged against him.

Kirk phoned Walker to say that their earlier meeting had left him with a sense of mixed messages. He wanted to know precisely where he stood. After receiving little encouragement from the chairman, Kirk decided to quit. He told Walker he would leave immediately after the weekend, on Monday 8 December.

The next morning, Friday 5 December, Kirk drove to work early. He planned to write the announcement for his departure, sort out his office and organise himself to be ready for Monday when the news would break. He sat at his desk overlooking a green park to compose his statement. An hour later he emailed it to Bruce Wolpe, a confidante and Fairfax's head of corporate communications. What followed was a scene that might have seemed at home in a television spoof.

Wolpe was in the middle of emailing a daily news summary to the Fairfax senior executive group. Reading over the two messages on his Blackberry — one from Kirk, the other a group mailing ready to send out — Wolpe pressed send. And with that, he accidently sent Kirk's statement to a dozen people at Fairfax. Panicking, he sent another message to recall the message and hit the phones. Those he could reach swore in blood that they would keep the secret and never leak, but Fairfax was a listed company and this was market information. When Kirk returned to his desk after fetching a coffee, he found Wolpe still frantically trying to retrieve the 'send', but it was obvious it was too late. Kirk rushed to find Walker and to gather the executive staff for an immediate announcement as the official statement was prepared for the stock exchange.

At 10 a.m. Kirk drove from the Fairfax car park for the final time, home to tell his children before they heard it all on the news. But it was not the last time Kirk would see his Fairfax colleagues. He had already scheduled a Christmas party for the following week, for all of Fairfax's top management, its news executives and the board of directors — at his own home. In a decision that floored everyone, Kirk decided to proceed with the party. When the news spread, there was slack-jawed speculation about who would attend and who would not. The Fairfaxes certainly would not come and probably most of the board would politely decline as well. After all, they had just knifed him.

In the end they all showed up: John B. Fairfax, his son Nicholas, the victor Brian McCarthy, and most of the board, barring those overseas. Some described it later as a funeral with the body still alive. Kirk in the end was a man with more personal stamina and pride than they had given him credit for, but it was hardly surprising. After all, he had captained a team to win the World Cup.

McCarthy was appointed as interim chief executive until a board meeting the following week, but it seemed like a *fait accompli*. The old Rural Press had been the darling of the stock market with its big share price and years of rich dividends. The markets had admired Kirk for a while and they had liked his style and his acquisitions at first. But when it all came down to it, McCarthy was their man. Kirk's departure on 5 December 2008 was two years, almost to the day, since his announcement on 6 December 2006 that Fairfax would merge with Rural Press. It had been a different time back then and a different world.

At precisely 9.04 a.m. on Wednesday 10 December, JB Fairfax pulled into the Fairfax underground car park at the wheel of a modest silver Audi, which he swung into an empty space amidst a row of Mercedes Benzes. Nick Fairfax was in the passenger seat. It was the morning after the party at Kirk's house and the Fairfax board was preparing to appoint the new chief executive. JB arrived on the fifth floor wearing a charcoal grey suit and blue striped shirt for the occasion. Finally, the man he trusted to put things back on track would be in the chief executive's office where he should have been all along. Walker, already in his own office, had chosen a pink shirt and navy tie with yellow polka dots. Julia King, a director since 1995 and a former boss of the Louis Vuitton fashion group in Oceania, wore a black dress, aqua beads and an Hermes bag slung on one shoulder. Executives from Rural Press strolled across the executive floor, confident in shirtsleeves.

Brian McCarthy had selected his own outfit with some care. He wore a yellow patterned tie that bore the word 'Goss', and a white shirt with blue stripes. Goss, he explained to a reporter who asked, was the manufacturer of the Fairfax presses. It was a tie McCarthy always wore proudly, a salute to his years in the newspaper industry. He was a print man. It was an insider's touch, far too subtle to be noticed by the board of directors about to make him the latest in a long line of chief executives, a line that had included for a brief time even young Warwick Fairfax himself.

CHAPTER NINE

PIRATE SMILE

Kerry Stokes popped to the surface of the blue waters off the coast of Ghizo Island in the Solomons, swam several strokes to the side of the boat and pulled himself up a ladder, water running from his wetsuit. He shrugged off his oxygen tank and dive mask. On the deck of *Antipodean*, the boat he had owned for 20 years, he set down the deep-sea camera that contained dozens of photographs of barracuda, schools of brightly coloured fish and tropical coral. He was working towards a book on diving in the Solomons, indulging a passion for underwater photography that he had pursued since the 1960s. It was a peaceful break from the busy madness of his sprawling business, embracing newspapers in Western Australia, the Seven Network and the earth-moving equipment firm Caterpillar. It was 8 July 2009, a balmy humid day and hot enough for a sun hat.

Suddenly the phone rang and Stokes answered to find Peter Gammell on the line. Gammell, one of his closest advisers, had

232

intriguing news: a line of shares in Consolidated Media Holdings had become available. This was James Packer's listed pay TV company, with its 25 per cent of Foxtel and 50 per cent of Fox Sports. Its other asset was 27 per cent of SEEK.

Kerry Stokes already owned 4.8 per cent of ConsMedia, bought a year earlier after a joint bid by Packer and Lachlan Murdoch to privatise the company had collapsed. A Packer selling anything always had Stokes' attention, and vice versa. Moreover, pay TV was a subject close to Stokes' heart. He had already fought and lost a bitter five-year, $200 million legal case against defendants including PBL, News Limited, Telstra, Optus, Channels Nine and Ten, the NRL and the AFL over the collapse of his pay TV service, C7 Sport. The case had wrecked his previous good relationship with the Packers, breaking down trust on both sides.

Now, in 2009, with world stock markets shaken by the financial crisis, rumours had spread like wildfire that James Packer was in serious strife over a rash of casino investments. The media had turned into a lynch mob baying for Packer's blood. Every detail of his financial distress was analysed and published, comparing him to his father's macho successes and superior business judgement and mocking his failure. The share prices of Packer's two big listed companies — the gaming company Crown and the pay TV company, ConsMedia — had fallen drastically. Stokes had closely watched Packer's travails through the early months of 2009 and had concluded he was on far more shaky ground than most observers realised.

Not long before, in December 2008, Packer had sold Consolidated Pastoral — the vast group of northern properties assembled by his father — for $400 million in the depths of the downturn. To Stokes, this smelled like panic. He calculated that Packer might not have the financial strength to defend ConsMedia, even though it was common knowledge he was deeply protective of his pay TV interests and SEEK. 'I think he's vulnerable,' Stokes told Gammell.

'I think we can get 12 per cent,' Gammell replied.

Within 24 hours Stokes had swooped, buying a total of 13.2 per cent of ConsMedia. A year before, the stock had traded as high as $4.50, in the grip of takeover fever as Packer and Lachlan Murdoch hammered out their privatisation plans. Now, Stokes' Seven Network paid between $2.50 and $2.60 a share. Within 24 hours Stokes was sitting on 18 per cent in Packer's company including the 4.8 per cent he already owned. He was in prime position. The one thing he didn't know was how wedded Packer was to staying in pay TV and whether he could shake something out of this.

James Packer was on his own boat, *Arctic*, anchored near the French Polynesian atoll Fakarava, an idyllic paradise of deep translucent waters and long white sandy beaches.

Stokes phoned him to announce that he had lobbed a ball straight into Packer's territory.

Packer was stunned. 'What are you going to do?'

'We haven't determined that,' Stokes told him.

When Packer recovered from the shock of the first phone call from Stokes, he became steadily more furious. He was not going to lose pay TV without a very big fight. He had created ConsMedia with two of his favourite investments: the Foxtel and Fox Sports stakes that he had pushed his father into after Super League, costing PBL a total of $226 million; and SEEK, which he had outmanoeuvred Fairfax to win, when he was still in the doldrums after One.Tel. Suddenly someone was trying to unseat him.

'I'm not a seller,' he warned Stokes.

In their next conversation, *Antipodean* to *Arctic*, Packer asked, 'Do you want to make a bid?'

Stokes replied, 'I'm not sure.' Stokes had kept buying. Within a week, he had 19.9 per cent.

Financially, Kerry Stokes was in good shape. He had sold half of his Seven Media Group to Kohlberg Kravis Roberts (KKR) after the falling out between Packer and George Roberts over the sale of Packer's media interests to CVC Asia Pacific rather than to KKR. Stokes had banked a more than satisfying $3.2 billion and paid down debt. He now had a public company, the Seven Network, with $2 billion in capital looking for a home.

Stokes was a self-made man in every sense of the word. He had made his mark with none of the silver-spoon background that characterised the privileged Packer and Murdoch families, much less the Fairfaxes, with their roots in early Sydney society and their patrician ways. Stokes shared one characteristic with the patriarch of the Murdochs, Rupert: he was a born scrapper, one eye always on the competition around him. He had emerged from the C7 case with a fierce reputation in the dog-eat-dog, rough-and-tumble world of the Australian media.

But Stokes had another side too. Beyond and beneath the black-and-white media portrayal of a buccaneer, the reality was far more nuanced. An adopted child forced to make his own way in the world when still a boy, Stokes had deployed some of his vast wealth assembling a breathtaking collection of art across many genres. He was constantly in the market for significant Australian military medals, which he donated to the Australian War Memorial; he had also collected the diaries of the explorer Ernest Shackleton and countless other historic documents. Stokes brought a meticulous obsession to preserving treasures of national identity.

By the start of 2009, James Packer was in as much trouble as he had ever been in. Even with all the media stories swirling about his disastrous foray into US casinos, few came close to exposing how truly rash his investments had been. By the time Stokes rang with the unwelcome news that he had raided ConsMedia, Packer had already spent six frantic months trying to salvage himself from a mess of his own creation — one that he had orchestrated in late 2007, like so many others his eyes wide shut to the debacle unfolding in the US. The decisions of 2007 had blown up in 2008.

Packer had agreed to buy, in whole or part, stakes in at least six US casino businesses, deals done in US dollars before the Las Vegas gambling industry had collapsed. The Australian dollar had crashed as well, adding 30 per cent to his costs in 2008. He had spent months flying back and forth to the US unravelling problems. His head was totally done in. He was emotionally shot, suffering depression and beating himself up under the weight of the same despair that had felled him after One.Tel. He had no idea when, or even if, things would stop spiralling down.

In March 2009, things suddenly went Packer's way after a deadly run. His US $1.75 billion investment in Cannery Casino Resorts was terminated after regulatory approvals dragged on for so long that a 15-month sunset clause in the deal was about to be triggered. Cannery owned casinos in both Pennsylvania and Nevada and Crown was required to go through vetting in both states. In January 2009, Packer had flown to the US to appear at the Nevada Gaming Commission, where Crown's licence was later approved. But the approval in Pennsylvania was caught up in a sidebar of legal action brought by Packer's sister Gretel and three trusts she was associated with, against the sellers of Cannery; Gretel Packer had also sought to withdraw from the licensing process citing privacy concerns. Crown issued a statement to say that neither Gretel nor the trusts were parties to the Cannery contract and they had not been required to be licensed in other jurisdictions where Crown operated. Eventually, the dispute continued for so long that the deadline on the deal ran out. It sparked accusations that a fix was in, but it could not have been better news for Packer. Cannery would still cost him a total of US $370 million to restructure, and he would end up with an almost worthless 24.5 per cent of the company, but he had avoided paying out another $1.5 billion in Australian dollars for a highly exposed business battling a recession. In the cascade of his bad bets, the delay in the US probity checks had saved him. (In 2011, Packer would finally receive regulatory approval for a stake in Cannery worth just US $45 million to Crown.)

Once Cannery had settled, the sale of Packer's pastoral assets and the big cheque that sale delivered in April 2009 relieved more pressure. He believed, finally, that he would get through. But he had sailed closer to the wind than ever before and he was determined to put his affairs in shape. He had been fighting on too many fronts. He kept Crown's gaming investments in Macau and wrote off the wreckage in the US.

Over 2008 and 2009, after converting his losses to Australian dollars including interest and fees, James Packer had lost $455 million on Cannery, $230 million in the Gateway joint venture with Macquarie Bank, $44.7 million in fees and costs for an option on land to build Crown Las Vegas, a dream that would never proceed, $347 million on Fontainebleau — by then a languishing development known as the largest unfinished building in US history and later bought by the investor Carl Icahn for less than US $S150 million — $172 million on Harrah's, and $268 million on Station Casinos. Another $78 million disappeared in interest payments on the original Cannery deal and in the termination of US dollar interest rate swaps. In London, where Packer owned 50 per cent of the high-end Aspinall's Club in Mayfair, he would write down a further $82 million by the end of 2009. Of the roughly $2.3 billion in Australian dollars that he invested outside Australia, James Packer had lost $1.67 billion in less time than it took a new driver to get off P plates.

The only spot of hope was Crown's $750 million investment in Macau with Lawrence Ho — the Melco Crown gaming business. This investment, however, was inextricably linked to the success of their City of Dreams: a massive project, built and financed during the global financial crisis after one of the biggest debt raisings anywhere in the world at the time. Melco Crown had listed on the US Nasdaq in December 2006 with the ticker symbol MPEL. It was owned one third by Lawrence Ho's interests, one third by Packer's Crown and one third by shareholders and it had a US $1.7 billion debt facility. By the end, City of Dreams would cost a heart-stopping $4 billion to build, using a string of capital-raisings that increased the exposure of its big shareholders. It was within months of opening and the question in such straitened days was, 'Would anyone come?'

Packer wound back drastically. The Packers' private company, Consolidated Press Holdings (or CPH), held the family's stakes of

38 per cent in each of the flagship listed companies, Crown and ConsMedia, as well as a vast array of other investments assembled by Kerry Packer over decades. James began selling whatever he could. CPH would no longer be a diversified conglomerate: a mass of odd investments, from abattoirs to skin care to aquariums, would end on the chopping block.

Kerry Stokes' raid on 8 July 2009 was a call to arms. An attack on pay TV, by Stokes of all people, was enough to blast Packer back into action. Within three days he had spent $50 million to increase his own stake in ConsMedia from 37.92 per cent to 40.77 per cent, just short of the minimum 3 per cent creep permitted by law without triggering a takeover bid. Packer called Matthew Grounds, now chief executive of UBS Australia, to the war room, assembling his guard. They commenced a series of manoeuvres that would give Packer room to embark on share buybacks to further increase his stake in ConsMedia.

Matthew Grounds was more than worried by the unfolding struggle. He had worked for Kerry Stokes on other market raids in the 1990s and he had seen the corporate metabolism at close hand. Stokes could raise his stake in ConsMedia, or creep under the takeover laws, by 3 per cent every six months. Or he could simply make a bid to force Packer into outright war — and on the defensive. Certainly the public signals from the Stokes camp were aggressive. Packer needed to build up his position on the ConsMedia balance sheet, to get to a controlling position of more than 50 per cent before Stokes could get there first.

On 25 August Packer bit the bullet, deciding to sell his holdings in a company he had never contemplated quitting, even in the worst of times in late 2008. SEEK was one of his proudest investments and he had been chairman since the float. Now SEEK would have to go. It was a decision he hated making on many levels. It was not just his affection for SEEK and its founders. This was a company that Fairfax had failed to buy in 2003, much less beat in the classified ad market where Fairfax had been the unchallenged leader. Packer had helped SEEK attack Fairfax, something that had given him great personal and professional satisfaction. Letting SEEK go meant publicly exposing his vulnerability in front of the hated Fairfax.

But cashing out ConsMedia's 27 per cent stake would give Packer the ability to fight Stokes with real financial muscle. It would also signal that he was back in the game. He was not going to deal with Stokes from a position of weakness. UBS was instructed to sell the SEEK shares in a block trade and there was a flurry of action, with UBS underwriting the sale. The shares would be sold before most of the market knew they were even in play.

Fairfax was among the companies offered James Packer's SEEK stake on 25 August. It was a moment in time when the past and the future collided. Fairfax had missed SEEK once already in 2003, looking the other way; now a very big block of shares was suddenly available in this market leader in online classified recruitment, which had already soaked up a portion of Fairfax revenue. But the timing of an immediate sale was too hard for a public company with no propensity for making lightning decisions. The shares were offered on the phone to Brian McCarthy, Fairfax's chief executive, who declined. Fairfax was neither willing nor able to make a commitment to write a cheque overnight before the market opened. Once again, Fairfax walked away. McCarthy said later:

I got a phone call about 6 p.m. They were offering it to everybody. They said, 'This parcel is going to be sold now, and if you're interested we need your answer in two hours.'

And I said, 'Well, we're a public company and we can't go through the processes in two hours.' I was excited by the opportunity, but I couldn't meet a two-hour deadline.

The following day, 26 August, was the date for Fairfax's latest results; if anything, the market surprise of snatching a very significant stake in SEEK would have rebranded Fairfax's commitment to a digital future, but it was not to be. The stake was offered to News Limited as well. But News, which already had a big online classified investment in realestate.com.au and support from a diversified international company in News Corp, said no too. The SEEK shares were on offer at $5.05. In what might have seemed to some like a doomsday prophecy, Fairfax shares closed at $1.54 on the day.

James Packer quit SEEK for $441 million. The sale was underwritten by UBS and sold to institutional investors. Packer was sitting in Macau, where he had been for a series of board meetings for Crown and ConsMedia. He had cut off the arm to save the body. Once it was done, he had an important call to make before the market opened at 10 a.m. He picked up the phone to ring Paul Bassat, a conversation that would end with Packer, always emotional, breaking down. He told Bassat that he needed a war chest to defend against Stokes if he had to go to war. He could not lose again, and he could not lose to Stokes.

I needed to load up to fend off Stokes so that I could send a message and have the firepower to fight back. Stokes

thought I was on my knees. Everyone did. And so I sold out
of SEEK, a company I loved dearly and felt incredibly proud
to be chairman of. And then I rang Paul Bassat and I burst
into tears. SEEK was my favourite company of anything
I had ever owned. I used that money from SEEK to take
my holdings in ConsMedia over time from 40 per cent to
50.1 per cent through buybacks. And that stopped Stokes.

Packer and John Alexander both resigned from the board of
SEEK on 26 August. As well as selling SEEK, Packer had sold
the building at 54 Park Street, Sydney, that for many years had
been the headquarters of the Packer empire, to AMP Capital for
$50 million. Selling SEEK might have made him weep but he had
no such affection for Park Street, although he would maintain his
offices there for years to come.

Now, ConsMedia had a touch under $500 million in the bank
and no debt. In the next step, also on 26 August, the board of
ConsMedia authorised a 10 per cent share buyback over the next
year. The effect of this, if neither Packer nor Stokes participated,
would be to reduce the company's overall issued shares in the
market; thus both Stokes' and Packer's shareholdings would
increase. It would get around the takeover rules that prevented an
accumulation of anything more than 3 per cent every six months
without a full bid.

Stokes had played his cards close to his chest, opaque as ever.
When asked by journalists about the sale of SEEK he declared
himself comfortable investing in a company — ConsMedia —
that had good money in the bank. At a briefing for analysts on
26 August, after the Seven results were announced, Stokes stated

calmly that ConsMedia was James Packer's company and he would wait to see what Packer wanted to do.

———————

By the first week of September 2009, Packer was back in Tahiti on board *Arctic*, staying as far from Australia as he could, with the press baying over his huge US casino losses, horribly exposed in Crown's annual results, which detailed $1.44 billion in write-downs for 2009. This was on top of $238 million written down in 2008, after the first wave of US losses. The whole fiasco amounted to losses of $1.679 billion. Ben Brazil, his old friend from Macquarie Bank, was with him. Brazil had worked for Packer's private company CPH in 2001 and again in 2008 before returning to Macquarie in 2009 after Packer's expansionary investment binge came to an abrupt halt.

The two were outside on the top deck of *Arctic* when Grounds phoned on 4 September to say he could sell Packer's stake in Challenger Financial Services immediately, with UBS underwriting the sale, which meant the money would be in the bank within days.

Challenger was a company Packer was close to. Part of its origins were to be found in the old FXF Fairfax Trust, a company set up in 1997. FXF Trust was 31 per cent owned and controlled by the Packers and it held their 14.9 per cent stake in Fairfax, assembled before Kerry Packer was ousted from Conrad Black's Tourang bidding vehicle in 1991. Later the FXF Trust changed its name to CPH Investment Corporation and in 2001 the Packers sold their Fairfax shares. In 2003, Challenger Financial Services, another company where the Packers already had a substantial shareholding, merged with CPH Investments and James Packer became chairman. Now Matthew Grounds proposed that Packer use Challenger to bolster his position against Stokes. The old FXF Trust, which had once held the Packers' trophy stake in Fairfax, and which had later morphed into Challenger, could be sold to protect ConsMedia.

Packer, who was no longer chairman of Challenger, agreed immediately. He did the deal on trust with Grounds on the phone. The block sale of Packer's 20.6 per cent stake in Challenger on 4 September fetched $396 million. He had already sold personal extravagances including a Boeing business jet, a brand new Mangusta 165 super yacht, and a London mansion once host to Winston Churchill's cabinet meetings for a further $150 million. He was preparing to sell a stake in the property developer Sunland for $20 million and a stake in the cattle and agricultural export firm Austrex for $28 million.

Packer had circled the wagons, cutting debt and freeing cash in his two public companies, Crown and ConsMedia. Crown had escaped from Cannery; in ConsMedia he had sold SEEK and 54 Park Street. In his private company, CPH, Packer had sold the farms in the north, the Challenger stake, and an array of planes and boats and homes. He was absolutely furious with everyone, but mostly with himself, for ending up in such a vulnerable position.

But he was ready for a game of cat and mouse. He was now in far better shape than he had been two months earlier when Stokes had commenced his raid. In Packer's circle, the talk was mostly about going to the mattresses against Stokes. But there was one close confidant who took a counterintuitive view. Matthew Grounds proposed to Packer that he turn the argument upside down. Why not look at the possibilities for engaging with Stokes rather than fighting him? Stokes was a crafty and experienced raider with a clear head; he was cashed-up and he had a fix on pay TV. He would not be easy to beat. Grounds pressed Packer to at least consider bringing Stokes into the circle in a way that conveyed trust — with board seats — rather than allow the animosity raging behind the scenes to prevail, particularly between the two alpha lieutenants, Peter Gammell and John Alexander, the executive chairman of ConsMedia.

It would be a big call for Packer to offer such a peace pipe. He had no wish to trust Stokes after their bruising encounters through the C7 case. But on the other hand, it could lessen the chances of Stokes mounting a bid for ConsMedia in which everyone would pay heavily, having to throw cash in the path of shareholders to pull them back and forth between the main bidders. A truce could deliver Packer control if it went the right way, and it could give Stokes 'face' and a true seat at the table.

Now that James Packer had a defensive cashbox secured inside ConsMedia after the SEEK sale, Stokes did not have Packer cornered, but he certainly had him on guard. Grounds offered to speak to Gammell, to test the waters and to put some conditions around any potential negotiation. In a nutshell, Packer wanted an understanding that this was his company and that he wanted to go to 50 per cent. It was a risky set of dominos for Grounds to line up and there was a chance they would fall the wrong way. It was a gamble at best. Other members of Packer's court told Grounds this was one of his worst-ever calls. James Packer, however, liked it. He was prepared to think about it now that he had reached a stronger position after the SEEK sale and cashed up his private company CPH with hundreds of millions from Challenger; that money would be in the bank on 9 September. He could defend ConsMedia from within and without if he had to.

On 7 September 2009, James Packer was on *Arctic* in Tahiti. Kerry Stokes was in Perth. Both picked up the phone at an agreed time and commenced a call that would change the course of their relationship and leave journalists who had covered the story dumbfounded, suspecting a double-cross somewhere beneath the surface. The hostilities, surely, could not be over.

It was one of the more remarkable peace pipes in an industry that regularly saw the richest and most powerful sultans swing clubs at each other and lose fortunes big enough to sustain small nations, before getting down to divide turf and light cigars.

'You've always been outside the tent,' Packer said. 'Why don't you come inside the tent and I'll give you a couple of board seats.'

This truce would mean more than cigars and reparations. For Packer, wary of Stokes since the C7 case, it would mean putting aside the past. It would mean the same for Stokes. Both would have to leave C7 behind. Seven Network would be granted two board seats and Stokes would consent to a standstill agreement wherein Seven would not buy shares in ConsMedia for the next 12 months; Seven would also not sell shares into the buyback. The deal was announced to the market three days later, on 10 September 2009.

There was plenty in the deal for Stokes. Packer's tremendous animosity since C7 had ostracised Stokes. He was on the outer with not just PBL, but News Limited, Telstra and Optus. If Packer reversed, other positions on the battlefield might relax too. Stokes would be given due respect.

The outcome of the deal was to enable Packer's stake in ConsMedia to rise to 50.1 per cent by 2010, cementing his control, and Stokes' shareholding to 24 per cent. Stokes' son Ryan Stokes and Peter Gammell joined the ConsMedia board. Ryan Stokes said later:

> We were not sure at the beginning of James' long-term intentions. The market was discounting all stocks and ConsMedia was trading well below the underlying value, which presented an opportunity. While not invited, we didn't approach it as a hostile transaction and the position enabled a genuine conversation. The agreement was important; it brought us inside and to be involved with him in his company, and with the standstills, it enabled James to increase his position. It was the foundation of a stronger relationship.

There was still one serious wrinkle left to be ironed out in the relationships between the Packer and Stokes camps, and this one harked back to much earlier days. It would also provide a very public demonstration of James Packer's fury at the media spotlight trained on his life and business dealings and his new determination to smash back at enemies, no matter the cost of revealing a temper that could rival his father's. This time, however, it was a strategic decision. Throughout the year, Stokes' Seven Network had broadcast a string of current affairs exposes about Packer's casino investments, his financial difficulties, his failed marriage and his connections to Scientology on both the nightly news and the prime-time show *Today Tonight*.

Packer had steamed with anger over these programs and most particularly over a recent dissection of his investments in Macau. His anger was directed at his old friend and mentor David Leckie, the one-time boss of Nine, now running Seven. Leckie had been fired by Kerry Packer when James was too weakened by One.Tel to defend him, but he had stood up for Leckie for years before that. Since his ousting from Nine, Leckie had taken Seven to big wins in the ratings. And he had greenlighted the stories on *Today Tonight*. Given the power of media proprietors everywhere, most believed the instructions to broadcast the Packer stories must have come directly from Stokes, or at the very least, been interpretations by Stokes' media executives of what the big boss would warm to. But Stokes and Packer had now healed their rift; it was Leckie's blood that Packer wanted, and it was very personal. Whenever the two were in the same social gathering Leckie was prone to greeting Packer with the matey warmth of old — and then another *Today Tonight* would go to air. Packer was stewing for a fight, looking for an opportunity to publicly repudiate Leckie. If he was loud enough, his message would reach all ears.

On Thursday 8 October 2009, during a party for Sam Chisholm's 70th birthday at the Sydney Opera House, a bristling Packer confronted Leckie. He shook his finger in Leckie's face, using every pejorative phrase he could think of, mostly starting with the letter 'f', as stunned witnesses later told journalists. Packer told Leckie venomously that his father Kerry had been right about him all along. He threw the *Today Tonight* programs in Leckie's face and told him to forget pretending to be friends.

The next day, the news was everywhere. *The Daily Telegraph*'s Annette Sharp — the former Fairfax columnist who had penned the 2007 *Sun-Herald* gossip on Kerry Packer's personal life straight after his memorial service — had the scoop. 'The casino magnate's face went red and hands started to shake as he greeted Mr Leckie with "f*** off",' Sharp reported. 'He is said to have told his former mentor: "You want to go outside now? Let's do it".'

Those with an eye for the symbols of war between kings would note that there were no further attacks on Packer in the vein of the brutal *Today Tonight* broadcasts after the public dressing down of Leckie. Packer and Stokes had found their own rapprochement and it was soon evident — with media reports of joint ski trips and photos of the pair happily seated together at functions in Stokes' Perth hometown — that a strong personal engagement followed the downing of weapons. ConsMedia's pay TV assets, which had begun life as a white flag between the Murdochs and the Packers after Super League, had delivered a truce after the C7 wars between Stokes and Packer.

CHAPTER 10

THE FAIRFAX CURSE

Brian McCarthy was boogying with his girlfriend in the living room, just the two of them shaking it together with the music turned up loud. Out on the deck, Fairfax managers exchanged office gossip looking over the garden and the tennis court below. Most of the company's top brass and the board of directors had made the drive to the Christmas party at McCarthy's Beecroft home in Sydney's northern suburbs, including the biggest shareholder, John B. Fairfax. At 10 p.m. the house lights were on and late-stayers drinking beer on the deck could see the chief executive grooving inside.

It was 9 December 2009 and there was exhausted relief among many of the Fairfax executives at the party that the year was finally drawing to a close. McCarthy had been appointed to the top job on 10 December 2008, exactly a year before. But if they had hoped that the fractures would heal after the departure of David Kirk and the installation of McCarthy, they had been stunned by what followed.

Fairfax had been torn apart publicly, month after month throughout 2009, as a ferocious battle raged in the boardroom. It spilled into the newspapers — a standoff between the independent directors on one side, and JB and his son Nicholas on the other.

Fairfax might have taken over Rural Press in 2007, but Rural Press was in the ascendancy by the start of 2009. There was no open gloating but there was a smugness that conveyed the message: we won and the city-dwellers lost. David Kirk was gone; the chief financial officer Sankar Narayan had quit; and Bruce Wolpe, the head of Fairfax corporate communications, had left too. Wolpe, an American with an optimistic 'why lose today if you can lose tomorrow instead' attitude to life, had finally judged that his own role would fall quickly under McCarthy's knife.

As he left Australia for a job on the staff of US Congressman Henry Waxman, Wolpe decided to deliver some unasked-for advice to both McCarthy and Fairfax's chairman, Ron Walker. Wolpe wanted to urge one man not to put the brakes on the company's growth — and he wanted to urge the other one to quit.

Settled into his seat on a United Airlines flight from Sydney to Dulles on 27 February 2009, Wolpe wrote two letters — a long one to McCarthy and a short one to Walker.

In his letter to McCarthy, Wolpe opened by wishing him well. He noted an earlier conversation between them and acknowledged McCarthy's view that one facet of his leadership would be judged a success or otherwise by integrating the Fairfax sales teams of print and online, while keeping the company's print base strong. And then he got quickly to the point, warning McCarthy that he was at risk of cementing a reputation for being unable to grasp the challenges of the online world, while implementing a narrow corporate strategy based mostly on cutting costs.

> The really hard part is that you have put the effort under the print publishers, which has created a perception that it looks like a defence strategy on print rather than an assertive strategy online. So you face criticism on both sides of the digital divide: the online guys aren't sure you are really with it in digital, and that you are still playing defence at the end of this decade just as Fairfax did ten years ago, and the newspaper staff doesn't believe management is credible with the defence of print because they think you will still eviscerate them with budget cuts and possibly more redundancies. Talk about a conundrum!

As far as the boardroom went, Wolpe agreed with a view McCarthy had expressed that more media experience was required. 'We see eye to eye,' he wrote. He undertook to write to the chairman about this. But he did not believe more operational newspaper experience was needed. 'You and the publishers have that and know it cold until kingdom come. But some newspaper people with new-media experience would be really great — and they would help change perceptions about you that it's newspapers first and digital second.'

But the real issue was 'where to from here?' Wolpe warned McCarthy that the critical path forward for Fairfax entailed diversification. He urged McCarthy to persevere with the acquisitions program, which had been the heart of Kirk's strategy, to expand the sources of revenue.

It's the only way to minimise the degrading of our prospects
as a result of weakness in the metro newspaper franchises. If
we don't, we'll be stuck, and I think there would be strong
prospects for breakup. That would be a tragedy. If we do
nothing, and just hunker down, and preside over a tightly
managed Fairfax with no perceived growth options, the sad
fact is that you will work like a dog year in, year out, and
not be any better off than you are today, and the shares will
be stuck between $1 and $2. And that is a painful prospect.

Wolpe urged McCarthy to consider selling Fairfax's radio stations
and merging with the Seven Network instead. He said he believed
the network's owner Kerry Stokes was interested.

TV is retro, but there will be one dominant network for
the next decade, and it is Seven ... I appreciate sharing
this with you. You may find it completely disagreeable. But
it is my honest view on the road ahead. I hope it is helpful
to your thinking. If not, I'll shut up and try to steer some
bailout money to you from Washington.

Next, Wolpe wrote to Ron Walker. If his advice to McCarthy had
been framed to at least encourage him to persevere with Kirk's
growth strategy, then his advice to the Fairfax chairman was far
more succinct: just get out while you can.

Wolpe had absolutely no doubt that the attacks that had so
damaged Kirk were only the beginning of a wider campaign by John
B. Fairfax, and that it would not stop until the clear-out was over. The
boardroom would be next. He wrote to Walker, painting a picture in

the starkest terms of what he expected to happen, which was a full-scale battle for control. He urged Walker to quit, well ahead of the company's annual meeting eight months later in November.

> This is written en route to Washington, with my departure fresh. There are many things we could talk about, but I just wanted to give you some very quiet and very direct advice: I believe you should get ahead of what I believe will come at you, and announce at the earliest moment, that you will not stand for re-election to the Board.
>
> After what was done to David, there is absolutely no doubt in my mind they will do it to you: orchestrate a campaign with the instos to get the votes against your re-election at the AGM. Once such a challenge emerges, it will be impossible to stop. And I don't think you can count on such a challenge not emerging. And for you to lose that fight would be a terrible way to go. You have been an outstanding champion for the company — it is your greatest attribute of service to the company.
>
> But I fear for you if you try to stay, and it is not worth the risk. Far better to leave with your head high, with opposition unformed and untested, and with your obligation to succession planning fulfilled. Ron, I always call them as I see them, and have always given you advice with the bark off, and I wanted to do it once more.

When he arrived in Washington, Wolpe sent the letters by airmail. McCarthy acknowledged receipt of the letter but nothing more, and Walker did not respond.

With the departure of David Kirk, Brian McCarthy's initial commitment to stay for just 12 months following the Rural Press merger had swiftly transmogrified into a desire to not just stay, but to entrench control. He began rapidly putting his stamp on things, but found himself hampered by the excessive bureaucratic structures of the much larger company, Fairfax. Having attained the CEO's job, McCarthy chafed at far deeper layers of management than he had been accustomed to at Rural Press, where the boss was the boss and managers were utterly loyal to him. Fairfax was not amenable to this type of control and there was more backbiting and less respect. McCarthy had been annoyed by the arrival of consultants to help bed down the merger between the two companies and his resistance was an early indication of tensions that would develop between himself and the board. He recalled later: 'We had a helper brought in to help get the synergies in the deal. I inherited him from Kirk, and I thought, "What the hell's he here for?" He used to monitor our progress.'

Still, for all the mismatch of the two companies, as each month went by it became clearer that the Fairfax culture was giving way to the Rural Press way of doing things. McCarthy had settled into the chief executive's office at Fairfax's Sydney building, but his old headquarters out of town was not forgotten. Rural Press management training courses became obligatory for the big metro managers, many of whom felt jolted back in time as they left the Fairfax building at Pyrmont, close to the city, and headed for North Richmond, where Rural Press was atop a green hill. Some returned aghast, with tales of country cousins and a rampant Rural Press identity that seemed like a cult.

They related staying at a local motel for the management course and later, as a treat, being taken up the hill for a tour of the Rural Press building. Sometimes this would end with a pizza dinner in the Mahogany Row boardroom, accompanied by warnings not to put anything on the big polished table without a coaster. Pizza boxes stayed on side tables. The culmination of the tour — the highlight — was ending up in Brian McCarthy's old office, where the Fairfax city types were encouraged to sit in the CEO's chair — 'Brian's chair' — so they could have a photo taken on their iPhones. Back at Pyrmont, the newsrooms were full of disparaging stories of the 'did you hear ...' variety about McCarthy's internet skills, which were said to include being unwilling or unable to use the Outlook online diary, in preference to a paper diary — a slur which could have been aimed just as easily at most journalists at the time. He continued to drive a car with the number plates RP1 and he had never allowed the Rural Press sign to be replaced on the gates at Richmond. Some executives from the old Fairfax regime — the pre-Rural Press regime — darkly referred to their new work colleagues as the dinosaurs, and in some cases, the Taliban.

But it was in the boardroom where the real divide occurred, in ways almost unparalleled in corporate sagas of dirty washing. From the very start, tension between the directors from Rural Press and everyone else had revolved around power, the company's debt, and whether making acquisitions for future growth had been the right or wrong strategy. Embedded in the argument were two deadly viruses: the anger left behind over Kirk's treatment, and the horrible downhill momentum of the share price.

For JB, the year was replete with more public revelations of his personal finances. He regarded such matters as no business of snooping journalists, but he was now forced to endure it, given his family name. For the first time, he was given a dose of the James Packer treatment.

In March 2009 *The Australian*, ever vigilant to Fairfax embarrassments, reported the news that JB had taken out a mortgage on his family's magnificent heritage harbourside property, Elaine. Nick Tabakoff, the journalist who had started the ball rolling on JB's margin loan in 2008, reported that NSW land titles documents showed that this historic 1870 Double Bay mansion had a registered mortgage taken out in January 2009 — for the first time in its history. The $30 million property had been in the Fairfax family for 100 years.

Tabakoff had joined the dots. The mortgage was held by the Commonwealth Bank and it covered not just Elaine but three apartments also owned by JB. The 2008 margin loan — used by JB to take over his siblings' stake in Marinya Media — had been with CommSec. JB had refinanced this after the uproar that followed revelations that it was pledged against his 14 per cent Fairfax shareholding. By the time that skirmish was over, the damage was done. Trust had been destroyed in the Fairfax boardroom and nothing would ever convince the independent directors that it was not JB's margin loan that had exposed Fairfax to the activities of short sellers pushing the share price down in the heat of the financial crisis.

JB was livid at the continuing exposés of his personal finances and *The Australian* quoted his spokesman as saying the mortgage was JB's private affair and no-one else's business. But suspicions that he was under financial pressure only increased after a heavily discounted $624 million Fairfax capital-raising in February 2009 — announced suddenly after months of denials that it was needed. JB took up less than 10 per cent of his entitlement to new shares, with the result that Marinya's stake was reduced from 14 per cent to 9.7 per cent of the company.

After all the excitement over the return of the Fairfaxes to Fairfax, and all the anticipation that this was a forerunner to the type of forthright direction and strong leadership accepted in media companies with a big controlling shareholder, pretty much the reverse had occurred. The boardroom was riven by suspicions and the big shareholder's stake had now been diluted. Worse, from JB's perspective, Marinya's holdings had tumbled in value from $1.1 billion at the time of the merger to under $300 million.

The collapse of trust in the boardroom, particularly between JB and Ron Walker, had descended to such lows that Walker warned that Fairfax's independent directors would boycott a board meeting if Marinya's investment chief, Patrick Joyce, attempted to attend. And yet, he was an alternate director for either JB or Nick Fairfax. JB recalled later: 'On one occasion when I was unable to attend a board meeting, the board refused to accept Patrick's attendance at the meeting, and while we had every right to insist he attend, in the interests of harmony, we relented and Patrick did not go to the meeting.'

By the start of September 2009, the Fairfax boardroom had disintegrated into total anarchy. Newspapers were soon filled with reports of the turmoil within: a stunning no-holds-barred attack by the Fairfaxes on Ron Walker for alleged failures of corporate governance by introducing unacceptable risk through acquisitions financed with debt; and counter-attacks on JB for failures of corporate governance by taking on a margin loan against Fairfax shares with no disclosure to the board.

Fairfax newspapers reported the unfolding debacle with almost as much gusto as News. The breakdown was irretrievable. On 19 September 2009, *The Sydney Morning Herald* catalogued accusations of infamy hurled back and forth from the boardroom. Walker, trying to cement his position long enough to set up the succession in the boardroom, had declared that he would step down from the board — but not for another year. In retaliation, JB and Nick warned they would vote their shareholding against Walker in an attempt to force him out earlier. Director David Evans hit back, publicly attacking JB over his margin loan and putting it on the record that not only had the loan not been disclosed to the board, but that other directors believed it had exposed the company to a raid by short sellers to smash the share price. Evans told *The SMH*:

> John B. Fairfax bought his brother and sisters' stock back from them, and then he had a margin call from CommSec for $400 million-plus. He secured a loan by pledging the Fairfax stock without disclosing this to the board. Shorts [short sellers] and hedge funds carved up the stock to the tune of $2. The board insisted he remedy that, he secured a loan from elsewhere to remedy it.

This was stunning news. And it was clear that the fight could only get dirtier, which it soon did when Marinya announced it would vote to unseat Walker at the annual meeting in eight weeks —

and made it clear it had the backing of several big institutional shareholders, including 452 Capital, in this plan. The Fairfaxes were determined to prevent Walker choosing his own successor, or taking the opportunity to feather the board with new directors. They wanted a new chairman and board renewal. A statement issued to the market by Marinya made it clear the company would be turned in a new direction: 'After years of under-performance, Fairfax Media has a new management team, a streamlined cost-base and is poised to rebuild some of the shareholder value that has been destroyed.'

Walker took a nanosecond to hit back, accusing JB of deception and a failure of corporate governance by not disclosing the margin loan. He told *The SMH*, which was rampaging freely through all the gory details in the exchange of hostilities: 'John B. Fairfax's comments about corporate governance are hypocrisy at its worst, when you consider that he deceived the board in not disclosing he had a margin loan on hundreds of millions of dollars' worth of shares that caused our share price to drop at the hands of hedge funds and short sellers.'

Within a week, as the fight ramped up and *The Australian* homed in with attacks on Walker, he switched course, announcing that he had sounded out institutional shareholders and that he would consider stepping down at the AGM. But he could not resist bashing the Fairfaxes as he commenced a round of exit interviews, telling *The Australian* that the Fairfax board had been ignorant of JB's margin loan until notified by sources at Goldman Sachs.

On 28 September 2009, one of the most remarkable publications ever to emerge from Fairfax was sent to the Australian Stock Exchange. It was a document issued by all five of Fairfax's independent directors, after a statement earlier that day from Walker to confirm he would not seek re-election at the AGM. If dirty washing had been hung out before, this time it was the full catastrophe.

Noting their deep regret at Walker's decision to go, they expressed support for the high standards of corporate governance that had been in place at the company. Concerned that the market had been ill-informed by the war conducted in the media blitz of recent weeks, the directors stated that any examination of the board minutes would prove several facts. The document was designed to show that JB had not only supported acquisitions since he had been appointed, but that these acquisitions had been funded mainly through equity, not debt. It was a stunning slap back at the Fairfaxes.

The statement was issued by Roger Corbett, David Evans, Julia King, Bob Savage and Peter Young. It said in part: that all directors had voted unanimously in favour of every recent acquisition; between 2004 and 2008, that the company had diversified away from metropolitan newspapers, funded mainly by equity not debt, and that the purchase of Rural Press, TradeMe and Southern Cross (all Kirk acquisitions) had been financed over 70 per cent by the issue of new equity; and that directors had discovered JB's margin loan not through disclosure by Marinya, but though market speculation.

It wasn't over, of course. A last-minute round of internecine plotting on the board dashed any hopes JB might have entertained of heading off the independent directors from putting their stamp on the chairmanship. The deputy chairman, Roger Corbett, was elected on 13 October. JB had tried to push the board into recruiting a chairman from outside, but had failed.

Walker left in November, as did Julia King — retiring after 14 years. David Evans was forced to quit after a regulatory inquiry into conflicts posed by his directorships of two companies with radio interests, Fairfax and Village Roadshow. The Fairfax share price closed at $1.58 at the end of November 2009.

Fairfax had been so consumed with the boardroom bloodbath that it had been virtually oblivious to the world around it. The wrestling match that had played out at the same time between James Packer and Kerry Stokes over Packer's ConsMedia between July and September 2009 had passed them by, although it had been covered in great detail in the company's newspapers.

In one of the great ironies, Fairfax had been unable to suspend its internal arguments long enough for an all-hands-on-deck move to snatch a large stake in SEEK, one of the most significant companies involved in the demise of Fairfax's business model. Had the company had a cohesive strategy with trust between management and board, this might have been possible. Instead it had not even been discussed. Packer's SEEK shares became available on 25 August 2009, but just as quickly as this mirage had appeared it was gone again.

Later, when McCarthy looked back at the impact of the online pure-plays in continuing to ravage Fairfax's classified advertising, he maintained that he had been well aware of the loss of the classifieds since before the agreement to merge Rural Press with Fairfax. With Kirk, he had examined the problems in considerable detail. But he had hoped to arrest the slide and to bolster the collapse of city advertising with a wider spread in Rural Press publications. McCarthy recalled:

We did okay with Domain but the other two, jobs and cars, went off so much more quickly. The classifieds were going off, newspaper circulation was going down; Kirk and Sankar Narayan had said there was not a lot left to lose on classifieds, but they also thought paid circulation had stabilised. We had a stuffed model because people read online, on the internet, and they had stopped spending in the GFC. There were a lot of challenges on revenues. Debt was a problem. Kirk had bought TradeMe, there was the radio deal and the earnings were in decline. Between the economic downturn and the structural downturn you'd never know which was bigger as both were operating at the same time. You'd hope the economy [was the bigger issue] because that would recover. But it was both.

The pure-plays had not emerged unscathed from the financial crisis, but they did come through with plans to capitalise on the even more deleterious position of newspapers. SEEK had been hammered as advertising volume dried up and, in April 2009, the Bassats had gone into the market to raise $100 million in cash as a bulwark against a falling share price — and to diversify further into education and training companies where they had already taken positions.

SEEK's share price had fallen from over $6 in March 2008, to $2.50 in March 2009. Ad volumes had halved. The Bassats had anticipated a downturn at some stage and they were determined to view it as an opportunity. As a start-up, they were used to operating in a more exposed environment than a mainstream media company, but they also had none of the vast array of fixed costs that hampered Fairfax and News. The Bassats planned to invest, not panic, and to manage their costs carefully without going overboard. What mattered most was continuing to take more business from Fairfax. By March 2010, as business optimism and jobs picked up, SEEK's share price had tripled to $7.50 and from there it just kept climbing.

The property market had been totally savaged in the downturn, and realestate.com.au — a company that had seen life at 7 cents a share way back in 2001 — fell from $6.00 to $3.90 between March 2008 and March 2009. But even with the collapse in the property market, the financial crisis proved a seminal moment. The way consumers husbanded resources in the downturn, watching what they spent, had established new and permanently altered patterns of behaviour in the aftermath. Every dollar mattered. Not only were online ads far cheaper than display and classified advertising in newspapers, they were simpler to update and alter. They allowed far more flexibility with photos and data. Within a year the share price of realestate.com.au had more than doubled to $10.60 as advertising volumes picked up and the market took notice.

Carsales had reached its own seminal moment on 10 September 2009. After years of building the business then joining forces with James Packer to bulk up against Fairfax, then agreeing to be sold in part to CVC Asia Pacific when Packer sold out of media, the carsales board finally decided it was time to float the business. Packer had always promised the carsales founders that he would support a float at a time of their choosing. So long as he had remained a big shareholder in the PBL Media joint venture with CVC this had been an easy promise to make. But once

Packer sold down, diluting his stake, his influence was reduced too. As the owner of 49.5 per cent of carsales, it would require CVC's agreement for this company full of wheelers and dealers from the auto industry to list on the stock exchange.

Packer had promised carsales' chairman Wal Pisciotta that he would take every step to shepherd CVC towards honouring his own earlier commitment on the float and he was as good as his word. To Pisciotta's relief, Adrian Mackenzie, chief executive of CVC, had agreed. Pisciotta recalled later: 'When Greg Roebuck and I finally went to see Adrian in July 2009 to say we wished to list the business on the ASX, they came back after 24 hours to say that was fine. James Packer was true to his word and so was Adrian.'

Carsales debuted on the Australian Stock Exchange on 10 September with a share price of $3.92, which settled back to $3.85. It was the biggest initial float on the ASX since the financial crisis and it valued the company at over $812 million. Within three years it would be worth $1.8 billion. After the float Greg Roebuck told the ABC business program *Inside Business* that Fairfax had had its chance to get its hands on carsales to ameliorate the falling volumes on its own online Drive site, but had failed. Recalling the discussions held with Fairfax in 2005 about buying 'all or nothing' of carsales, Roebuck recalled:

> They were our second largest shareholder and I guess they
> had the opportunity to increase that stake at that time and
> they left us alone. We ended up doing a deal at the time
> with PBL and acquired the online assets of ACP Magazines
> and grew our scale. That was their best opportunity and

they've certainly known who we've been, all the way back
to, even to, I would say, the late 90s, early 2000. They knew
who we were, and allowed us to get to where we got to,
without really trying to stop us.

On the day carsales floated at $3.92, Fairfax shares closed at $1.64.
Carsales had fared reasonably well through the financial crisis.
Consumers had not stopped buying altogether, but they had scaled
back their ambitions — from buying brand new cars to buying
near-new cars, and from buying near-new cars to buying used cars
from car dealers.

Carsales' display advertising, offering more sizeable ads, picked
up dramatically, taking more business away from print. The overall
advertising pie might have shrunk as many consumers stayed with
the old car in the garage, but carsales took a bigger share of what
advertising was available. When the pie grew again along with
the economy after the financial crisis, it was that increased market
share that enabled Greg Roebuck's bunch of troublemakers — by
now a big company with a powerful market position — to grow
faster and further than their struggling brothers in print. And after
that, carsales just went from strength to strength.

Foxtel, where Fairfax's rival News Limited had a substantial
investment, had come out of the financial crisis in exceptionally
good shape. The 2008 and 2009 years would deliver record sales
as customers flocked to sign up for pay TV. With people staying
at home more, rather than taking holidays amidst all the gloomy
economic talk, a new term was developed — the 'staycation' —
to describe stay-at-home vacations. Foxtel ran a campaign to take
advantage of these cautious times, exhorting customers to stay

home and save money. The government stimulus package had helped too.

In 2010, a series of dominos began to fall at Fairfax. While the first one to drop seemed harmless enough, it would not be long before all had fallen, revealing that the second coming of the Fairfax family back to Fairfax had entirely reversed course.

From mid-2010, Marinya began looking for its own exit strategy. This was an extraordinary development after such a short space of time, but the first sign came with the announcement by JB that he intended to retire from the board in November 2010 at the annual meeting. Moreover, Marinya, acknowledging its reduced ambitions with only 9.7 per cent of the company, would not push to maintain two seats on the board after his departure. During the knife fight between Marinya and Walker the year before, some Fairfax directors had turned a light on the Fairfax family's position on the board, arguing that with less than 10 per cent of the company, two seats was one too many.

The departure of Walker and two other directors had not been followed by any improvement in the share price or the reorientation of the company that Marinya had anticipated and the mood in the boardroom remained one of cold mistrust. The ghastly ructions among directors in 2009 had also left in its wake an untrusting environment between most directors and the chief executive. McCarthy, always viewed as a Rural Press man, had not been able to shake off the taint. McCarthy made it clear he thought most of the board were galahs and in turn some on the board had reached the worrying conclusion that the CEO was out of his depth.

The new chairman, Roger Corbett — a former boss of Woolworths — had turned out to be more hard-headed and wilier than Walker. In May 2010, Corbett had brought in the consultants Bain & Co to produce a major strategic review for the board — and to assist and corral a chief executive who wanted to do things his own way. McCarthy resisted at every turn. He was furious to find consultants forced on him, and his relationship with Bain soon became poisonous. McCarthy recalled later: 'I had a rule that I never used consultants. It was my view that management was paid to run the business and make decisions, and so why would you use consultants?'

The markets had begun to turn on their one-time favourite newspaperman. There was pointed criticism from analysts about Fairfax's future direction, querying whether momentum in diversifying the revenue had stalled. It said something about analysts and the pundits that Kirk had been railroaded for making too many acquisitions in the name of new revenue, and two years later McCarthy was under a cloud for not branching out of newspapers. Those same pundits who had lauded McCarthy's cost-cutting prowess in 2008 were now pessimistic about the breadth of his vision and the narrow scope of his past experience: running a company with small publications and operating in monopoly rural markets not yet attacked by the internet. McCarthy suddenly seemed unsuited to the big metropolitan markets with their multi-media platforms making the transition to a digital age.

JB Fairfax later blamed the board: 'From mid-2010, it was a nightmare. Marinya didn't think the board had grasped the gravity of the company's predicament and the compelling reason to focus on shareholder value. The CEO was fighting with the board and they had lost confidence in him in the final six months. I encouraged McCarthy to stay when he wanted to get out.'

On 11 November 2010, John B. Fairfax stood down from the Fairfax board. Whatever hopes he might have entertained for a dynastic revival in the company appeared to have been dashed. His son Nick remained on the board, but with just 9.7 per cent of the company and a share price of $1.45 there appeared little prospect that the wealth they had sunk into the company could be rebuilt under their direction. JB bid his personal farewell with a politeness that belied the fight that gone on before. He noted that he believed Fairfax was better placed than other media companies in the world to tackle the challenges of the information age.

At the end of November, Brian McCarthy finally released his future strategy paper at the Fairfax investor day, where he outlined a five-year overhaul of the company. He had held back the announcement while he rewrote Bain & Co's input to the document. When it finally came out, McCarthy found himself facing bright headlights. The response of analysts was swift and harsh: the strategy was light on detail, narrow in scope and lacking in vision. It fell so flat that it sealed McCarthy's fate. He said later that he had read the tea leaves already and that he was not prepared to tolerate the board hiring consultants to clip his wings and usurp his role.

> There were signals already that my future was not looking too bright and that if it came to a showdown, I'd lose. A couple of directors had told me. But I never changed my view that most of the directors had no media experience, so why would I listen to them? And my view was that I wasn't going to work in a compromised situation.

On Wednesday 1 December, the Fairfax board — including Nick Fairfax, but without McCarthy — met for dinner at the Royal Sydney Yacht Squadron at Kirribilli ahead of a board meeting the next day. McCarthy's performance at the investor day was roundly criticised, and after a long discussion they resolved to fire him. They considered whether there should be a period of transition and the best way to handle the whole unpleasant situation. It was agreed that McCarthy should leave on the day and that Corbett should tell him this at the conclusion of their meeting.

One board member was asked if he would stand in as acting chief executive once McCarthy was gone. Greg Hywood had become a director of Fairfax just two months before, on 4 October 2010. He had been chief executive of Tourism Victoria for a number of years, but as far as the Fairfax board was concerned, and Corbett in particular, Hywood had a more interesting history on his CV than his tourism credentials.

In a past life, Hywood had been both editor-in-chief and publisher of each of the three Fairfax flagship mastheads — *The Sydney Morning Herald*, *The Age* and *The Australian Financial Review*. Tall and slim, he was a marked physical contrast to the short, nuggetty McCarthy and their backgrounds too, could not have been more different. McCarthy had run his own show at Rural Press with its flat management structure and hundreds of small papers; Hywood knew the big newspapers, and was a creature of Fairfax's Machiavellian culture. He had been fired by Fred Hilmer in 2003. His appointment to the board in 2010 had immediately sparked rumours in the newsrooms that he was being positioned to replace McCarthy.

Nick Fairfax, who had agreed with the decision to let McCarthy go after the fiasco of the investor day, was asked by the board to sit in on the termination meeting between the chief executive and Corbett. He would be there to support the chairman. But Nick also felt that he should face McCarthy, who had worked for his family for 30 years. He planned to support both men.

On Friday 3 December, McCarthy received a call from Corbett's office to let him know the chairman wanted to see him on the following Monday in his Pyrmont office. McCarthy said later, 'I knew things were not good, but I didn't know I was going to get shot.'

McCarthy arrived at lunchtime on Monday 6 December 2010, and was surprised to find Nick Fairfax in the room with Corbett as well. Corbett got quickly to the point. He told McCarthy that the board had lost confidence in him, particularly after his poor performance at the investor day. The share price had fallen further and the board had taken the view that McCarthy should leave.

As the news sank in, McCarthy decided that he should stay for a proper handover to his successor. He had forgotten, perhaps, the speed with which Kirk had left. 'What do we do now?' he asked Corbett, suggesting that six months might be the right amount of time. Corbett made it clear it would have to be sooner. McCarthy recalled later:

So then I said three months and Corbett replied, 'Sooner than that.'

And I said, 'Do you mean by Christmas?'

And he said, 'I want you out of the building in fifteen minutes.'

Finally, Corbett laid two press releases on the desk. He told McCarthy that he could choose between two endings: one would mean finishing on a harmonious note; the other would mean a fight. The first version announced that McCarthy was leaving because he could not commit to another five years in the job. The second version announced that McCarthy had been terminated. He chose the first one. Nick Fairfax made no comment at all during the meeting except to tell McCarthy that he had agreed with the decision of the board.

Corbett later disputed McCarthy's recollection of their conversation about the timing of his departure. He said that it was McCarthy's own decision to leave on the spot. 'Whilst it was the board's decision that the separation should take effect immediately, it was McCarthy's decision to go and get his keys and leave within minutes.'

As Fairfax prepared to issue the announcement that McCarthy had grown too tired to continue, he left the building. He drove out of the Fairfax garage precisely two years and one day after Kirk had quit on 5 December 2008. He went home, packed a bag and left as quickly as he could, before the press hounds could start in pursuit. He did not want to be photographed as a loser. He had said good luck to Corbett and then departed. His things would be packed up on the weekend. McCarthy noted that the Fairfax share price was $1.50. It had been $1.36 when Kirk left two years before, not much between the two.

Hywood, who was waiting at a hotel across the road, received a call from Corbett and arrived soon after. He was appointed on an acting basis, the first former journalist to lead the company in many years, and would be appointed permanently two months later.

Eleven months later, on 10 November 2011, the final act began with an order from the Marinya investment committee to the investment bank Goldman Sachs to commence selling Fairfax shares. By the next morning, John B. Fairfax had sold out. The experiment was over. He had sold Marinya's 9.7 per cent stake — 232 million shares — for $193 million, at 85 cents a share. It was all gone, except for a small handful of shares, perhaps for old time's sake. It had been worth $1.1 billion on paper in April 2007 at the moment of the merger. Like his second cousin Warwick in 1987, JB had now ventured and lost a fortune in the name of Fairfax.

Afterwards, JB and Nick (who would resign from the Fairfax board three weeks later), together with Patrick Joyce and the Goldman's team who had handled the sale, headed to a bar at the top of the Intercontinental Hotel to celebrate with French champagne. JB sent a text message to his wife to let her know where he was, but accidentally sent the message to a journalist at *The AFR* instead. He texted a second message a minute later to say, 'That was not for you,' but it was too late. The fact that JB was at the Intercontinental had rocketed through the busy newsroom, close to deadline, like a flash. A reporter and a photographer had been despatched on the spot.

When the journalist assigned to the story arrived in the Intercontinental bar, JB, whose family had made their fortunes and their fame from media, sent him packing. But the reporter hung around, watching and hoping for a break, until eventually the Intercontinental staff offered to call security to have him removed — an offer JB declined.

Later, when the champagne was finished, JB, Nick, Patrick and the bankers headed for the hotel's lifts. They stepped in, and as the doors closed for their descent to the ground, the doors on another lift, directly opposite, opened to reveal a photographer from Fairfax toting camera gear. As the photographer stepped out on one side of the foyer, the doors opposite closed on JB and his group.

JB Fairfax was finally out of the company. The experience had been purgatory at times, but now it was done. They all went for dinner at a restaurant on Bridge Street and in the middle of the meal, JB's wife, Libby, called to let him know there was now a photographer from *The Australian* standing in the street outside their home. He was determined not to leave until he got his picture. Equally resolved to avoid another brush with the press, JB returned to his office after dinner. He picked up a toothbrush and left to spend the night at Nick's.

The last member of the Fairfax family to play a significant role in the company had been young Warwick. A recluse from Australia since his disastrous foray of 1987, Warwick had since lived far from the long lens of the Australian media. But he had been in Australia for a rare visit exactly one year before to celebrate his 50th birthday at his mother's mansion, Fairwater, on the edge of Sydney Harbour at Seven Shillings Beach, side by side with the old Fairfax mansion, Elaine, which had been rented out for years. As the Fairfax board met to terminate Brian McCarthy's employment, young Warwick was blowing out the candles at Fairwater. Now, one year on, John B. Fairfax had turned the lights off for good.

CHAPTER 11

ESCAPE TO NEVERLAND

Gina Rinehart was a woman who knew how to make her presence felt, with her untamed long hair, diaphanous outfits, shining pearls and the hard punch that came with $20 billion worth of pure power. The richest person in Australia, and known for her confident, combative nature, Rinehart could select her prey with the ease of a fox in a closed hen house. When she chose Fairfax, the uproar was deafening. After assembling a tiny stake in the company at the end of 2010 and sitting quietly on the sidelines, Rinehart let fly in January 2012 with a full-scale raid that shot her to 14 per cent of the company within days, and 19 per cent within months. And then, with the Fairfax boardroom exhausted after the years of jousting with JB Fairfax — culminating in the resignation of David Kirk in 2008, the retirement of Ron Walker in 2009, the ousting of Brian McCarthy in 2010, and the sell-off by JB himself as a major shareholder in 2011, just two months earlier — Rinehart and the board went to war.

JB had sold out at 85 cents. On 31 January, Gina Rinehart started accumulating shares at 81.5 cents, adding to what she already owned. Rinehart made it clear she was aiming high. Almost immediately speculation ran wild about the likelihood she would demand a board seat once she hit 15 per cent — if not two board seats. Within 24 hours, the company's response had started to form. The chairman and the chief executive, Roger Corbett and Greg Hywood, refused to comment; but sources described as 'close to the company' told journalists that Gina (as she was almost universally known) would have to abide by the principles of independent journalism. She could not interfere in the newspapers. The term 'sources close to' Fairfax was a giveaway for anyone in the industry. It suggested the company was already briefing reporters either at the management level or through public relations operatives, but maintaining its distance and deniability through anonymity — at least until it worked out which way the wind was blowing.

On the second day after Rinehart's raid, well-argued concerns about editorial interference were filled out by a long-time media commentator at *The Australian*, columnist Mark Day. He raised the matter of the Fairfax Charter of Independence, a document initially framed in the years after young Warwick Fairfax's disastrous privatisation, and which had later seen service in the vanguard of a campaign by Fairfax journalists to block the aspirations of Kerry Packer and Conrad Black in 1991. When Black won Fairfax, the document was revised and formally adopted by the board in 1992, however unwillingly by Black. It was rarely mentioned in the intervening years although its existence remained an underpinning of the Fairfax culture — treasured by many with a belief in strong and independent journalism with Fairfax as the standard-bearer, and disparaged by detractors who thought it was the work of a bunch of lefties.

Mark Day summed up the tenets of the campaign about to unfold against Rinehart — and in defence of Fairfax. 'The notion of the nation's richest individual thinking she can covertly pull the editorial strings of a television network or a major publishing house behind a blanket of secrecy invites derision,' he wrote on 2 February 2012. He predicted that Rinehart's bid to suppress details of a riveting legal action already underway with her children was unlikely to be met, given an imminent decision by the High Court. He tied this together with Fairfax.

'Not even full ownership of Fairfax could prevent this being reported in detail. So, what are her motives? If it's influence, she's wasted her money. If it's a play to make money, she needs her head read. Mining, which may yet make her the richest person on the planet, is a much better prospect than media, where the digital age is turning pounds into pennies.'

Day summed up an array of views Rinehart was said to harbour, including some probably inherited from her father, who had an interest in the use of nuclear explosions to blast open mines. She had campaigned on the back of a flat-bed truck against the Labor Government's mining tax, startling east coast critics who regarded Gina's politics as the antics of an extremist.

The big strike against Rinehart in Fairfax eyes were the lawsuits with her adult children, with a parade of expensive silks chasing suppression orders at the exact same moment Rinehart was buying stock in a media company reporting on the events. It fuelled suspicions that Rinehart would try to interfere in the newspapers; after all, one objective in her legal battle was to shut down information. Before long, the Fairfax boardroom had girded itself for a fight. This time the enemy was not inside the boardroom, and directors made it their business to see that it stayed that way; unless Rinehart made a commitment to the Charter of Independence there would be no invitation. Not for two seats; not even for one. Outraged at being told how to behave by the board of a company with a market capitalisation of just $1.7 billion and sinking, Rinehart refused. It became a standoff.

Already Rinehart was dabbling in other media. She had taken 10 per cent of the Ten Network in late 2010, where she became a shareholder alongside Lachlan Murdoch and James Packer, with 9 per cent each. She had a seat on the Ten board. The investment of all three had seemed initially like a collective rush of blood to the head, and by the middle of 2011, Packer seemed to have lost interest. He had joined the Ten board, settled some scores with old foes at the top of the company, and then quit the board on 2 March 2011, following a short-lived tiff with Murdoch — who as a Ten director had poached a favoured executive from Kerry Stokes' Seven Network, placing Packer in an invidious position. Packer was close to Murdoch but he had quit in protest, signalling to a furious Stokes that he took his side.

It was a reflection of where Packer's bets were placed. He and Murdoch had an initial investment of $127 million each in Ten, but Packer and Stokes had an investment of $1.5 billion in ConsMedia, the holding company for 25 per cent of Foxtel and 50 per cent of Fox Sports. The tussle reflected the conflicted deals and relationships at the top of the media world and it reminded Packer again of one reason he had sold his father's Nine Network after Kerry died. Stokes and Packer had developed a warm friendship — perhaps to the surprise of both, as neither could be called a pushover and pride had been on the line in the chess game for ConsMedia in 2009. But James Packer also had major plans for his Burswood casino business in Western Australia, and Kerry Stokes was the proprietor of not just the Seven Network but Western Australian Newspapers. When it came to media power, Stokes owned Perth. The last thing Packer needed was a fight with the proprietor of the leading newspapers when he was trying to push an expanded casino business over the line.

There was another factor too. By early 2012, Packer had begun framing an idea that could reshape his empire, quitting media for good aside from retaining a plaything in Ten. His casino business was at the forefront of his plans and he was focussed on increasing his Crown stake from 45 per cent to a controlling 50.1 per cent. This was the tipping point. After the fiasco of the financial crisis and the write-downs on his US investments, Packer did not want to raise more debt to increase his shareholding in Crown; he wanted to use cash. He had sold most of his major non-core assets to get to 50.1 per cent of ConsMedia. Now, he hoped that ConsMedia could help him reach 50.1 per cent of Crown.

In March 2012, James Packer raised with Kerry Stokes the idea of selling ConsMedia, perhaps to the Murdochs if they were interested. Stokes was a 25.3 per cent shareholder in ConsMedia, having increased his original stake of 24.4 per cent through share buybacks over time. Seven had two directors on the ConsMedia board, including Kerry's son Ryan, and Packer's proposal would be his to support or wreck.

Kerry Stokes held his cards close to his chest. He told Packer that he would be a good partner to him, conveying the notion that he understood Packer's objective of building his stake in Crown and that this would be kept in mind when decisions were taken on Seven's strategy. Stokes was non-committal about the opportunities he might see in the deal for himself. Packer raised it with Ryan Stokes as well. After all the dramas of years gone by, he wanted, as much as anything, to get through with no fights and the good relationships, which had been hard-won, still intact.

The merry-go-round of media had been spinning since 2006 when the Howard government had announced new media laws. But a sale of ConsMedia could reshape the whole landscape, delivering a significant plank of Foxtel and Fox Sports to a new owner — quite possibly News Limited, which had never been happy about carving off half of its shareholding for the Packers in 1998 and 1999, even though it was not worth much at the time. ConsMedia was now valued at almost $2 billion; Packer owned half, Stokes owned a quarter, and the rest was in the hands of small shareholders. For Packer, this would be an audacious play and it would see him walk away from media entirely. But suddenly, before he could take another step, an opportunity for a vastly different media investment materialised.

Gina Rinehart invited Packer to dinner in a private suite at the Four Seasons Hotel in Sydney on 6 March 2012. They were both shareholders in Ten and they knew each other through the Western Australian mining mafia, where Packer was friends with another resources billionaire, Andrew Forrest. Over dinner, Rinehart put her cards on the table. She wanted Packer to join her as a shareholder and partner at Fairfax, where she owned almost 15 per cent of the company, and to help drive a huge cost-cutting operation aimed at reducing the staff of 11,000 employees by almost half, to rationalise costs and lift the share price. Rinehart had been watching operations at other media companies, and she believed that Fairfax was way over-staffed and living beyond its means. But Packer was not interested. His stake in Ten — his only shared financial interest with Rinehart — was a small investment riding beside his gaming empire, and it was more a co-share with Lachlan Murdoch than anything else. He was annoyed at the implication that he could be easily dragooned into helping to run Fairfax, a company he loathed and which was rife with problems; he left the dinner abruptly, making it clear to Rinehart that the answer was no.

Aside from any other considerations, Packer knew that buying into Fairfax would be guaranteed to raise the hackles of the Murdoch family and in particular Rupert. The younger generation at News might be on a digital wavelength, but Rupert was always watchful on all media fronts and particularly anything to do with the old enemies at Fairfax. 'I was not interested in going back into print. And I had no interest in competing with the Murdochs in newspapers,' Packer said later.

Rinehart's Fairfax proposal was over almost as quickly as it had been made. James Packer's father might have jumped at the chance, but James had said no to Fairfax each time it had come his way in the years since Kerry Packer had died. He had plans to divest himself of his remaining media interests instead.

A week later, on 13 March 2012, Packer and Kim Williams met at Packer's Park Street office. Williams had only recently been appointed chief executive of News Limited — on 5 December 2011 — succeeding John Hartigan, who had held the job since late 2000, himself following in the steps of Lachlan Murdoch. Williams had been Foxtel's chief executive until three months before, so he understood the benefits for News in bolting together two 25 per cent shareholdings in Foxtel — one owned already by News and the other by ConsMedia — and he could see the synergies. If Packer was prepared to be sensible on the price, then News was open to action.

A string of meetings followed: Matthew Grounds and Williams met to discuss the value of the Foxtel business before Packer and Williams met again at Williams' Holt Street office to strike a preliminary agreement. It had been Lachlan Murdoch's office in the old days, when he had been chief executive of News and had fought the Super League wars in the late 1990s, culminating in a truce which had allowed a deal to split the Murdoch's Foxtel holdings with the Packers. Now News was negotiating to buy that stake back. Lachlan's old war room was still intact, entered through a tall door set in a wall of bookshelves. Packer had settled on a price for ConsMedia of $3.50 a share. 'If you can deliver $3.50, I'll sell,' he told Williams.

On Tuesday 12 June 2012, the directors of News Corp gathered in Italy for a board meeting, to be held at the Milan headquarters of Sky Italia. ConsMedia was just one line item on a very long agenda. Rupert Murdoch was preparing to take the first significant steps of a remarkable strategy to split his company in two, to unlock the value of his film studio and cable assets for investors. By floating them in a separate company, the film and cable divisions would be freed from the drag of traditional media.

News Corp's third quarter results had been released in May, and they had highlighted stark contrasts in the health of different sectors of the company. The lag was in the newspaper divisions, with their high fixed costs and low revenue, compared with the cable division where earnings were roaring ahead.

Not only were the newspapers pulling on earnings, but the London papers had dragged Rupert Murdoch through the mire as well. In mid-2011, Murdoch's UK newspaper empire was engulfed in an unprecedented scandal that had its roots in years of failing ethical standards at hard-charging tabloids that crossed all boundaries. Revelations of phone-hacking by News employees in London had laid bare a shocking culture at a leading Murdoch tabloid, the *News of the World*. For the journalists involved, the use of phone-tapping to obtain information had usurped the skills of real journalism. Many had lost sight of what journalism was even about. The scandal enveloped not just News; it had dragged in the British Government, Scotland Yard and other 'red tops' — as the British tabloids with their celebrity obsessions and their red mastheads were known. News was forced into countless financial settlements; dozens of arrests were made and Murdoch himself was summoned before a savage parliamentary inquiry and grilled on what he knew. News Corp and its UK arm, News International, were slaughtered by competitors, with exposés in the London media led by *The Guardian* newspaper. Murdoch ordered the *News of the World* closed. The disease was not confined to News alone, but it was News publications that had been its most aggressive and brazen proponents. For Rupert Murdoch, so used to thumbing his nose at the Establishment, the scandal was a watershed.

When News Corp directors and top executives met in Italy, their task was to decide which assets would go into each of the two new companies after the split: one company with News' huge US film studios and cable networks as its main assets, and the other for the newspapers owned mainly in Australia, the US and the UK. There was considerable debate about which assets would go where. Splitting the company would be irrevocable. Once something was put on one side of the books, it could not come back. For Murdoch, many of these decisions challenged the core of his ethos. While he had created an empire of film studios and biting cable news able to terrorise politicians, Murdoch remained a newspaperman at heart. Yet now, his newspapers would have to learn to stand on their own two feet, without the cross-subsidisation from 21st Century Fox (as it would be known) and the Fox News network in America, which had enabled many of his influential favourites to prosper without the need to turn a profit. But he intended to ensure that News Corp, as the new publishing company would be known, would be buttressed by other growth assets worth billions of dollars, and with enough cash for significant new acquisitions. Murdoch had no plans to turn his beloved newspapers into orphans.

The proposal to buy James Packer's ConsMedia was approved in Italy, and within a week a bid would be launched. If it succeeded, News would own Australian pay TV interests valued at close to $4 billion, becoming an equal 50 per cent partner in Foxtel with Telstra, and opening the way to deals that could range from news and sport on phones, to partnerships in a string of other digital and broadband Telstra plays. This would all be plugged into the side of the 'new News'.

But there was another Australian-based investment for the News Corp board to consider, and this one had flown mostly under the radar. REA had barely been noticed by the bean counters in New York, despite having been owned 61 per cent by News for more than a decade. With its realestate.com.au property website, REA had been a stunning success, but it had nestled in the books without drawing attention to itself. In June 2011, Macquarie Bank had approached News to probe its interest in selling. At the time, the shares were trading at $13.30 and the market capitalisation was $1.77 billion. Lachlan Murdoch, a director of News Corp, had headed off the sale. REA was his baby, and he had maintained a watchful eye throughout the years; he was convinced there remained considerable growth in this company he had nurtured from early days.

REA had become a substantial digital advertising company and it was number one in the Australian classified property market by a very big margin. In the News Corp boardroom in Italy, where everything was shaken for its financial potential — and whether it should stay or go — News' president and chief operating officer Chase Carey and James Murdoch, the deputy chief operating officer and Rupert's second son, had their eyes on REA. They considered it to be a non-core asset and with the share price surging, they pressed to take the money off the table — in other words, to sell. Lachlan intervened. He argued to his father that there was huge value yet to be had from growth in REA and that it was the best pure-play digital business held globally by News Corp. Lachlan then took his arguments into the boardroom, arguing the same points he had made to his father. By the time the discussion was over, he had killed the push to sell.

A year later, by June 2013, REA had more than doubled in size to a market capitalisation of $3.9 billion. Of this, $2.35 billion belonged to News. The REA story emboldened News executives in New York to consider replicating the business model globally; already REA's sister site, casa.it, was number one in Italy. Casa had started life in 2001 as a small regional business in the northeast of Italy; in 2006, it was bought by REA in a joint venture with Sky Italia. Then it went national and in 2011 REA bought Sky out. Casa had gone from a loss leader to number one with good profits. Another online property site bought by REA in Luxembourg in 2007 was already growing rapidly.

Rupert Murdoch rued the fact that News had got its hands on only one of the major Australian digital pure-plays back in the day when they were start-ups. He was delighted to have REA, although he expressed surprise that the original investment had never been cleared with him. He recalled: 'We got one of them. In hindsight, we should have got more of them. REA cost us two and a half million dollars and a bit of other stuff. And I don't remember Lachlan even asking me about it.'

The companies News decided should become foundations of the 'new News' were the newspapers, the Australian pay TV businesses — the 50 per cent of Foxtel and 100 per cent of Fox Sports — REA, the book publisher HarperCollins, and a digital education company, Amplify. The newspapers included the UK papers, the Australian newspapers and *The Wall Street Journal*, which was not just a prestige business where Murdoch had poured in resources, but a dynamic front in the fight to transform newspapers into digital businesses.

Murdoch had for years attacked companies such as Google for taking content from traditional media and running it online for free.

In October 2009, at a world media summit in Beijing, Murdoch had declared the aggregators to be 'parasites' and 'kleptomaniacs' and warned they would soon have to pay. Murdoch was sick of any company — be it an aggregator or a traditional media company — waving the flag of the new world in its own defence as it snatched expensively produced information for free. This 'Philistine' era would soon come to an end, he warned. His *Wall Street Journal* had been the first major newspaper in the world to introduce a paywall — in 1997. Subscribers had been undeterred by the cost due to the power of this world brand.

A day after the News Corp board meeting on 13 June, Kim Williams and Chase Carey finalised the details of the bid for ConsMedia — an approved, non-binding conditional offer and shareholder scheme of arrangement. They spoke by phone as Carey hurried to a meeting in Rome with Mario Monti, Italy's Prime Minister.

On 19 June 2012, News announced a full takeover offer for ConsMedia at exactly $3.50 a share. It was a 13.6 per cent premium to the closing price of $3.08 and it was dependent on final clearance from the board of News Corp and the approval of two regulators: the Foreign Investment Review Board and the Australian Competition and Consumer Commission (ACCC). Packer issued a statement to say that ConsMedia and News would discuss the details of the offer and that subject to these talks, his own private company CPH (which held his stake in ConsMedia) believed the offer was fair and would support the bid — in the absence of a better cash offer from elsewhere. What no-one could guess, however, was what Kerry Stokes might do.

By the end of June, Stokes had begun to position himself for the final play. A week after News announced its bid, media reports conveyed the clear impression that the Stokes camp was keeping its options open: they might agree to sell Seven's 25.3 per cent of ConsMedia to News, but then again they might not. Stokes could possibly launch his own bid. With his own shareholders in mind, Stokes took the matter to the ACCC, asking the regulator to review a proposal for Seven Group to acquire the shares in ConsMedia it did not own. This unleashed a wave of anticipation that Stokes could play the wild card and come in with a better bid.

Amidst the growing media reports that he planned to upend the deal, Stokes moved quietly behind the scenes to lay these suspicions to rest. On 26 August 2012, Stokes phoned Kim Williams. He assured Williams that he had made a decision. He had explored a variety of ways into and around the deal, and while he would love to remain a shareholder, he believed it could not work. He intended to sell his shares to News, but he was in no hurry to announce this; he would make his plans known when it suited him best.

Packer too, was rattled by the media coverage suggesting that Stokes planned to cut across News. The background stories in the papers appeared to have come directly from Seven. Stokes assured Packer that his camp was not leaking. He could cause mayhem if he wanted to, but his delays in backing the deal hinged on waiting for the regulator's findings. Stokes just wanted some clarity for his own shareholders. He recalled later:

I had said to Kim earlier, given the offer as it was outlined [of $3.50], if that proceeded in the manner indicated, we would be supportive. And we would make the announcement when legally the documents reached the point that allowed that. James was aware of our position because we were supporting his position. We just wanted to go through the processes because we were a public company and we didn't want to be seen as not supporting the process. There were some articles written at the time that were mischievous, but we told James that we were supporting him.

The Federal Labor Government had been constantly at war with Murdoch-owned newspapers in Australia over what many angry ministers regarded as biased political reporting. An inquiry had been established into press standards, using the long bow of phone-hacking in Britain, although no local examples had been found in any media company. It was a move described by many as a 'get-Murdoch' strategy. But the deal for News to dramatically increase its control of pay TV was not politicised. The Communications Minister Stephen Conroy — known for his friendly relations with both Stokes and Packer and for having joined both to ski or snowboard in Colorado — had been a vociferous critic of News Limited reporting. But when it came to the sale of Packer and Stokes' $2 billion pay TV holdings to the Murdochs, no political objections were raised.

While Packer negotiated the carve-up of pay television with News, Fairfax had maintained a bitter standoff with its new major shareholder, Gina Rinehart. Now Rinehart struck back. In the same week that the News Corp board met in Italy to sign off the bid for ConsMedia, Rinehart electrified Fairfax. On 18 June 2012, she lifted her stake to 19 per cent. Already she had made a solid loss on her investment. Fairfax shares bought in February had traded at 81 cents; by mid-June, they closed at 59.5 cents. It had not deterred her advance.

On the same day that Rinehart increased her position, Fairfax acknowledged that the financial crisis and the challenges posed by social media and online advertising had gutted the company's income. Greg Hywood, chief executive for just 18 months, had watched the share price fall from $1.43 to 60 cents.

Hywood grasped the nettle, declaring that structural challenges and the cyclical environment left him with no choice. He announced drastic changes, never countenanced before, but which were not far short of what analysts wanted to see, and even went some way to meeting the criteria Rinehart had privately outlined to James Packer in March. Hywood announced sweeping changes: a redundancy program that would see 1900 employees leave; the big metropolitan daily papers turned tabloid-size; and major printing presses in Melbourne and Sydney closed. Paywalls would be introduced on the metro papers to stop readers getting everything for free. *The Financial Review* had already had a paywall for years; that newspaper now was moving to loosen this and to reduce online subscription fees after discovering that years of too-tight control had strangled digital growth. Hywood flagged the possibility that newspapers in the group could eventually close if they became unprofitable, but he played this down, for the short term at least. 'I would expect there to be a print product around for some considerable time,' he told shocked journalists.

News Limited would soon follow with its own significant program of redundancies, but there would be no headline numbers to focus on. The cuts throughout News' Australian newspaper businesses would be carried out quietly as the company sought to avoid feeding the story, by contrast with the noisy realpolitik at Fairfax.

Rinehart was not mollified by news of the huge Fairfax redundancy program. Undeterred, she commenced a series of skirmishes with the board that soon gave way to raging hostilities. Rinehart wanted three board seats and, newspapers reported, she had demanded the right to hire and fire editors. Damon Kitney reporting for *The Australian* revealed that Rinehart had asked for the deputy chairman's position and wanted alternate directors — but who would not be first vetted by the board. It was more than a shot across the bows, rather a blast into the side of the ship. For the Fairfax board it may have felt as though the incendiary years just passed had been little more than a practice run.

Politicians from both sides weighed in against Rinehart. The Liberals' Malcolm Turnbull described the board's reluctance to offer board seats as understandable given the absence of any commitment from Rinehart to editorial independence. Labor's Stephen Conroy attacked Rinehart head-on, warning that she would traduce the credibility of the Fairfax mastheads. 'If you start turning it into just a pro-mining industry gazette, well, I don't think you would say the rest of the shareholders in Fairfax would be too excited about the collapse in readership'.

On 20 June, *The Australian* published a breathtaking feature story, based on an interview with former Fairfax chairman Ron Walker. In the article, Walker questioned whether the Charter of Independence had relevance for directors. When he had become chairman in 2005, directors had been asked to sign the charter but had refused 'on the grounds that their word should be their bond,' he said. Walker argued, too, that Rinehart could be a positive influence on Fairfax's strategy and financial position and he predicted she would act in the interests of all shareholders. This was an amazing proposition to journalists at Fairfax, but for the board it was a step too far. Walker had provided what seemed like a reference for Rinehart.

In a phone call to Walker late that morning, Roger Corbett expressed his disquiet that Walker had given the interview at all, telling him that it was not his place to interfere and nor did he know all the facts.

Several days later, Corbett decided that Walker must have spoken directly to Rinehart. He called Walker again. This time the phone call was brief. Corbett asked Walker if he had spoken to Rinehart, and Walker hesitated. He was driving and he said he would call back. Corbett was by then furious. He told Walker that it had become clear that Walker had been speaking to Rinehart. 'Don't bother ringing me back,' he said before hanging up the phone.

Corbett said later: 'Ron had not told me that he had talked to Gina Rinehart, and it was very unhelpful. I rang him up and I said, "What are you doing?" I think some of Gina's misunderstandings came from Ron.'

Walker believed that as the largest shareholder in the company, Rinehart was entitled to the same privileges that had been extended to John B. Fairfax with his 14 per cent of the company in 2007 delivering two seats. Walker said later that he had neither met nor spoken to Rinehart before she called him one day, quite out of the blue. 'Gina rang me and she wanted to know if I had signed the Charter of Independence — not to interfere. And I said, "No, but I gave my word to the journalists not to interfere."'

On 29 June 2012, Gina Rinehart aimed her guns directly at Corbett. In a letter released to the media, she demanded Corbett resign as chairman if he was unable to reverse what she described as 'the five-year decline in paid circulation and in revenue of the Fairfax mastheads' by the time of the 2012 annual general meeting. Rinehart raised concerns about the three-year time frame for the company's massive redundancy program and the impact on staff left behind. It was important, Rinehart wrote, that remaining staff knew where they stood in order to run the enterprise without years of uncertainty and potentially, disputes and strikes. 'Such a sprawling time-frame can lead to staff demoralisation and a lack of focus on a strategy for recovery,' she said.

The Fairfax board retaliated before the day was out, declaring in a statement of its own that the dispute was really about editorial control and a single shareholder attempting to gain control of the whole company without paying a premium. 'If Mrs Rinehart wants control of Fairfax then she must make a bid. Mrs Rinehart's letter today has once and for all unmasked her motives for her continual attacks on the company and its board. Our readers are telling us that if Mrs Rinehart succeeds in this personal crusade they will abandon us.'

The statement pilloried Rinehart for the share price at the Ten Network since she had joined its board, citing a fall of 63.4 per cent compared with Fairfax, which was down only 60.6 per cent. It was a comparison that hardly seemed worth bragging about but everyone was down in the mud now. Suddenly on 9 July 2012, Rinehart sold 3.7 per cent of her Fairfax stake for 58 cents a share. Rinehart's company Hancock Prospecting announced that the sale was related to potential problems with director's insurance, and further, that she was not about to launch a bid. She still owned 15 per cent of the company.

Six weeks later, Fairfax's bleak financial position was confirmed with the release of the 2012 results. It was a sea of red ink and write-downs, with the headlines focussing on a $2.7 billion loss and a write-down of $2.8 billion on the value of the mastheads, goodwill and customer relationships. It was hardly a surprise given the surging advertising pure-plays outside Fairfax and their impact on the business.

On 15 August 2012 *The Australian Financial Review* published a short piece by the paper's media writer, Ben Holgate, titled 'New media stocks put on weight'. The article was accompanied by a graphic sourced from Bloomberg statistics showing the market capitalisation of traditional media, online companies, and pay TV. That graphic marked a fork in the road between the old and the new.

At the top of the list was SEEK at $2.2 billion. Next was Packer's ConsMedia at $1.9 billion; REA was third at $1.7 billion and carsales was fourth at $1.6 billion. In fifth place, Seven West Media at $1.4 billion was the first traditional media company in the top ten. Fairfax followed it at $1.3 billion, then TradeMe in sixth place at $1.1 billion. 'Dedicated digital companies have taken over the media sector, recently moving into three of the top four spots as measured by market capitalisation,' Holgate wrote. It was a remarkable chart, revealing as it did the impossible position for traditional media. The pure-plays had become the leviathans.

It was over a year since SEEK's market capitalisation had eclipsed Fairfax. On 15 June 2011, SEEK was worth $2.25 billion and Fairfax, once the king of the hill, was worth $2.21 billion.

Now Fairfax had fallen to $1.3 billion. The big $9 billion brute of 2007, bulging after the merger with Rural Press, was a shadow of itself. The muscle of its advertising had been eaten away. Online advertising was a huge and sprawling business, growing bigger and spreading tentacles overseas. It was cheap and it was strategic. It could go where print publications with their community identities could not. The fears of Fairfax and other media companies a decade before that the start-ups would cannibalise their print classifieds had been truly borne out.

Fairfax had been dealt a deep blow. Hamstrung by debt and with earnings falling, Hywood had been forced into radical change. On 16 December 2012, Fairfax announced that it would sell its remaining stake of 51 per cent of TradeMe for $616 million. It had listed 35 per cent of the company in an IPO in November 2011 to pay down debt, reaping $291 million. A further 15 per cent had been sold in June 2012, netting $160 million to help fund redundancies. TradeMe had cost Kirk $625 million and it had proved a cash cow for Fairfax. Now it would be a cash cow to pay down debt.

By the close of 2012, all of James Packer's plans came together. Kerry Stokes had announced on 11 October that he would sell Seven's stake in ConsMedia to News Limited. The ACCC had ruled that Seven would not be allowed to bid itself, citing the risk that Seven would have an advantage over other free-to-air networks to pitch jointly with pay TV for sports rights. Instead, Stokes would take a profit of $140 million for his stake, held since 2009. The Murdochs' News Limited would end up with a combined 50 per cent of Foxtel and 100 per cent of Fox Sports to go into the new News Corp. The three big families of media — the Murdochs, the Packers and the Stokeses — had done well out of this.

The last of James Packer's media assets would soon be gone. His share of the cheque, for his 50 per cent of ConsMedia, was $970 million. The cash would enable him to increase his stake in Crown. He had begun the year with 45 per cent of Crown, crept to 48 per cent before the sale of ConsMedia and now he could reach a takeover-proof 51 per cent. He was driving to the airport when Guy Jalland phoned with the news that Stokes would sell. When he arrived in Melbourne, Packer met his mother for breakfast at Crown's Conservatory restaurant in the casino complex. The family business was gaming now, far from media, which had been its lifeblood for so long. Ros Packer told her son that she was happy to see that he was his own man now.

Packer's new boat *Seahorse* sailed through the Sydney heads on 3 November, the day after the second court hearing to finalise the sale of ConsMedia. On Monday 5 November John Alexander arrived for a meeting with Packer on the boat, with its three decks and its communications apparatus springing from the top like sculpture. Alexander stood ramrod straight in the prow of a glossy white tender, a figurehead in a black suit, as it whisked across the waves of Rose Bay. He had been the executive chairman of ConsMedia since 2007, but with the sale to News, that had come to an end. He remained executive deputy chairman of Crown, but for virtually for the first time in his adult life, he had no role in media.

John Alexander had packed up the art and antiquities in his office at Park Street, a collection that included Khmer sculpture dating back to the 5th century, antique Aboriginal shields, a cabinet of miniature ivory and gold Buddhas, black and white Max Dupain nudes and stylised landscapes by the Japanese photographer Hiroshi Sugimoto. The *pièce de résistance* was a massive floor-to-ceiling display case filled with rare, stuffed Australian birds and wildlife from an exhibition in London in the 1850s. Alexander, with the rapier wit that had terrorised journalists at Fairfax 15 years before, had been known to joke that it was filled with his ex-staff members.

On 28 November 2012, after the year from hell, Fairfax employees from across the many divisions of the company gathered to shed their stress at the office Christmas party. The emailed invitation seemed to anticipate the mood: 'Escape to Neverland', it declared, and 'never grow up'. The dress code was 'fairy tales'.

Party or no party, unanswered questions about Gina Rinehart's intentions and the countless redundancies had tamped down the old loco Fairfax spirit. Newsrooms once full of court reporters rushing in with breathless tales, noisy political writers with their exclusives, eccentrics and ambitious young things from general rounds, ponderous elders with their advice and investigative journalists with their occasional visits to the news pages had become more sombre. So much was hanging in the balance. The wave seemed to have arrived suddenly, and yet it had risen quietly for more than a decade before breaking across the company.

On Friday 30 November, two days later, another Christmas party was held, this time at Kirribilli House. The Prime Minister's drinks was an opportunity for leaders from business and the arts, newspaper editors, titans and moguls to rub shoulders, spilling across the lush lawns that ran down to the harbour. James Packer and his wife Erica were walking along the veranda, enjoying the scene, when they passed a small knot of people talking and laughing. Fred Hilmer was in the group. Spying Packer passing by, Hilmer greeted him jovially and referred to the carnage unfolding at Fairfax. 'I got out at the right time,' he told Packer. Erica Packer, who had stood by James through all the bad days since One.Tel, looked away. Packer recalled in a flash the relentless Fairfax coverage of his life and he turned on Hilmer. The former chief executive's off-the-cuff comment seemed to eschew any responsibility for Fairfax's woes. It pressed a red button. 'Don't come up and try to be my friend,' Packer hissed. 'The damage had already been done by the time you got out, Fred. Fuck off.'

CHAPTER 12

THE SMOKING GUN

Guests mingled on the forecourt of the Museum of Contemporary Art at Circular Quay, overlooking the gleaming sails of the Sydney Opera House as water taxis navigated a choppy swell on the harbour. Street artists performed for tourists down by the water — a silver-painted man standing on a box, a didgeridoo player, an entertainer with performing dogs. Waiters hovered with drinks as the in-crowd from the corporate set rubbed shoulders with the journalists who were their hosts. Camera crews jostled on the perimeter waiting for their quarry; finally, in a sign that he had arrived, his mother, his sister and his wife materialised in the crowd.

In a high-ceilinged room beyond the MCA lobby with its signature work by Imants Tillers, the final preparations had been laid for a dinner with James Packer. The evening was a moneymaking event for *The Australian Financial Review* — and a sell-out, given the guest speaker. All the Fairfax big wheels were present, and the room would soon be wall-to-wall with chief executives and chairmen. For Packer, this was a singular public coming-out that his father would have caustically dismissed at the first mention. Now the whole family was here. James Packer had become increasingly public, appearing at conferences and conventions after years of hating even a mention in the press. This time he would be on stage, talking about himself. It was part of his campaign to pressure community opinion and the New South Wales government as he sought to expand his Melbourne, Perth and Macau casino interests to Sydney, his home town. He had successfully lobbied the federal government a year before to abandon its reform of poker machines, exercising a blend of charm and threat inherited from his father. This was the equilibrium of life, the yin and yang: conceding his privacy brought rewards for his business.

It was Thursday 25 October 2012 and Packer's sale of ConsMedia to News Limited was about to close, bringing him to the end of an almost year-long strategy to leave media behind and focus all of his energy on building his gaming empire. But in the way of the world, an unexpected diversion was about to fall across his path, and once again it involved the relationship between the Packers and Fairfax.

Packer was seated at the top table, between Fairfax's chief executive Greg Hywood and the chairman Roger Corbett. Given everything that had gone before — the Goanna, One.Tel, and all the years of venom — Packer's presence between two Fairfax bosses was astounding, no matter his motives.

After his talk — a mix of frank and witty reflections on his life, some soft sell on his love for Sydney, and the hard sell on his plans for a high-roller casino — Packer had the room in his hands. He returned to his table, where he fell into conversation with Corbett. They were old friends. Corbett had offered private words of support to Packer in his broken days after One.Tel and even now, more than a decade on, Packer remained appreciative. Now it was Corbett who had trouble at his door. They discussed the events of the year at Fairfax and the general newspaper industry woes. They agreed to get together again soon to continue the conversation.

Five weeks later, in the balmy mid-evening of 29 November, Roger Corbett stepped from the wharf at Mosman Bay onto a white tender, to be taken out to the huge boat anchored in Lavender Bay. When Corbett climbed aboard *Seahorse*, Packer greeted him with affection. Drinks arrived and they sat down for a private dinner *à deux*. Packer, who had given considerable thought to their previous conversation, announced that he had a solution to Fairfax's woes: the company needed new blood in the boardroom, and it needed sound media experience to buttress the chief executive, who remained the only director with a history in the business. It was an old refrain expressed over many years by journalists at the company, market analysts and shareholders. But Packer had gone one further: he had a candidate and he had a plan.

Packer proposed John Alexander. With his historic links to Fairfax, where he had been on both the editorial and the commercial side of the company, then all of his subsequent years at PBL, Alexander had the right background and experience. Moreover, he could become a factor in Corbett's succession planning. Starting as a copy boy on the Sydney *Sun* in 1968, Alexander had more than 40 years in the media industry. For all his sharp personal style, he was a potential chairman who could be ready to step in when Corbett wished to retire. He could join the board immediately and Corbett could leave the company in good hands.

Alexander had turned the Packers' ACP magazine division into a thumping financial success before it was sold in James Packer's big move out of media. He had been central to a purge that had brought the Nine Network all the wrong headlines in 2006 but this rout was one blip on an otherwise remarkable career for a man who had once hankered to become a sports reporter. He had been chief executive of PBL under both Kerry and James Packer. He had spent five years as executive chairman of the pay TV holding company ConsMedia, where he had been at the pointy end of the takeover defence against Kerry Stokes in 2009. He understood the dynamics of media war. Now, after the sale of ConsMedia to the Murdochs, he was free. 'I'd put John on,' Packer said.

It was an extraordinary suggestion. Alexander had been a Packer man since 1998. He had been an ally in James Packer's SEEK deal in 2003 and he had been central to his strategy at carsales.com.au, which had all but destroyed Fairfax's auto classifieds. He had been on the boards of both companies. He understood print and digital media inside out, and he had actively and enthusiastically supported Packer wreaking personal vengeance on Fairfax by attacking the classifieds business. After his own years at Fairfax when he had presided over newspapers with huge profits on the back of advertising, Alexander had been right in the middle of the payback which had left Fairfax so exposed. To return 14 years later would be not just vindication for Alexander. It would be a signal that Fairfax acknowledged its mistake in losing him.

There was another factor that could tip the scales. Given Alexander's long association with Park Street, appointing him to the Fairfax board could easily be construed as giving James Packer a voice on the board, with no shareholding. There would be uproar in some quarters. Fourteen years earlier, in 1998, the dramatic move by Brian Powers — chief executive of the Packers' private company Consolidated Press Holdings and executive chairman of PBL — to quit for an appointment to the board of Fairfax had caused a storm. Powers' breathtaking appointment as chairman of Fairfax 11 days later had sparked a full-scale inquiry by the media regulator. Later, no-one was found to have breached the law, although the whole situation seemed like something from a novel. John Alexander was fired by Fairfax four days after Powers' arrival, notwithstanding their convivial relationship. He had fallen victim to endless power plays inside the company and white-anting from outside. Alexander was a complicated cat. He was an editor who stood out, but he took risks. Amongst his crimes was a weekend cruise in Fiji in March 1997, at the invitation of Powers on a boat owned by the Packers. At face value, the trip seemed hardly controversial. Powers and Alexander had known each other since Powers' first stint on the Fairfax board as a director in 1992. But anything involving the Packers, with their 14.9 per cent stake in Fairfax, provoked suspicion. Alexander's own senior journalists had forced the story of the cruise into *The Sydney Morning Herald*. It was a year before Alexander was fired from Fairfax, but the trip had left a cloud that never lifted.

From James Packer's perspective there was a further political dimension that would have to be handled with care and respect, and this involved another media family. Appointing Alexander to the Fairfax board would attract the notice of the Murdochs. It would add media muscle in the Fairfax boardroom and a layer of new relationships. Packer told Corbett he had no wish to precipitate any fights. Just the week before, News Limited had cut James Packer a cheque for a billion dollars for his share of ConsMedia. It was a deal that had been done with no war and little stress. He wanted no battle with the Murdochs. Before any appointment of JA to the Fairfax boardroom, Packer would need their blessing to proceed.

Corbett was noncommittal. He told Packer he was grateful for his advice and that it was intriguing enough to take to the Fairfax board. And that was where it would stand or fall.

Packer promised Corbett that he had no plans to back his proposal with a hostile play for Fairfax — even though it would be spare change to buy 5 per cent of the company for $50 million at the prevailing 50 cents a share. He could join forces with Rinehart if he chose, or another media player; they could nominate Alexander as their director in a bid to force change if the idea took his fancy. Packer had hated Fairfax for so long that there was a temptation, grounded in all the old history and his father's training, to get entangled again. But he had formed a good relationship with Hywood and they planned to ski together in Aspen in the New Year of 2013. He had not forgotten Corbett's kindness after One. Tel; these factors would stay his hand.

Corbett in turn told Packer that if Fairfax rejected the olive branch of JA — in other words, if the Fairfax board decided it looked more like a Trojan horse than a gift — then he would release Packer from his word. Their friendship would survive.

It was an extraordinary conversation and even more remarkable as a sign of how times had changed. Sitting on the deck of *Seahorse*, out on the dark waters of the harbour with the lights glowing on land, the head of the Packer family and the chairman of Fairfax had discussed appointing one of Fairfax's most high-profile former executives to the board. It was 14 years since Alexander had been thrown out of the company for sins that included suspicions of friendly relations with the Packers. It was ironic that Hywood, now chief executive of Fairfax but back then editor-in-chief of *The Australian Financial Review*, had been one of the strongest voices advocating that JA be disciplined for consorting with the enemy.

Rumours about JA hit the newspapers even as Packer and Corbett were having dinner. *The Australian* reported online at 7.28 p.m. that same night, 'widespread rumours' that Alexander was on the comeback trail to Fairfax. The paper canvassed Alexander returning not only as a director but possibly making a push for the chairmanship. Phoned for a comment, Alexander had declared that he had held 'zero conversations with anyone at Fairfax'. Nor had he had any conversations with shareholders of media organisations, he said. *The Australian Financial Review*'s Rear Window column simply called it the 'Second Coming'. Clearly someone, somewhere had sprung a leak.

The Fairfax board decided overwhelmingly on 6 December 2012 that John Alexander should not be invited to become a director. Roger Corbett was circumspect about the whole affair, leaving the secrets of the boardroom where they belonged, but appearing to leave the door open to revisit the issue.

He said later: 'John Alexander is held in high regard by James Packer, whose judgement I respect, and I hold John in high regard also. But the board took the view that at this time there wasn't a situation available. That shouldn't imply any criticism of John. I consider James as a good personal friend and I took his advice on John very seriously.'

For the second time, Alexander was lost to Fairfax. His years with the Packers might have left the board fearful of precipitating a return to internecine wars from the past, but there seemed at least an argument that his experience could have strengthened a boardroom grappling with Rinehart and other shareholders, whose voices became louder by the day.

Just five months later, Kerry Stokes showed none of the reservations of the Fairfax board when he personally recruited Alexander to the board of his own Seven West Media on 2 May 2013. A tough operator with all the confidence of the self-made mogul — and one who had clashed with Alexander in the past — Stokes declared himself delighted with the new appointment.

James Packer later pinned the Fairfax board's reluctance to bring JA on board on the historic rift and suspicions between his own family and Fairfax. And yet it was over 11 years since the Packers had sold out of their Fairfax shareholding, netting $436 million after selling for $4 a share, a sum the current board could only dream of.

> Roger asked me for my advice and I said he should appoint JA to the Fairfax board. I thought it was simple: you put someone in who knows a lot about journalism and a lot about media generally. I made the offer, and I told Roger I wouldn't go hostile and start buying Fairfax shares if he didn't want to do it. But I said to him, 'You're mad if you don't take him, because he's one of the best media executives in Australia.'

Roger later said they didn't want to do it. The board was not interested because they thought John was too close to me. It was the old drama of Fairfax and the Packers. I could get over it but they couldn't.

———————

James Packer had been called a moron by the media for so many years that he almost anticipated the charge whenever he picked up a newspaper. His old bugbear — that Fairfax papers focussed unduly on his business — was easily fed by an index that was featured daily in the business 'comment & analysis' section of smh.com.au. On a rolling basis, the site listed the names of business identities ranked by the number of articles published about them. Packer was always on top of the index. By June 2013, over a thousand items of comment or analysis about his life and business were available on the site. Australia's most important global business figure, Rupert Murdoch, was second with 790. Murdoch had been through a tumultuous period, with phone hacking and the split of his global empire. He had not been a shrinking violet nor out of the news, and yet he came a distant second. The chief executive of Qantas, Alan Joyce, was almost neck and neck with Murdoch on 747; former BHP Billiton chief executive Marius Kloppers, who had left BHP in May 2013, came in fourth at 652; and Kerry Stokes was in fifth place with 592 items published.

These were meaningless numbers with no context, and given Packer's high profile and his controversial play for a new casino licence in NSW with no competitive tender, the focus on his interests was not surprising. His dispute with Fairfax, however, was that he was always on top of the index, year in and year out. Success had not given Packer a thicker skin.

After the period between 2006 and 2008 when Packer had gambled his fortune on expansion in the US casino business, run headlong into the financial crisis, then scrambled to survive, he had reoriented his companies away from debt.

He had invested $2.3 billion in Australian dollars offshore in the worst of times in 2006 and 2007, lost $1.6 billion of this in the US, and then seen the $750 million he had invested in Macau turn into a shareholding worth approximately $4.5 billion. By mid-2013 Crown had a market capitalisation of $9 billion. Packer's Melbourne and Perth casino properties were poised to make more money than the three free-to-air television networks in Australia combined. He was on a sound footing.

That was certainly not the case for the Nine Network. Packer had been labelled a genius when he sold to CVC Asia Pacific for $5.5 billion after his father's death and a fool after his $1.6 billion US casino losses. But he had ended up in better financial shape than he had begun.

The same could not be said for the masters of the universe. By September 2012, debt from the acquisition had overwhelmed Nine. In late 2012, US hedge funds ousted CVC and took 100 per cent ownership of Nine, while leaving the Australian management in place.

Kerry Packer's treasured Nine had been sold by his son to private equity, lost by private equity to hedge funds and held together as an Australian icon by the public face of its blokey Australian chief executive David Gyngell, best man at both of James Packer's weddings and the son of Bruce Gyngell, the man who had helped Sir Frank Packer to establish Channel 9. Gyngell senior had famously appeared on the small screen in its earliest days in September 1956 to declare, 'Good evening, and welcome to television.'

The halcyon days of the Australian media were gone. The obligatory 6 p.m. news, the morning papers, the classifieds on Saturday for jobs and cars and property had been swamped by the internet, with its real-time news and citizen journalism, and the digital pure-plays who had trounced everyone, seizing the rivers of gold.

In all of this, Fairfax had taken the biggest beating, perhaps because it had the most to lose. In the mid-1990s, John Fairfax Holdings had been Australia's premier media organisation. It had not been oblivious to the developments of the internet; it had simply been unable to frame the right strategy at the right time. It had not been willing to aggressively change course to entrench its dominance. Fairfax had seen the rise of the internet and commenced early forays. It had watched the jostling by free-to-air networks to get into pay TV. It had been in pole position for first-mover advantage in all of this. And yet it had ended up with no winning position in the new wave of pure-plays or pay TV. In 2013, it was still identified mostly as a newspaper company — 18 years after the first nerdy young computer techs and dreamers had put wires and data into computers in garages and small offices to create SEEK, REA and carsales.

Both the Murdoch and Packer families had produced a younger generation switched on to the internet, or at least keen to give it a go. Through hubris and inexperience, James Packer and Lachlan Murdoch had bungled early investments like One.Tel with catastrophic costs, both financially and for their reputations. Theirs had been an unexpectedly symbiotic relationship. Both had persevered with the internet and they had ended up with major stakes in all three of the pure-plays that made it to number one.

Packer had deployed his investment in carsales into the creation of PBL Media — internet dust to sprinkle over the Nine Network for the $5.5 billion sale to private equity. His SEEK stake had been cashed in to defend his pay TV interests, and those pay TV interests in turn had delivered a $1 billion bonanza. Lachlan Murdoch's $2.2 million REA investment had become a $2.3 billion pipe to plug into his family's new News Corporation. Packer would later describe Lachlan Murdoch's initial REA investment as the best deal in Australian media for the last 25 years.

The Fairfax family, meanwhile, had produced as its highest-profile offspring, young Warwick Fairfax, a man whose legacy was to leave the company in administration, saddled by debt. His second cousin John B. Fairfax had returned to the company 18 years after that disaster, merging his own Rural Press into the bigger newspaper firm that bore his name. He took his place in the boardroom after an investment of $1.16 billion in April 2007 but by the time he sold out in December 2011, this stake was worth just $193 million.

In the mythology bred into the children of the other major Australian media dynasties from their earliest days, Fairfax was not only arrogant but seemingly a fortress. Lachlan Murdoch recalled the formative training from a father who raised him to see Fairfax as the competition:

From the earliest lessons in our family, which began sitting around the breakfast table dissecting every newspaper — from editorial to layout to advertising — we were taught about the value of strong classified revenues, the so-called rivers of gold and the near monopoly Fairfax held on them which we never had enjoyed, and likely never would. And we were taught that this almost impregnable revenue stream was a massive strategic benefit, owned lock, stock and barrel by our competitor at Fairfax.

Fifteen years after the pure-plays got going in their suburban garage empires, the great Fairfax cash flows had evaporated. Fairfax had failed to replicate online the power of even one of its vertical classified advertising streams. The company was proud of its independent journalism and the important role this played in a democracy and it had promoted and fostered the expensive competitive news-breaking spirit between its independent mastheads. And yet it had allowed the business that underpinned all of this to be chipped away.

Fairfax had failed to pursue SEEK when the company was worth $120 million in 2003 and it had said no to a second opportunity to buy Packer's stake in 2009. It had declined REA when the share price was 20 cents and the company had been rescued by Lachlan Murdoch instead. It had been outmanoeuvred by James Packer at carsales, starting out with a stake of 11.6 per cent and ending with nothing.

Fairfax had gone from having a $9 billion market capitalisation in 2007 after the merger with Rural Press to a market capitalisation of $1.1 billion by June 2013. In that same time SEEK had gone from a market capitalisation of $2.1 billion to $3 billion; REA had ranged between $680 million and $740 million through 2007, then soared to $3.6 billion. Carsales — which had not been listed in 2007 but had an imputed value in the sale to CVC of $400 million — was worth $2.1 billion by the middle of 2013.

Greg Hywood had inherited this legacy when he came in as chief executive in 2010. In June 2013 he echoed the words of David Kirk a full five years before, when he declared to an investor briefing that business conditions were 'pretty tough'. He expected Fairfax earnings to fall by up to 39 per cent in the second half of the 2012–13 financial year. Total revenue in the June half year had fallen by between 9 and 10 per cent. The big falls, as they had been for some years, were in the newspapers. Radio was looking better and the Domain online property business was the star, increasing revenue by 16 per cent in the same time frame.

The Domain business was worth only a fraction of its rival, the number one site, REA. But given its growth, Domain was moved into a separate profit centre, rather than remaining subsumed in the bigger, and less healthy, picture. Hywood announced that the metro newspapers would almost immediately shift to a digital paywall model — following *The AFR*, which had operated behind a paywall for several years. The new model would allow readers to gain access to a number of free articles before they had to pay, a system that had been successfully trialled in numerous big papers overseas. But there was also more cost cutting and more jobs would be lost.

James Packer had remained scathing about Fairfax long after his support for carsales and SEEK had helped those two companies to back Fairfax into a corner. It remained a point of considerable resentment that he had been pilloried for his own failings, yet Fairfax had implied for years that its position as the central pillar of journalism in Australia was the crux of its business model — an argument Packer dismissed as hubris. After his own retreat from the brink of disaster, he could never resist a swipe at Fairfax, deriding the company's failure to understand the internet and playing up his own role in undermining the business. 'My view was that Fairfax had a classifieds business and we were going to steal it. Fairfax thought they had a journalism business. No-one at Fairfax got it. Look at the amount of classified revenue lost at *The Sydney Morning Herald* and *The Age*. And yet they did nothing to protect it.'

Fred Hilmer had been at the wheel of Fairfax through many of the years which showed early signs that the traditional newspaper classifieds model was under threat and that a new model — a strategy to defend king and country — was needed. He had supported his digital managers in creating CitySearch, the website for general listings and entertainment, later sold for a considerable loss to Telstra. But he had not fought for SEEK. Hilmer instead had strengthened the fort with more newspapers. Looking back seven years after he had left the chief executive's position, Hilmer said he believed no amount of strategic reorientation could have averted the coming catastrophe. The evaporation of the business model for print newspapers could not have been stopped, and it would have been a better strategy to simply sell the newspapers and create a new business.

The problem at Fairfax was that the bleeding of the classifieds at *The Age* and *The Sydney Morning Herald* was going to overwhelm anything you could do with online classifieds, and the only thing you could have done was sell *The Herald* and *The Age*, and start again. In hindsight, almost anything you did would have been better than keeping them. When you have a business as threatened as this, you should get out and start again.

Hilmer had fired Greg Hywood in a different era in 2003 and by the time Hywood returned to the company as CEO, Fairfax had had two more chief executives. They could not have been more different. David Kirk had started the company's diversification into internet pure-plays in a serious way with TradeMe, and then left in the face of concerted resistance from the Fairfax family. Brian McCarthy had put his foot on the brake in the financial crisis, leaving Fairfax more or less stalled for the two years before he was fired. He had cut costs, but he had not invested. When Hywood returned, the failings of the past had caught up and the company was in a tailspin.

Hywood's warning during an international news media conference in New York in May 2013, that at some time in the future Fairfax would be entirely digital — or predominantly digital — in its metropolitan markets, amplified earlier comments he had made in 2012. His prediction antagonised not just old-time readers with their affection for newspapers, but at least one big competitor who was trying to sustain the idea that print would survive. Rupert Murdoch, always with his antenna tuned to Australia, said later:

I think Fairfax have damaged themselves with this public
outspokenness about their problems and closing their
print works and going around putting themselves at a
disadvantage really. They're saying well, in 18 months' time,

the papers will all be digital for Saturday ... They've done a lot to destroy everybody's revenue by talking about the future of print, publicly, time and again. But it hasn't hurt us as much as they've hurt themselves.

Murdoch's own global newspapers were now boxed inside a new business together with high-value businesses like REA and Foxtel designed to support the share price. After all the corporate plays of recent years in Australian media, one thing had become clear. News Corp had husbanded new-media resources in the good times that would provide the framework of its defence in the teeth of the downturn. After interviewing a range of analysts on the eve of the News Corp split, the media specialist Ben Holgate reported that together, the Australian pay TV business Foxtel and the online site REA would make up close to 50 per cent of the value of the new News.

Greg Hywood had to make do with what he had to reshape Fairfax. The Rural Press newspapers bought by David Kirk had been a mainstay in sustaining revenue. TradeMe had been sold to slash debt and Hywood had created a balance sheet to fit the new modish austerity. Most of the classifieds business was history. Drive was closed as a classified listings business, and jobs listed on the MyCareer site became free in 2013. The Domain online and print property business was cordoned off to highlight its value away from the papers. The conundrum for Fairfax, for newspapers everywhere, was this: if no-one paid for newspapers, then who paid for journalists?

As 2013 unfolded, Fairfax staff began clearing their desks as they prepared to move to new workspaces. Throughout the five floors of the Fairfax Media building, tradesmen reshaped newsrooms and executive offices. By the end of this transformation, the whole top management of the company as well as newspapers and reporters would be relocated or reconfigured in dizzying moves up and down the building. Everyone was hot-desking. Hywood, his chief financial officer David Housego, and the general counsel Gail Hambly would share a pod, demonstrating to grouchy newspaper reporters how it was done. By the end of it all, a vast empty floor had been created.

Hovering with a red pen over costs, Hywood had resolved to give up space to another paying tenant, a tenant moreover who personified the enemy. Google was possibly the most powerful of the digital forces that had reshaped the world of information, going head-to-head with the content creators as it sucked in vast, unfathomable quantities of news and opinion, general listings, maps, video, anything in its path, and churned it all out again in a free, ever-moving whirligig. Google's arrival inside the portals of Fairfax seemed somehow to sum up the new age. The enemy was inside the tent.

James Packer and Lachlan Murdoch had not killed Fairfax off. They had taken their revenge, extracted in blood, for sins never forgotten between the dynasties. They had helped to raise the pure-plays. The three new media stocks in Australia that they had been involved in — SEEK, carsales and REA — were worth a combined $9.85 billion by June 2013. They had reversed position entirely with Fairfax, which fluctuated uncertainly between $1.1 billion and $1.3 billion. But in the end the damage done to Fairfax had been inflicted by Fairfax on itself. It had said no to everything. The internet had brought science fiction to life but Fairfax had closed the book. It had had a monopoly the envy of its competitors and an opportunity, years earlier, to pursue and hold each of the online leaders in the field. It had refused, stood back, or sold out of all three.

If there had been a moment to consider its future, a *memento mori* for Fairfax, it might have been the day Paul Bassat stood on a suburban street and wondered how much easier it would be to look a house up on the net. Or the afternoon Martin Howell decided a customer needed three clicks and no more to find something online. Or perhaps the day Greg Roebuck had rushed in with a printed copy of the Drive lift-out emblazoned with the words 'carsales.com.au', and said 'Let's register that.' It could have been the day a young Lachlan Murdoch said yes to a meeting with a friend about a dying website, or it may have been the day that James Packer told the founders of SEEK that they had won the game.

NOTES

Quotes included in this book are from interviews conducted by the author unless otherwise indicated. Sources below include interviews provided for this book with the exception of interviews granted on a confidential basis.

Prologue

James Packer and Lachlan Murdoch, author present, Rockpool restaurant, Hunter Street Sydney, 16 August 2012

Ben Holgate, 'New media stocks put on weight', *The Australian Financial Review*, 15 August 2012

Chapter 1: Seek and ye shall find

Paul Bassat, author interviews and emails to author, October–December 2012, February 2013

Andrew Bassat, author interviews and emails to author, November–December 2012, February 2013

James Packer, author interviews, November–December 2012, January 2013

Daniel Petre, author interview, 19 December 2012

Nigel Dews, author interviews, 10 and 24 January 2013

Alan Revell, author interviews, 3 and 4 January 2013

Brian Powers, author interview, 19 December 2012

Fairfax board strategy and budget overview memorandum,
    'Further acquisition opportunities', 25 and 26 June 2003

Barry Davies, author interview, 17 January 2012

Barry Davies, email to Alan Revell, 23 July 2003

Alan Revell, email to Barry Davies, 25 July 2003

Barry Davies, email to Alan Revell, 30 July 2003

Barry Davies, email to Alan Revell, 1 August 2003

Allan Revell, email to Barry Davies, 2 August 2003

Jeff White, email to Barry Davies, 7 August 2003

Jeff White, author interview, 13 February 2003

Fred Hilmer, author interview, 6 December 2003

Allan Revell, email to author, 17 May 2013

Andrew Bassat, email to Paul Bassat, 15 June 2011

Chapter 2: A property too good to refuse

John McGrath, author interview, 27 November 2012

Lachlan Murdoch, author interview, 9 November 2012

Greg Duncan, author interview, 3 January 2013

Peter Macourt, author interview, 4 February 2013

David DeVoe, author interview, 23 January 2013

Karl Sabljak, author interview, 1 February 2013

Simon Baker, author interview, 29 January 2013

Martin Howell, author interview, 5 May 2013

Andrew Barnes, author interview, 24 January 2013

ASX announcement, 'Realestate.com.au, admission to official list',
    29 November 1999

ASX announcement, 'Realestate.com.au and ninemsn enter exclusive deal', 30 November 1999

ASX announcement, 'Becoming a substantial shareholder from MBL', 6 December 1999

ASX announcement, 'Discussions with f2 terminated', 10 October 2000

Sam White, author interview, 6 February 2013

New Limited media release, 'Takeover offer for realestate.com.au at $2 per share', 1 August 2005

ASX announcement, Realestate.com.au ASX, 2 August 2005

John Niland, author interview, 22 January 2012 and 1 January 2013

Nigel Dews, emails to author, 2–7 February 2013

Wikipedia, The Free Encyclopedia, http://en.wikipedia.org

James Packer, email to author, 24 January 2013

Warren Lee, author interview, 24 January 2013

Ron Walker, author interview, 4 February 2013

John-Paul Drysdale, Hubb Financial Group, email to author, 6 February 2013

Chapter 3: Drive baby drive

Wal Pisciotta, author interviews, emails, October 2012–May 2013

Greg Roebuck, author interviews, emails, 23 November 2012–May 2013

Drive section, *The Sydney Morning Herald*, 1 August 1997

Gregg Haythorpe, author interview, 26 November 2012

Alan Revell, author interviews, 3 and 4 December 2012

Jacquie Murray, email to author, 17 May 2013

James Packer, emails to author, 20 February 2013

Alan Revell, email to Greg Roebuck, 18 July 2005

David Kirk, Fairfax Annual General Meeting, address to
shareholders, 18 November 2005

Chapter 4: Channelling Foxtel

Alan Ramsay, 'Hayman homage to Murdoch, the maker of kings',
The Sydney Morning Herald, 22 July 1995

Mark Booth, author interview (phone), 13 February 2013

Mark Booth, email to author, 12 March 2013

Lachlan Murdoch, author interviews, 14 November 2012 and 25
March 2013

Rupert Murdoch, author interview, 11 April 2013

Dawn Hayes, 'Mark Booth — a hand of steel to hold up Sky', *The
Independent*, 1 February 1998

Mark Furness, 'ABC, Fairfax, Foxtel to form pay-TV alliance', *The
Australian Financial Review*, 28 July 1995

Kim Williams, author interview, 13 November 2012

Lindsay Gardner, author interview, 10 April 2013

Doug Halley, author interview, 9 April 2013 and emails to author,
3 and 4 March 2013

Sue Lecky, 'News vetoes pay TV deal at last minute', *The Age*, 29
July 1995

Glenda Korporaal, 'Lights on at Australia's pay TV powerhouse',
The Sydney Morning Herald, 24 February 2005

Richard Aedy interview with Kim Williams, *ABC Sunday Profile*, 1
July 2012

Kim Williams, email to author, 28 March 2013

Helen Meredith, 'Murdoch wins Sydney showground', *The
Australian Financial Review*, 21 July 1995

Mark Furness, author interview, 6 March 2013

Ben Potter, author interview, 10 March 2013

Mark Furness, 'ABC, Fairfax, Foxtel to form pay-TV alliance', *The Australian Financial Review*, 28 July 1995

Sue Lecky, 'AIM nears joint venture target', *The Sydney Morning Herald*, 28 July 1995

Ben Potter, 'Pay TV venture close to signing a deal with Foxtel', *The Age*, 28 July 1995

From *The New York Times*, 'Murdoch victory in Fox foreign ownership fight', *The Australian Financial Review*, 28 July 1995

Glenda Korporaal, 'We'll get TV deal', *The Sydney Morning Herald*, 11 August 1995

Glenda Korporaal, 'Price the key to AIM's prospects', *The Sydney Morning Herald*, 12 August 1995

Bruce McWilliam, author interview, 28 February 2013

James Packer, emails to author, May 2013

James Packer, email to author, 28 March 2013

Bruce Wolpe, author interview, 15 March 2013

PBL media release, 'PBL announces exercise of option to take a 25% interest in Foxtel', 29 October 1998

PBL media release, 'PBL today announced that as previously foreshadowed, it has exercised its option to acquire a 50 % interest in Fox Sports', 6 October 1999

Brigid Glanville, 'News Corp, PBL accused of misusing power within Foxtel', *ABC PM*, 13 September 2005

Mark Westfield, 'Wide impact anticipated in proposed Foxtel–Optus deal', *ABC 7.30 Report*, 23 May 2002

Chapter 5: Turn off the TV

James Packer, author interviews, December 2012–March 2013

David Gonski, author interview, 21 March 2013

Lloyd Williams, author interview, 21 March 2013

David Gyngell, author interview, 4 March 2013

Memorial service for Kerry Packer, DVD, 17 February 2006

Matthew Grounds, author interviews, March 2013

Ron Walker, author interview, 4 February 2013

Wal Pisciotta, author interviews, November 2012–April 2013

Lisa Murray, 'PBL wants full control of Carsales website', *The Sydney Morning Herald*, 22 May 2006

'The SEEK prospectus: blue sky for who?', 12 April 2005

AAP, 'Fairfax takes swipe at SEEK', 14 April 2005

Katherine Murphy, 'Murdoch turns up the heat on changes to media laws', *The Age*, 27 June 2006

AAP, 'Murdoch named most influential Aussie', 26 June 2006

Janet Fife-Yeomans, 'Home James', *The Daily Telegraph*, 30 June 2006

Janet Fife-Yeomans, 'James has fun while Nine staff left fuming', *The Daily Telegraph*, 30 June 2006

'Nine's ones to watch out for', *The Daily Telegraph*, 1 July 2006

Ben Brazil, author interview, 16 November 2012

Nicholas Moore, author interview, 17 April 2013

Matthew Grounds, email to James Packer, 20 August 2006

James Packer, email to author, 17 May 2013

PBL, ASX statement, 'PBL expands online and gaming interests', 25 September 2006

Lisa Murray, 'Packer may sell Nine and ACP', *The Sydney Morning Herald*, 16 October 2006

Lisa Murray, 'PBL set to sell Nine, magazines', *The Sydney Morning Herald*, 17 October 2006

'PBL share trading halted', *abc.net.au/news* 17 October 2006

Lisa Murray, 'Packer first to act on media laws', *The Sydney Morning Herald*, 17 October 2006

Lisa Murray, 'It's PBL Media, $6b predator', *The Sydney Morning Herald*, 18 October 2006

PBL, 'PBL's $5.5 billion recapitalisation and establishment of Australia's largest diversified media group, PBL Media', 18 October 2006

Lisa Murray, 'The big media carve-up', *The Sydney Morning Herald*, 18 October 2006

Michael Evans, 'Taking part in the great non-activity', CBD, *The Sydney Morning Herald*, 18 October 2006

Stephen Mayne, 'The carve-up of John Fairfax has begun', *Crikey*, 20 October 2006

Brad Norington and Jane Schulze, 'Packer eyes Fairfax at right price', *The Australian*, 24 November 2006

James Packer, chairman's address, PBL annual general meeting, 26 October 2006

Fairfax, 'News Corporation 7.5% acquisition of Fairfax is an investment only', *ASX*, 20 October 2006

Matthew Ricketson, 'Seven stake heightens Fairfax speculation', *The Age*, 6 December 2006

Rupert Murdoch, author interview, 11 April 2013

Chapter 6: Rivers of red

Ron Walker, author interview, 24 and 26 April 2013

David Kirk, author interview, 24 April 2013

David Kirk, author interview, 5 March 2011

James Packer, emails to author, 26 April and 15 May 2013

Annette Sharp, 'Lonely time for Packer intimate', The Diary, *Sun-Herald,* 19 February 2006

Sam Morgan, author interview, 13 May 2013

Ron Walker, letter to James Packer, 20 March 2006

Helen Westerman and Lisa Murray, 'Fairfax spends big on internet expansion', *The Age,* 7 March 2006

AFP, 'Myspace purchase a "huge mistake": Murdoch', 21 October 2011

Wendy Frew, 'Fairfax hit the spot INL chairman says', *The Sydney Morning Herald,* 18 June 2003

Tom Mockridge, emails to author, 15 and 16 May 2013

John Lyons, 'Stop press', *The Bulletin,* 26 August 2003

Roger Colman, 'NZ: is this Fairfax's Vietnam?' CCZ Equities Research, 23 May 2003

Roger Colman, author interview, 21 May 2013

Macquarie Research, 'SEEK: where the jobs are hiding', 5 August 2003

Macquarie Research, 'Classified information: will online dry up FXJ fivers of gold?' 13 August 2002

Macquarie Research, 'Still SEEKing classified', 6 August 2003

Eric Beecher, author interview, 10 April 2013

Eric Beecher, 'The state of the Fairfax business model', 23 June 2004

Roger Corbett, author interview, 31 May 2013

Fairfax board strategy pack, 1 June 2006

James Packer, email to author, 25 February 2013

Ron Walker, author interview, 4 February 2013

Michael Evans, 'Taking part in the great non-activity', CBD, *The Sydney Morning Herald*, 18 October 2006

Fairfax Media, 'Statement to the Australian Stock exchange', 20 October 2006

Stephen Mayne, The carve-up of John Fairfax has begun', *Crikey*, 20 October 2006

David Kirk, 'Annual general meeting, address of David Kirk', Fairfax Media, 10 November 2006

AAP, 'Seven buys stake in Fairfax', 5 December 2006

Chapter 7: A big future for newspapers

Ron Walker, author interview, May 2013

Michael Evans, 'Taking part in the great non-activity', CBD, *The Sydney Morning Herald*, 18 October 2006

John B. Fairfax, email to author, 17 May 2013

John B. Fairfax, author interview, 3 May 2013

Andrew Sayers, director National Portrait Gallery, author interview, 7 December 2006

Perpetual Limited archive

Brian McCarthy, author interview, 9 May 2013

David Kirk, author interview, 9 April 2013

Pamela Williams, 'John B. home after 19 years', *The Australian Financial Review*, 7 December 2006

Alan Kohler, 'Fairfax snaps up Rural Press', *Inside Business*, transcript, 10 December 2006

James Packer, author interviews, April–May 2013

PBL, ASX/media release, 'PBL and CVC complete recapitalisation and establishment of Australia's largest diversified media group, PBL Media', 7 February 2007

Colin Kruger, 'Fairfax, Rural Press deal gets court approval', *The Sydney Morning Herald*, 23 April 2007

John B. Fairfax, email, 17 May 2013

Peter Sikora, Standard & Poor's, *AAP*, 23 April 2007

Lisa Murray, 'Stokes quietly lets stake in Fairfax go', *The Sydney Morning Herald*, 24 April 2007

Fairfax Media, 'Patrick Joyce appointed as alternate director on Fairfax board', *ASX* 17 December 2007

Fairfax Media, 'Correction to investment report on refinancing risk', *ASX*, 19 December 2007

David Kirk, email to author, 2 June 2013

John B. Fairfax, email to author, 26 May 2013

Patrick Joyce, author interview, 23 May 2013

Chapter 8: Party like there's no tomorrow

Reuters edition US, 'A dozen key dates in the demise of Bear Stearns', 17 March 2008

Arnold M. Knightly, 'Crown buys into Harrah's, station', *Las Vegas Review-Journal*, 21 February 2008

James Thomson, 'The ace up Packer's sleeve', *Business Spectator*, 20 February 2008

Vanda Carson, 'Buyer interest in Packer's Macau casinos', *The Sydney Morning Herald*, 1 February 2010

James Packer, author interviews, April–June 2013

Fleur Leyden, 'James Packer and Lachlan Murdoch win market approval', *Herald Sun*, 23 January 2008

Peter Smith, 'Lachlan Murdoch's CMH buyout collapses', *Financial Times*, 7 April 2008

Miriam Steffens, 'Buyers shun CMH after deal fails', *The Sydney Morning Herald*, 9 April 2008

Nick Tabakoff, 'Fairfax's Marinya denies margin call', *The Australian*, 25 June 2008

Miriam Steffens, 'Fairfax moves to unwind margin loan', *The Sydney Morning Herald*, 27 June 2008

Nick Tabakoff, 'John B. Fairfax takes a $300 million hit on shares', *The Australian*, 12 November 2008

Wikipedia entry for Lehman Brothers

Ron Walker, author interviews, April–May 2013

Brian McCarthy, author interview, 9 May 2013

David Kirk, author interviews, April–June 2013

John B. Fairfax, author interview, 3 May 2013

John B. Fairfax, email to author, 26 May 2013

Patrick Joyce, email to author 3 June 2013

David Kirk, email to author, 5 June 2013

Fairfax Media, 'address of David Kirk', Annual General Meeting, 13 November 2013

Steven Bartholomeusz, 'Fairfax situation critical', *Business Spectator*, 20 November 2008

Robert Gottliebsen, 'Year of the media merger', *Business Spectator*, 17 November 2008

Malcolm Maiden, 'Crunch time for Fairfax as it faces its debt, cutting dividends', *The Age*, 6 December 2008

Bruce Wolpe, author interview, 16 May 2013

Brian McCarthy, author interview, 10 December 2008

Pamela Williams, author notes, 10 December 2008

Chapter 9: Pirate smile

Kerry Stokes, author interviews, 22 March 2013 and 5 June 2013

Peter Gammell, author interview, 30 April 2013

James Packer, author interviews, March–June 2013

Guy Jalland, author email, 4 June 2013

Ryan Stokes, author interview, 6 June 2013

Neil Shoebridge and Damon Kitney, 'Packer cashes up for Stokes battle', *The Australian Financial Review*, 27 August 2009

Steven Bartholomeusz, 'Packer, Stokes and all that cash', *Business Spectator*, 26 August 2009

Miriam Steffens, 'Packer buyback may foil Stokes' CMH raid', *The Sydney Morning Herald*, 27 August 2009

CMH, media release and statement to ASX, 'CMH announces successful completion of underwritten sale of its shareholding in SEEK Limited to institutional investors', 26 August 2009

Annette Sharp, 'Packer explodes over Seven's knocking', *The Daily Telegraph*, 9 October 2009

Chapter 10: The Fairfax curse

Nick Tabakoff, 'Troubles hit home for John B. Fairfax', *The Australian*, 18 March 2009

Bruce Wolpe, letter to Brian McCarthy, 27 February 2009

Bruce Wolpe, letter to Ron Walker, 27 February 2009

Dan Oakes and John Huxley, 'Battle lines drawn in fight for Fairfax', *The Sydney Morning Herald*, 18 September 2009

Malcolm Maiden, 'Fairfax directors and investors take sides', *The Age*, 19 September 2009

ASX announcement, Fairfax Media 28 September 2009

Wal Pisciotta, email to author, 24 May 2013

Greg Roebuck, email to author, 25 May 2013

Andrew Bassat, email to author, 24 May 2013

'Carsales float revved up for first trading day', AAP, 10 September 2009

'Fairfax asleep at the wheel', AAP, 14 September 2009

Neil Shoebridge, 'JB Fairfax to quit board', *The Australian Financial Review*, 20 July 2010

Brian McCarthy, author interview, 9 May 2013

John B. Fairfax, email to author, 16 June 2013

Kim Williams, email to author, 10 June 2013

John B. Fairfax, text message to author, 10 November 2011

Pamela Williams, 'Executive stress in a digital age', *The Australian Financial Review*, 11 December 2010

Pamela Williams, 'Board dinner seals McCarthy's fate', *The Australian Financial Review*, 7 December 2010

Ben Butler, 'John B. Fairfax sells out of company that bears his name', *The Sydney Morning Herald*, 11 November 2011

John Durie, 'Goldman sells last of JB Fairfax stake at deep discount', *The Australian*, 10 November 2011

Roger Corbett, author interview, 16 June 2013

Chapter 11: Escape to Neverland

James Chessell, Neil Shoebridge and Sarah Thompson, 'Rinehart poised to snare 15pc of Fairfax', *The Australian Financial Review*, 1 February 2012

Mark Day, 'Gina Rinehart can't buy a voice at Fairfax', *The Australian*, 2 February 2012

Terry McCrann, 'James Packer, Lachlan Murdoch split over Ten', *Herald Sun*, 3 March 2011

James Packer, author interviews, 13 October 2012, 5 November
   2013 and 20 March 2013

Kerry Stokes, author interview, 22 March 2013

Ben Holgate, 'Packer rethinks Foxtel prospects', *The Australian
   Financial Review*, 7 May 2012

Ryan Stokes, email to author , 18 June 2013

James Packer, email to author, 14 June 2013

Kim Williams, author interview, 21 November 2012

Rupert Murdoch, author interview, 11 April 2013

James Thomson, 'Why News Corp's bid for Consolidated
   Media tells us where James Packer and Rupert Murdoch are
   heading', smartcompany.com.au, 20 June 2012

Kirsty Simpson, 'Gina Rinehart lifts stake in Fairfax to 15% as
   pressure for board seats builds', *The Sydney Morning Herald*,
   15 June 2012

Damon Kitney, 'Gina Rinehart asks for three seats on Fairfax
   board', *The Australian*, 18 June 2012

Kirsty Simpson, 'Fairfax to shrink jobs, newspapers', *Canberra
   Times*, 19 June 2012

Ashley Hall, 'Fears for job cuts at News Limited', abc.net.au/am,
   20 June 2012

Damon Kitney, 'Former Fairfax chair Ron Walker backs Gina
   Rinehart', *The Australian*, 20 June 2012

Ron Walker, author interview, 26 March 2013

Roger Corbett, author interview, 31 May 2013

Gina H. Rinehart, 'Open letter to Roger Corbett, Chairman,
   with copies for Fairfax directors', 29 June 2012

Fairfax Media 'Statement', 29 June 2012

ABC, 'Rinehart sells partial stake in Fairfax', abc.net.au, 9 July 2012

Fairfax Media, '2012 results announcement', 23 August 2012

Ben Holgate, 'New media stocks put on weight', *The Australian Financial Review*, 15 August 2012

Colin Kruger and Gareth Hutchins, 'Fairfax shares jump on TradeMe sale', *The Sydney Morning Herald*, 17 December 2012

Fred Hilmer, email to author, 21 June 2013

Chapter 12: The smoking gun

James Packer, author interview, 21 December 2012

Roger Corbett, author interview, 30 May 2013

Anne Davies, 'Editor's Packer boat trip "disturbs"', *The Sydney Morning Herald*, 6 March 1997

'Will John Alexander rejoin Fairfax?', *The Australian*, 29 November 2012

Joe Aston, 'Second Coming', Rear Window, *The Australian Financial Review*, 30 November 2012

Darren Davidson, 'Seven West Media appoints John Alexander to board', *The Australian*, 2 May 2013

James Packer, 6 April 2013

Lachlan Murdoch, author interview, 25 March, 2013

Malcolm Maiden, 'Fairfax restructure gives a new home for Domain that will make its value more explicit', *The Age*, 4 April 2013

Fred Hilmer, author interview, 6 December 2012

Rupert Murdoch, author interview, 11 April, 2013

Clive Mathieson, 'Fairfax chief Greg Hywood sizes up the end of newspapers', *The Australian*, 1 May 2103

AAP, 'Newspaper execs embrace online news', 25 June 2013

Ben Holgate, 'New News Corp shares could access REA', *The Australian Financial Review*, 28 May 2013

ACKNOWLEDGEMENTS

Shona Martyn at HarperCollins understood what I wanted to write about from our first phone call and she gave me unstinting support for a project that always looked as though it could go easily awry. In a nutshell, the idea was about what had happened to Fairfax with the rise of the internet and how this had intersected with the old wars between media dynasties in Australia. I was fascinated by the idea that not only had the internet sparked a new 'war of the worlds', but that the old media families of Australia were up to their necks in it — and that it gave them new ways to settle old scores.

The story depended on a huge range of sources, many of whom helped on the basis of anonymity. James Packer and Lachlan Murdoch, whose lives have been intertwined with Fairfax since birth, were prime amongst those on the record and I am immensely grateful for the time each made — as well as their patience with endless rounds of fact-checking. Neither put conditions on their interviews. Fascinating for me were the stories from the online advertising pioneers who founded and fostered the three big winners: SEEK, carsales and realestate.com.au. I would especially like to thank Paul and Andrew Bassat, Wal Pisciotta and Greg Roebuck, and Martin Howell and Karl Sabljak for their incredible insights and recollections. So many people tolerated being interviewed dozens of times and then receiving a torrent of emails for fact-checking.

At HarperCollins, Catherine Milne was simply amazing. She gave me endless encouragement and I am sure she kept secret from me the pressures she was juggling at her end as the manuscript got later and later. She obviously decided the carrot of enthusiasm and kindness was better than the stick. Sally Collings edited the book (from Palo Alto) with such careful attention that she has immeasurably improved my writing. She always managed to ask that extra question that sent me off on two days of research to fix half of a sentence where I had tried to skate over something. Belinda Yuille's careful proofreading added a final layer of protection from my own errors and inadequacies.

It hardly suited Michael Stutchbury and Brett Clegg to have me on leave from the newspaper for six months and I am so grateful to them both for agreeing to this crazy plan — particularly given the subject matter of the book. I started work as a reporter on *The Australian Financial Review* on Monday 31 August 1987 — the same day young Warwick Fairfax launched his bid to privatise Fairfax. Alan Kohler, then editor of the paper, put me on six months' probation to see how it worked out. Whether Warwick or I worked harder on that first day I'll never know, but I got through the probation and he did not.

I want to thank so many people who generously gave time and insights. They include John Alexander, Andrew Barnes, Mark Booth, Roger Corbett, Barry Davies, Nigel Dews, John B. Fairfax,

ACKNOWLEDGEMENTS

Peter Gammell, Matthew Grounds, Doug Halley, Fred Hilmer, Guy Jalland, Patrick Joyce, David Kirk, Peter Macourt, Brian McCarthy, John McGrath, Hamish McLennan, Rupert Murdoch, Jacquie Murray, John Niland, Daniel Petre, Brian Powers, Allan Revell, Kerry Stokes, Ryan Stokes, Ron Walker, Kim Williams, Lloyd Williams and Bruce Wolpe.

My friends as ever were my backstops. Jenni Hewett (the woman for whom the words 'how does she do it' were invented), Judith Hoare and Marian Wilkinson know how much they mean to me. They kept a roster of gossip and news rolling in from the outside. To Jenny Brockie, Leigh Sales, Lisa Millar, Jim Crawford, Margot Saville, Monica Attard, Alexander Michael and Tony White (who sent ice cream, amongst other cruelties), Lis Sexton, Hilary Russell and David Uren, plus the AFR Chicks group — thank you for always being there. And to my mother Barbara Cameron, who put up with no phone calls. Warren Scott read the manuscript all the way through and improved it in so many ways with his independent and intelligent eye, always posing a question I had not even thought of. He made sure the author never starved and put up with me raving on and on about Fairfax.

And to Fairfax: long may she survive!

INDEX